"The nonviolent approach does not immediately change the heart of the oppressor. It first does something to the hearts and souls of those committed to it. It gives them a new self-respect; it calls up resources of strength and courage that they did not know they had. Finally, it reaches the opponent and so stirs his conscience that reconciliation becomes a reality."

— Dr. Martin Luther King, Jr.

To Jeffrey:

a role model in education and group organizing in the black community. Without your efforts, generations to come would not benefit from your tireless efforts.

Best wishes,

6/97

Martin Luther King, Jr., December 1964

Reflections of the Dream

1975-1994
Twenty Years
Celebrating the Life of
Dr. Martin Luther King, Jr.
at the Massachusetts Institute of Technology

Edited by
Clarence G. Williams

The MIT Press
Massachusetts Institute of Technology
Cambridge, Massachusetts
London, England

Published by the MIT Press.
All rights reserved. Reproduction or translation of any part of this work beyond that permitted by Section 107 or 108 of the 1976 United States Copyright Act without the permission of the copyright owner is unlawful. Requests for permission or further information should be addressed to:

Dr. Clarence G. Williams
Massachusetts Institute of Technology
77 Massachusetts Avenue
Room 3-221
Cambridge, MA 02139-4307

Photo credits: front cover, frontispiece, facing page 1, pages 36, 42, 54, 62, 72, 80, 88, 112, 126, 136 (top), 136 (bottom), 146, 162 (top), 162 (bottom), 192, 204, 214 (top), 214 (bottom), 222, 234 (top), 234 (bottom), 244, 254, 266—Wide World Photos; pages 6, 66, 74, 79, 83, 93, 121, 135, 187, 198, 203—MIT News Office (Calvin Campbell); pages 12, 24, 53, 61, 71, 87, 111, 125, 175, 182, 213, 233—MIT Museum; pages viii, x, 25, 31, 239, 243, 253, 260, 265, 271, 274, 277, 278, 288—MIT News Office (Donna Coveney); Page 27, 29, 32—L. Barry Hetherington; page 28—Don Dixon; page 30—Atlantic Photo Service, Inc.; page 35—Sandy Middlebrooks; page 41—Boston University Photo Services; page 98—St. Paul's A.M.E. Church; page 191—Brooks; page 221—Katherine Huff; back cover—African Technology Forum.

Acknowledgments and Permissions

"Mother to Son" by Langston Hughes
from SELECTED POEMS by Langston Hughes
Copyright 1926 by Alfred A Knopf Inc and renewed 1954 by Langston Hughes
Reprinted by permission of the publisher

"Far Music" by Earl Marlatt
from CATHEDRAL: POEMS BY EARL MARLATT
Copyright 1937 Harper & Brothers

WILD, WILD WEST by M. Dewese
Copyright 1987 Zomba Songs Inc.
All Rights Reserved
WARNER BROS. PUBLICATIONS U.S. INC., Miami, FL 33014
Used by Permission

Printed in the United States of America
Design and Layout by African Technology Forum

ISBN 0-262-23187-5 (hardcover)—ISBN 0-262-73115-0 (pbk.)

Library of Congress Catalog Card Number: 94-77837

Contents

Contents

Foreword

In January 1994 the Massachusetts Institute of Technology held its twentieth annual observance and celebration of the life of Martin Luther King, Jr. Two decades of commemorations on our campus have kept the dream alive and have reminded us of the true meaning of the national effort to secure social justice for all of our citizens.

Those of us who lived during the King era know why we continue to praise his legacy to America and the world. But it would be meaningless to continue these observances without reminding ourselves of his legacy and passing it on to our younger generations, and without reaffirming our own commitment to eradicate the root causes of discrimination and poverty in our society. Too many of us, given the pace of our everyday lives, quickly forget that the struggle against racism remains a lingering American dilemma and a major societal problem.

There is still reason for hope, however. This was brought home to me in Dr. King's last book, *Chaos or Community: Where Do We Go From Here?* The term chaos has more than one meaning, of course, one of which is particularly fitting for us at MIT. That has to do with the new science known as "chaos" theory, which was pioneered by Ed Lorenz, a professor in our Department of Earth, Atmospheric and Planetary Sciences. This new science deals with nonlinear and irreversible events. For example, there is the butterfly effect—where a small disturbance becomes amplified to generate a major change. This means that, literally, the beating of a butterfly's wings can initiate a chain of atmospheric motions that becomes a huge storm. One might say that Martin Luther King, Jr. demonstrated this effect in the social and political realms: for if ever one man's life—and life's work—changed an entire society irreversibly, it was his life.

This book contains two decades of speeches at MIT by local and national leaders who gave us their insights not only on some of the events of the past twenty years but on those times during which Dr. King made his major civil rights triumphs. The issues have not changed as much as we would like over these twenty years. Yes, we have made some progress on our campus. The intellectual and social map of MIT, and the world in which MIT operates, is marked by an increasing diversity. Yet, while these changes are the source of renewal and growth, they are also the cause of discomfort and tension. The message of cooperation is simple, but its implementation is not, for we seem to have fragmented along every conceivable fault line—fragmented by intellectual discipline, by race, by gender, by class.

It will not be easy to resolve our differences and tensions, but if we are to build the future we want for ourselves and our children, we must build it together. To do that, we must have mutual respect and we must hold common values at the deepest levels. This will require courage, commitment, and faith—and the wisdom and inspiration of men and women such as those whose messages are contained in this book. The lessons are there. It is up to us to act on them.

Charles M. Vest
President, MIT

•

Realization of the dream of Martin Luther King, Jr. has not, unfortunately, been achieved. But the ideals he espoused and the opportunities before us now compel us to continue, indeed to strengthen, efforts to build racial harmony and equal opportunity for all. This volume documents twenty years of annual observances of the birth of Dr. King held on the MIT campus, beginning in 1975 with the inaugural presentation by Hubert E. Jones and concluding with the presentation in 1994 by Coretta Scott King. The twenty-year history of the MIT celebrations of Dr. King's life and contributions goes well beyond the twenty formal presentations documented in this book and includes numerous workshops, programs for members of the minority community at MIT, musical contributions, and scholarly efforts determined to make progress toward the ideals reflected in the life of Martin Luther King.

The programs at MIT have been ones which have involved a core group of individuals from across the Institute, including especially the Martin Luther King, Jr. Committee, who have devoted enormous effort to lead and coordinate MIT's Martin Luther King celebrations over these past twenty years. Obviously, the principals whose keynote addresses are contained in this volume have played a catalytic role in deepening and sharpening our understanding of the dream of Dr. King, and in inspiring our efforts to achieve that dream. I am grateful to all of these individuals for their work, their presence, and their persistence in the MIT community.

As Provost of MIT, it has been my privilege to participate in several of the Martin Luther King celebration events and to meet the keynote presenters. Every one of these people has had an important message. Each has been a message with lasting relevance for our lives and each has been presented with personal feeling and sharing uncommon in this science and technology-focused university. Re-reading these presentations in their edited form here revives that glow of excitement and conviction I felt after hearing the presentations in Kresge Auditorium on this campus. Dr. Clarence G. Williams, editor of this volume, has effectively captured twenty riveting presentations, and we are grateful for the creativity he has demonstrated in presenting this volume and for the hard work expended on our behalf in completing this important project.

In my interactions external to MIT it is common to be on the receiving end of compliments expressing surprise that we have a major commitment to community-building programs. But our resolve is not false, not a forced fit, and not unnatural: this is a learning institution involving people. Science and engineering education and research are done by people. Achieving diversity among our student body, staff, and faculty has been, and continues to be, a key objective, and President Vest and I have concluded that MIT's continued success as the leading academic institution focused largely on science and technology is possible only if we are successful in building diversity.

Dr. Martin Luther King, Jr. has inspired our efforts to recognize and enhance the contributions of minority scholars and to enhance the representation of members of minority groups on our campus. Two recent tangible manifestations of this are the establishment of the Martin Luther King, Jr. Visiting Professor Program in January 1995, and the Robert R. Taylor Professorship. The Visiting Professor Program is intended to bring more minority scholars to MIT to contribute fully to the intellectual life of the Institute. This program is one initiated by our Martin Luther King, Jr. Committee—an example of their leadership and good work. The Robert R. Taylor Professorship is a new, fully endowed senior professorship announced by President Vest on the occasion of Coretta Scott King's visit to MIT in February, 1994. The Taylor Professorship is named in honor of MIT's first African-American graduate who became a distinguished architect, and this professorship is intended to honor the contributions of African Americans. Dr. Marcus Thompson of Music and Theater Arts was named the first holder of the Robert R. Taylor Professorship in January, 1995.

I am proud to be associated with an institution dedicated to remain at the forefront, and our programs and policies to build a learning environment that encourages inclusiveness are ones we value and will sustain. As noted above, MIT is a learning institution. The accounts in this volume are ones from which we can learn. Read them, learn from them, and act on them. Martin Luther King's dream is very much alive, and individuals, as he has so clearly shown, make all the difference in this world.

Mark S. Wrighton
Provost, MIT
(now Chancellor of Washington University)

Acknowledgments

I began collecting information for this publication nine years ago, and many people have collaborated to bring it to fruition. Special acknowledgment goes to MIT's President Charles M. Vest and former Provost Mark S. Wrighton. Without their support, both for this editorial project and for MIT's ongoing activities in recognition of Martin Luther King, Jr., this volume would not have been possible. Furthermore, former Presidents Jerome B. Wiesner and Paul E. Gray, now Chairman of the Corporation, through their shared leadership of MIT provided the vision and unanimous strong support for the origin and survival of this historical event.

Our primary debt, of course, is to the speakers who took the time to come to our campus and share with the MIT community their thoughts on the life and work of Dr. Martin Luther King, Jr. These twenty-six speakers, including six lecturers, provided words of insight and wisdom about the past, present, and future of America. Generously, they shared their expertise and the fruits of their experience and reflection.

I also wish to thank the following individuals and groups for invaluable assistance in the preparation of this publication. Ms. Denise Brehm edited twenty-two speeches after they were transcribed, collected relevant supporting data, and laid the groundwork for additional input by the speakers and lecturers, readers, and technical writers. African Technology Forum, an MIT-affiliated organization, did the technical editing, design and production preparation, and developed marketing strategies. Special thanks go to Mr. Mawuli Tse and Mr. Michael Kobina Owu, who led a team of student supporters consisting of Ms. Khaitsa Wasiyo, Mr. Clarence G. Williams, Jr., and Mr. Kwabena Ofori-Tenkorang. Mr. Philip N. Alexander assisted with the final stages of editing.

I am grateful to several individuals whose experience in logistics and financial matters—and attention to detail—proved essential. They are: Mr. Roy Charles, Mr. Robert Dunbar, and Ms. Josephine M.

Bartie (over ten years of service to MIT's Martin L. King, Jr. activities), my former Administrative Assistants, and my present Administrative Assistant, Mr. Stephen Charles; Ms. Doreen Morris, Assistant Provost for Administration; and Ms. Nan Henderson, Ms. Pearl Mosley, Ms. Margaret Daniels Tyler, and Ms. Shannon Anderson, document readers. Also supportive were staff of the MIT News Office, especially Mr. Kenneth D. Campbell, Director; Ms. Joanne Miller, Editor of *Tech Talk* and Assistant Director; and Ms. Chandra Wilds, Receptionist. Articles in *Tech Talk* written over the years by Mr. Robert C. Di Iorio, Associate Director of the News Office; Mr. Charles H. Ball, Senior Assistant Director; and other staff members were beneficial in developing perspectives on speakers and events. Although Mr. Robert Byers, former Director of the News Office, is no longer at the Institute, he deserves recognition for his successful effort in 1981 to reproduce an unpublished speech by Dr. Martin Luther King, Jr., discovered on tape at MIT. Mr. Nelson Armstrong, former MIT Associate Director of Admissions and Area Director of the Alumni Fund, and presently Director of Alumni Relations at Dartmouth College, earned special praise for his committee work and especially for organizing our Marches from Lobby 7 to Kresge Auditorium for many years. Mr. Richard J. Frye, Manager, and Ms. Jean G. Caloggero, Administrative Assistant of the Graphic Arts/Purchasing Office guided and advised on printing and publication decisions. Mr. Michael T. Leonard, Associate Director of Operations at the MIT Press, offered wise counsel on writing protocols. Staff of the MIT Museum, especially Mr. Michael W. Yeates, Associate Director for Collections, patiently identified important historical documents and photographs. Professor Kenneth R. Manning provided sound, helpful advice.

During the past twenty years, numerous members of the MIT community have given unstintingly of their time and service to the work of the Martin Luther King, Jr. Planning Committees. Their commitment has helped to ensure the success of the annual celebrations. Committee co-chairs included Dr. Isaac M. Colbert, Professor Michael S. Feld, Professor Royce N. Flippin, Jr., Ms. Yvonne L. Gittens, and Professor Leo Osgood. Professor Robert W. Mann chaired a committee, appointed by President Paul E. Gray in 1988, to review the program and to consider ways in which the Institute could further promote recognition of the life and work of Martin Luther King, Jr. This committee's recommendations prompted a renewed commitment at MIT to principles and activities dear to Dr. King. Committee members included Mr. Ronald S. Crichlow, Professor Carl W. Garland, Ms. Yvonne L. Gittens, Dr. James E. Hubbard, Jr., and Professor Frank S. Jones. Professor Royce N. Flippin, Jr. joined in the latter stages of the committee's deliberations. The 1994-95 Martin Luther King, Jr. Planning Committee worked diligently to move the program forward. Its members were: Ms. Kristy G. Bellamy, Ms. Maureen Costello, Mr. Ronald S. Crichlow, Mr. Robert C. Di Iorio, Professor Michael S. Feld (Co-Chair), Professor Jerome I. Friedman, Reverend Jane Gould, Mr. Arnold R. Henderson, Professor Melvin H. King, Ms. Evette M. Layne, Professor Philip Morrison, Professor Leo Osgood (Co-Chair), Ms. Ann Davis Shaw, Ms. Margaret Daniels Tyler, and Professor Cardinal Warde. Other members who have served since the first Presidential Committee in the 1990-91 academic year were: Mr. Squire J. Booker, Mr. William B. Buckner, Reverend Bernard J. Campbell, Mr. Kenneth D. Campbell, Ms. Naomi F. Chase, Professor Ellen T. Harris, Ms. Judy Jackson, Professor Willard R. Johnson, Dr. Vincent M. McNeil, Ms. Barbara M. Nichols, Reverend Scott Paradise, and Professor Frank Solomon.

My deepest gratitude is to my wife of thirty-four years, Mildred Cogdell Williams, a constant source of encouragement and support in all of my work. She transcribed nearly all of the speeches and played a key role throughout the editorial process. Our son, Alton L. Williams, contributed by urging that all of the speeches—and the documentation surrounding them—be preserved in the MIT Archives and Special Collections.

C. G. W.
Cambridge, Massachusetts
January 1996

Martin Luther King, Jr. in 1958

Introduction

Clarence G. Williams

The legacy of Martin Luther King, Jr. remains as one of the major agents of change and awareness in society in the past decades. It provided that clarion call to America to address the concerns of oppressed minorities, women, and other interest groups. The 20-year period of Martin Luther King, Jr. celebrations at MIT includes lectures, youth conferences, and visiting scholars. While these speakers address a broad range of King's life, a brief summary is presented here.

•

THE LIFE OF MARTIN LUTHER KING, JR.

Dr. Martin Luther King, Jr. was assassinated on April 4, 1968 in Memphis, Tennessee at the early age of thirty-nine. Dr. King was America's most influential African-American leader and the most celebrated American Civil Rights leader in the country. In 1955, King came into national prominence when he was elected by community leaders in Montgomery, Alabama to lead a boycott against the city's public transportation system. The success of the Montgomery Bus Boycott convinced King that his mission in life was to lead black people to freedom from discrimination and racial injustice. He was well-educated to meet the challenge: a bachelor's degree with top honors from a historically black institution—Morehouse College; a theology degree from Crozer Theological Seminary, where he was the top academic student in his class; and a Ph.D. from Boston University. As a student, King constantly searched for solutions that would help his people overcome the problem of segregation in American society. Through reading and research, particularly the writings of Henry David Thoreau and Mahatma Gandhi, he became convinced that Gandhi's approach of nonviolent resistance would work in America. King firmly believed that if it could work for the people of India who used it to win freedom from British rule, it could be used by blacks in America to fight peacefully against discriminatory practices in education, housing, employment, and other public accommodations.[1]

1

King had come to Memphis to support striking Negro garbage workers who were fighting for equal pay. He took on the hopes and fears of many who were fighting for social and economic change. Thus, it is no surprise that following King's assassination, there were several days of unrest. Much of what remains in our urban cities—blocks of dilapidated buildings and garbage strewn streets—are the aftermath of his death.[2]

Out of frustration and disillusion—of a dream yet unfulfilled—riots flared up in 110 cities, and 39 people were killed, most of them Negroes. More than 75,000 federal troops and National Guardsmen patrolled America's streets. The hardest hit was Washington, DC, where 711 fires blazed against the sky and 10 people died, among them a white man who was dragged from his car and stabbed.[3]

During this period of slightly over a decade, King single-handedly and courageously led our country from a segregated society to a more open and integrated America. He was either directly or indirectly responsible for:

- Integrating public accommodations, schools, colleges, hotels, housing, and other general services;
- Teaching the country, especially African Americans, the powerful technique of protest through nonviolence;
- Signing the Civil Rights Bill on July 2, 1964 as the national leader of the Negro Revolution;
- Striving to help the poor in his latter days of 1968 by promoting jobs and income for everybody;
- Speaking out against the war in Vietnam during the mid-1960s because the country was spending its resources on this war rather than on the "War on Poverty" at home.[4]

Martin Luther King, Jr. made us more aware of and responsive to the problem of racism in America. His legacy remains one of the major agents of change, so we celebrate the legacy of Dr. King. As Judge Margaret A. Burnham said in 1992, "Dr. King's vision—what school children have been taught to call the King dream—was meant to be a yardstick against which we might measure our progress . . . as a people, and as a nation."[5]

20 YEARS OF MLK CELEBRATION AT MIT

The Massachusetts Institute of Technology began celebrating the life of Dr. Martin Luther King, Jr. seven years after his assassination. A celebration was held in honor of Dr. King in 1975, although it was not designated as an official Institute holiday by the Academic Council, the Institute policy-making body, until 1976 under the leadership of President Jerome B. Wiesner and Chancellor Paul E. Gray. In 1976, a week-long series of public events to commemorate the birthday of King was established, and from that year on the Office of the Special Assistant to the President for Minority Affairs (in 1984 changed to Special Assistant to the President) engaged in extensive planning to celebrate the life of this great American.

This volume reproduces the messages of 26 speakers during a 20-year period, 1975 to 1994—messages conveying the life and times of a great American to the MIT community. We invited both national and local speakers because King not only committed himself to issues of national prosperity but to the common person in the local community as well. These annual celebrations enunciated and compared: (1) the times of King's life with the present, (2) the progress of civil rights of African Americans, and (3) their economic status during and after King's era. As the chairman of the Planning Committee and coordinator of the first 14 annual programs, and as a member the following 6 years, I became familiar with all these speakers and their backgrounds. It seems appropriate to share some brief comments about each of them, giving the reader an additional perspective on their speeches.

Hubert E. Jones (1975)

Hubert E. Jones, our first speaker in 1975, was a visiting professor in the Department of Urban Studies and Planning at MIT. I was asked by President Jerome B. Wiesner and Chancellor Paul E. Gray to plan a program for an Institute memorial service in honor of Dr. King. Since there was not enough time for long-range planning, we immediately looked within our own ranks to select a speaker who could emphasize a connection with the local Cambridge/Boston community. With his professional background in social work and urban community involvement in the Boston metropolitan area, Hubert E. Jones had an ideal profile to serve as our speaker.

His strong commitment to improving the socioeconomic conditions of disadvantaged groups, especially in such areas as the welfare of children, urban education, economic and political well-being of people of color, provided an excellent model for our future speakers. Jones later became a professor in Urban Studies and Planning at MIT and subsequently was selected as the first African-American Dean of the School of Social Work at Boston University. Since retiring from that position, he remains an active leader in his roles as a popular Boston TV commentator, political analyst, and lecturer at the University of Massachusetts, Boston.

Walter J. Leonard (1976)

Walter J. Leonard, with whom I became acquainted shortly after we were selected by our respective presidents at Harvard and MIT as Assistants to the President, was the second speaker for our celebration of Dr. King's life. He had served earlier as Assistant Dean and Assistant Director of Admissions and Financial Aid at the Harvard Law School. A fiery African-American lawyer and Affirmative Action Officer, with the responsibilities of coordinating, developing, and implementing the Harvard University Plan for Affirmative Action, Walter Leonard provided insight not only from his own personal contact with King but from memories of that era. One of the reasons for selecting Leonard was to recognize his recent efforts in affirmative action: a conference that he organized in October 1974, entitled "A Step Toward Equality: Affirmative Action and Equal Employment Opportunity," and his involvement with the civil rights movement as one of the founders of the Southern Christian Leadership Conference, with which King was very much associated during the 1960s.

After several years at Harvard University, Leonard went on to become President of Fisk University in Nashville, Tennessee and a faculty/administrator at Howard University. He recently retired as Executive Director of Cities In Schools, Inc. in Alexandria, Virginia.[6]

Muriel S. Snowden (1977)

Muriel S. Snowden, along with her husband Otto Phillip Snowden, maintained a high profile in the black community as co-founder and co-director of Freedom House, Inc., an African-American community advocacy organization in Boston. In her role on various key Boston committees and boards of corporations, she impressed Chancellor Paul E. Gray as an outstanding African-American woman during their collaborations in several of these activities. Her affiliations included: New England Aquarium, National Shawmut Bank, Museum of Science, Babson College, Associated Harvard Alumni, and the National Council of Negro Women (life member).

Our association developed into a very positive relationship through my involvement on the board of Freedom House, Inc. and in programs to encourage black youngsters to pursue science and engineering careers. This created a strong link between MIT and Freedom House. Mrs. Snowden was well prepared educationally as one of the few African-American women of her generation to be educated at Radcliffe College. She graduated from Radcliffe in 1938 and pursued advanced work at New York School of Social Work from 1943 to 1945.

Before her death on September 30, 1988, she was recognized as an outstanding Boston community leader. She received the Radcliffe Alumnae Achievement Award; an honorary doctor of law degree from the University of Massachusetts; and jointly with her husband, the Most Distinguished Citizens Award of the Massachusetts Department of Jewish War Veterans.[7]

Jerome H. Holland (1978)

Jerome H. Holland was a member of the MIT Corporation (1969-1985) when he was our speaker for the 1978 observance. He was the first African American to serve on the MIT Corporation. One of my prime mentors, he gave me my first job in higher education. I knew him extremely well. This educator and diplomat contributed in many areas: sports, education, government, and business. His exceptional talents and prowess began as an undergraduate at Cornell University, where he was an honor student and became the first All-American black football player in 1939. He received his Ph.D. in Sociology at the University of Pennsylvania in 1950, and served as President of two historically black universities, Delaware State College and Hampton Institute (now Hampton University, Virginia).

1978 MLK King Celebration. From left to right, Jerome B. Wiesner, Jerome H. Holland, Clarence G. Williams, Paul E. Gray, and Walter A. Rosenblith.

After serving in these leadership positions, he became in 1970 the first African-American United States Ambassador to Sweden. By 1972, Dr. Holland was connected to many Fortune 500 corporations, serving as a director of several major companies and governing boards of national organizations such as the New York Exchange, the Foreign Policy Association, and the American Management Association. He also served on the board of the American Arbitration Association, the Johnson Foundation, New York Hospital, Save the Children Foundation, and as Chairman of the American Red Cross. He was featured in *Newsweek* magazine during this period as the black who had received the most corporate directorships in the country.

"Brud" Holland, as he was often called by his friends, served on the MIT Corporation Visiting Committees for the Center for International Studies and the Department of Humanities and Social Sciences. He was chairman of the latter from 1972 to 1976. His speech in 1978 carried the substance of a cosmopolitan, wise, educated, and rare human being: an African American, a dynamite educator, a successful U.S. diplomat, an influential businessman, a socially conscious leader, and a star athlete. He served as a role model for hundreds of young people, especially African Americans, and his name is inscribed on buildings at Cornell University and the University of Virginia. Dr. Holland was "truly a man for all seasons."[8]

Melvin G. Brown (1979)

Melvin G. Brown, a young local Cambridge minister, was selected as our fifth speaker. He was the Senior Minister of the Union Baptist Church in Central Square, about two blocks from MIT's main campus. A number of MIT black employees are members and some of our students are actively involved in the church. The Union Baptist Church is significant because it is known as one of the churches where Dr. King preached while he was attending Boston University.

A native of Norfolk, Virginia, Reverend Brown was educated at the University of Arkansas at Pine Bluff, where he received his B.A. *summa cum laude* in philosophy and religion, while serving as president of the student government. He received his master's degree in Divinity from Harvard University in 1977. At the time of his presentation, he was a member of the Board of Directors of the Cambridge Community Center and the United Baptist Convention of Massachusetts and Rhode Island. Reverend Brown—high spirited and well-connected with the younger generation—was a very provocative speaker. He is currently pastor of the Greater New Hope Baptist Church in Washington, DC.[9]

Anthony C. Campbell (1980)

Anthony C. Campbell, the pastor of the Eliot Congregational Church in Roxbury, Massachusetts, was the keynote speaker for our sixth observance honoring the late Dr. King. Reverend Campbell reminded us of the old traditional ministers who would not allow the congregation to remain uninvolved with the message that he wanted to convey. With a charismatic personality and excellent singing voice, he aroused the audience in a most unusual way, prompting responses in a manner that will not be fully appreciated merely by reading his speech. Perhaps Reverend Campbell revealed some of his Southern and predominantly black educational background in his ministerial style. He received his B.A. in history and sociology from Howard University, and the M.S.T. degree in theology and history from Boston University.

Before being called to the Eliot Church in 1974, he was a field consultant for the College Service Bureau. He organized workshops and seminars aimed at encouraging institutional development at 26 colleges in the South and East. At the time of his sermon at MIT, he was a board member of the Boston Ministers' Alliance, a member of the Boston Housing Commission, and a chaplain of the Boston Police Department. Reverend Campbell left us with much to ponder. He is currently a Professor of Theology at Boston University.[10]

Samuel D. Proctor (1981)

Samuel D. Proctor, Professor in the Graduate School at Rutgers University and Senior Minister at New York's Abyssinian Baptist Church, was the first person selected to deliver our newly created Martin Luther King, Jr. Memorial Lecture in 1981. Well known in the educational arena and well acquainted with King and his family, Dr. Proctor was a superb candidate for our lecture on "King: What Progress Since the Dream?" He did not disappoint us. His lecture reproduced in this volume speaks for itself, but hearing and seeing the man deliver his message is a unique and invaluable experience. He came to the podium with outstanding credentials and wide experience. He was formerly president of Virginia Union University and of the North Carolina Agricultural and Technical State University, both predominantly black institutions, and had held key administrative posts with the Peace Corps in Nigeria and Washington, DC, the Office of Economic Opportunity, the Institute for Services to Education, and the University of Wisconsin.

Dr. Proctor had been involved in many other governmental and community affairs as a member of the Advisory Committee on Recombinant DNA Research of the National Institutes of Health, and on governing boards of the United Negro College Fund, Meharry Medical College, and the Overseas Development Council. His speech was so well received that he was invited to come to MIT in 1982 to give our opening keynote address for the "First National Conference On Issues Facing Black Administrators at Predominantly White Colleges and Universities." Dr. Proctor is now Professor and Minister Emeritus, but he continues to enlighten and thrill audiences throughout the United States, and is also associated with the Divinity School at Duke University.[11]

LeRoy Attles (1981)

LeRoy Attles continued the tradition at MIT as our seventh speaker in 1981. The Reverend Dr. Attles of St. Paul's A.M.E. Church, a few blocks from the campus, continued what was a long and very close relationship between the church and MIT. Many employees and students have historically participated in its services and activities. Although Dr. Attles had been at St. Paul's Church for only four years, his influence in and out of the church was rising rapidly as a young theologian who knew how to make a difference in the community. He came to Cambridge well qualified for the job. A native of Newark, New Jersey, he received the B.A. in sociology and religion from Wilberforce University and Payne Theological Seminary in Wilberforce, Ohio. He went on to obtain his Ph.D. in the sociology of education from Rutgers University.

At the time of his presentation, Dr. Attles was the chairman of the board of examiners for the New England Conference of the A.M.E. Church, which certifies candidates for ordination; and vice chairman of the board of Christian Education for the First Episcopal District, encompassing the Northeast and Bermuda. He served on several community boards and committees in Boston and Cambridge. His speech was well received at MIT, and he and the St. Paul's A.M.E. Church continue to be a major religious resource for many of us in the community.[12]

Charles S. Brown (1982)

Charles S. Brown came to MIT highly recommended as our eighth speaker. An Associate Professor of Practical Theology at Yale University Divinity School, he had served earlier as a teaching Fellow in Human Relations in the College of Business Administration and an instructor in Human Relations in the Metropolitan College at Boston University from 1963 to 1966. He became a full professor at the United Theological Seminary, during his tenure there from 1968 to 1979. He served as Director of Training at the Opportunities Industrialization Centers of Greater Boston, Inc. and was also director of Urban Witness and Strategy Program for Southwestern Ohio seminaries. Reverend Dr. Brown served as Associate Pastor and Pulpit Associate at Bethel Baptist Church, Dayton, Ohio; Minister of Youth and Assistant Pastor at Ebenezer Baptist Church, Boston, Massachusetts; and several other pastoral positions. He is currently pastor at Bethel Baptist Church, Dayton.

He received his B.A. in 1956 from Morehouse College, Master of Divinity *cum laude* in 1962 from United Theological Seminary, and Doctor of Theology in 1973 from Boston University. A native of Plant City, Florida, Dr. Brown has traveled and taught in Nigeria and served on a number of distinguished boards and societies. He has received many awards and honors.[13]

A. Leon Higginbotham, Jr. (1983)

A. Leon Higginbotham, Jr., a judge of the U.S. Federal District Court in Philadelphia, was the speaker at our ninth commemorative service on January 13, 1983. I had heard Judge Higginbotham speak at a conference the previous year and was convinced that his presentation would be well received at MIT. At the time that he was asked to come to the Institute, his popularity was extremely high due to his bestselling book, *In The Matter of Color*. As one of only six black Americans to reach the Federal Appellate bench, Judge Higginbotham tells us in this book how the law itself contributed to inflicting injustice on millions of Americans, solely on the basis of their color. In praising his book, Eugene D. Genovese in the *New York Times Book Review* proclaimed, "If this book helps, as it should, to bring home [an] urgent truth to white Americans, it will richly deserve all the acclaim and honors it seems destined to win." John Hope Franklin, an eminent Professor of History at the University of Chicago at the time, indicated "Leon Higginbotham has brought to this subject the skills of a great legal scholar and the sensitivity of a great humanist. He establishes quite clearly that the law has played a major role in the degradation of black Americans." And finally, Dr. King's widow, Coretta Scott King, said that "Judge Higginbotham's book . . . should be read by all Americans who believe in justice and dignity for all."

His speech at MIT illustrated why so many scholars recognized him through his intellectual work. We already had firsthand knowledge of him. He had delivered a major presentation at the highly successful "First National Conference on Issues Facing Black Administrators at Predominantly White Colleges and Universities," held at the

Massachusetts Institute of Technology in 1982. Although a reading of his text in this volume will attest to his eloquence, his voice and gestures will be missed. He was truly one of our great orators.

The judge is a graduate of Yale Law School and, at the time of his presentation, held sixteen honorary degrees. He had taught at Yale University and several prestigious institutions including the law schools of the University of Michigan and the University of Pennsylvania. His speech will encourage those who have not read his book and his other writings to do so. Now retired, he remains active as an attorney and a lecturer in the struggle to keep King's ideals alive.[14]

Price M. Cobbs (1983)

Price M. Cobbs, a distinguished psychiatrist and author, and a senior partner in Pacific Management Systems, was MIT's Dr. Martin Luther King, Jr. Lecturer in January, 1983.[15] Dr. Cobbs was recognized as an excellent choice because of his research and involvement in racial issues. We expected that he would assist the MIT community to better understand and deal with such issues. He did not disappoint us. His lecture was outstanding, as was the workshop he led on "Developing and Maintaining a Positive Ethnic Image or Identity in a Predominantly White Environment." The workshop content, although not included in this document, can be gleaned from the lecture. Dr. Cobbs's presentation was so well received that he was invited to be a major speaker for the "Second National Conference on Issues Facing Black Administrators at Predominantly White Colleges and Universities," at MIT in 1984.

Dr. Cobbs is a graduate of the University of California, Berkeley, and of Meharry Medical College. He is co-author of *Black Rage* and *The Jesus Bag*. From my perspective, *Black Rage* (1968) is a must-read for anyone interested in understanding the frustration of African Americans. United States Senator Fred R. Harris (a member of the National Advisory Commission on Civil Disorders, 1968) acknowledged this in the book's foreword:

"This book is crucially important because it . . . goes to the heart of the matter. I can only hope its message is heeded. That message is simple—that despite the passage of five Civil Rights Bills since 1957, despite the erosion of legal supports for segregated institutions, both public and private, it is still no easy thing to be a black person in America. . . . The authors as psychiatrists can easily see that white perceptions of Negroes, and the historical inculcation of these perceptions in the minds of Negroes themselves, are at the root of our present troubles. They demonstrate beyond challenge the crippling effects of white American culture on the attempts of Negro Americans to do here what all people everywhere must do if they are to develop fully to find an identity, a sense of worth, to relate to others, to love, to work, and to create. Black rage is the result of our failure, after 300 years, to make these human values possible. . . .

Ann A. Poussaint served as coordinator of the 1983 workshop "Developing and Maintaining a Positive Ethnic Image or Identity in a Predominantly White Environment."

Without question the hour is late and the message of this book is grim. But the restoration of domestic tranquillity to this land depends on our understanding and heeding it."

Dr. Cobbs's writings help us grapple with and understand problems of race in our society.

During the 1983 MLK activities, a workshop on "Developing and Maintaining a Positive Ethnic Image or Identity in a Predominantly White Environment" was held for the first time. Dr. Ann A. Poussaint, a noted local clinical psychologist, served as the workshop leader.

Helen G. Edmonds (1984)

Helen G. Edmonds, a distinguished historian, professor and dean emeritus of North Carolina Central University in Durham, and my life-time mentor, was the speaker for MIT's Dr. Martin Luther King, Jr. Lecture Series. As a scholar who had lived and taught black college students in the South during the King era, and who had motivated many black students to go on to higher achievements, she was a perfect choice to lecture on the topic, "The Legacy of Martin Luther King, Jr.: The Path of Human Dignity and Freedom." Dr. Edmonds possessed the knowledge of a worldly traveler who examines life from a wide perspective. She is a graduate of Morgan State University (A.B., 1931), Ohio State University (M.A. and Ph.D., 1938 and 1946 respectively), and the University of Heidelberg, Germany (post-doctoral, 1954-55). She still speaks German fluently.

Dr. Edmonds has received "Woman of the Year" awards from various civic organizations over the years; held six presidential appointments (including international assignments in countries of Africa, Europe, South America, and the Middle East); and occupied, at the time of her presentation, positions on numerous national committees and boards of directors (including the United Negro College Fund and the United Research and Development Fund). Dr. Edmonds has authored numerous articles and the widely acclaimed book, *Black Faces in High Places* (1971), and is currently writing a book tentatively titled *The American Black Woman in the Political Process Since 1980*. She exquisitely engaged the topic, "The Legacy of Martin Luther King, Jr.," in her presentation. Dr. Edmonds brought to this celebration her independently achieved beliefs and wide respect for constructive charting of the future. This is an excellent speech to digest and reflect on for our present and future endeavors.[16]

John R. Bryant (1984)

John R. Bryant was the tenth speaker for our memorial service. At the time, he was the pastor of Bethel African Methodist Episcopal Church, one of the largest churches in Baltimore, Maryland, with a congregation of over one thousand. Dr. Bryant had been a major religious leader in Cambridge prior to 1972, as the pastor of St. Paul's A. M. E. Church. He had served as guest lecturer and minister at more than 25 colleges and universities around the country; preached on five continents; served as a faculty member of Boston University's School of Theology; led study tours to West Africa, Jamaica and Haiti; conducted workshops on World Poverty and Hunger at the World Conference on Evangelism in Truro, England; and authored papers in four published books.

It is significant to note that a very highly regarded female African-American assistant dean of students had been dismissed at MIT just a few months before Dr. Bryant's presentation. Minority students had been protesting to the MIT administration that the dismissal was unfair. Those who worked or studied at MIT, and were familiar with the turmoil on campus surrounding this unfortunate and (to many) unjustified dismissal of a popular administrator, sensed that Dr. Bryant's comments supported the students' position. Before the program was adjourned, approximately 10 students who were leading the demonstration mounted the stage of Kresge Auditorium and made a number of demands. With this background, one can read Dr. Bryant's speech with additional understanding and appreciation of the historical role of religion for African Americans. Dr. Bryant is currently a Bishop in the Tenth Episcopal District, A.M.E. Church in Dallas, Texas.[17]

John H. Adams (1985)

John H. Adams, one of the nation's leading churchmen of our times, was our eleventh annual celebration speaker. One of his friends and colleagues, historian Helen G. Edmonds, a visiting scholar in the Department of Humanities-Writing Program, assisted the planning committee and was instrumental in bringing the program to fruition. As Bishop of the Second Episcopal District of the African Methodist Episcopal Church, Dr. Adams administered all affairs of churches in Washington, DC, Maryland, Virginia, and North Carolina. He was and continues to be included in a list of America's greatest black preachers published by *Ebony* magazine annually. He graduated from Johnson C. Smith University (A.B.); received theology degrees from Boston University School of Theology (S.T.B. & S.T.M.); and received doctorates from Payne Theological Seminary (D.D.) and Paul Quinn College (H.H.D.). He served as a Professor at the Payne Theological Seminary; President of Paul Quinn College, Waco, Texas; and Senior Pastor of several churches before his selection as a Bishop.

Bishop Adams received numerous awards from several national organizations, including Man of the Year awards from the National Urban League (Seattle and Northwest area) and the B'nai B'rith Northwest. He did not disappoint the MIT audience. His ministerial and oratorical presence was extraordinary, and the content of his speech was outstanding in its scholarship, informed by firsthand knowledge of King and his family, and by a deep familiarity with the South. Dr. Adams is currently a Bishop in the Seventh Episcopal District, Columbia, South Carolina.[18]

•

In 1985, the MLK Celebration included a panel in addition to the lectures. Three panelists addressed the theme, "The Unfinished Agenda of Martin Luther King, Jr. Within the Context of the 1980s." Brief comments about them follow.

Julius L. Chambers (1985)

The Honorable Julius L. Chambers, former Director and Counsel of the NAACP Legal Defense and Educational Fund, Inc., focused on legal and judicial issues. He was well qualified to speak on legal matters. Chambers had graduated *summa cum laude* in history from North Carolina Central University, and was mentored there by Dr. Helen G. Edmonds, the panel moderator. He received his master's degree from the University of Michigan, J.D. from the University of North Carolina School of Law, and M.L. from Columbia University School of Law. He has taught at a number of law schools, including Columbia University, Harvard University, the University of Pennsylvania, and the University of Virginia. His memberships in key law societies and national civil rights organizations are too numerous to list here.

When you read his paper, keep in mind that his words spring from extraordinary experience in the South during a time when segregation was endemic. Yet, he became the first black editor of the *University of North Carolina Law Review*; established the first integrated law partnership firm in Charlotte, North Carolina; and won several landmark civil rights cases before the Supreme Court. His involvement in civil rights litigation led to the bombing of his home in North Carolina. His words in these proceedings stand for justice and peace. Attorney Chambers is currently Chancellor of North Carolina Central University.[19]

Leo Marx (1985)

Leo Marx, William R. Kenan, Jr. Professor of American Cultural History in MIT's Program in Science, Technology, and Society, was asked to discuss the theme from a humanist's perspective. Recognized throughout the profession as one of our most distinguished scholars in American Studies, he traced King's cry of "I Have A Dream" in his famous speech of 1963 back to "the failure of the American people to carry out the agenda of 1863." He cited poets, famous American political figures, and proclaimed democratic principles to make cogent points regarding King's unfinished agenda for this nation. Perhaps the key point that Dr. Marx makes is that we all need each other if the agenda is to be completed. When we look back now nearly a decade, it appears that he was in the vanguard of a new generation.

King gave his life trying to help us address our social problems. According to Dr. Marx, all races of people in this land need each other if we are to solve these social problems, and all of us must "shake off our dangerous and discouraging lethargy." While you cannot here experience his eloquence, style, and manner, you can appreciate the content of his presentation. Dr. Marx is now Professor Emeritus of MIT.[20]

Michael R. Winston (1985)

Michael R. Winston, Vice President for Academic Affairs at Howard University, provided an excellent and scholarly paper on the theme as it relates to higher education. He ably discussed the historical perspective and assisted the audience in understanding the nation's unfinished educational agenda. In his analysis of the state of affairs in higher education, he projected quite clearly the consequences of the nation's failure to sustain a commitment to African Americans in higher education.

Dr. Winston has authored several books, including *The Negro in the United States*. A historian, he was trained at Howard University (B.A.) and the University of California (M.A. & Ph.D.). As a Woodrow Wilson scholar and recipient of many awards and honors in education, he has much to offer those who cherish a true professional using mastery of historical research skills to bring insight to social problems and issues.[21]

Respondents to the panel presentations were Attorney Herman Hemingway, Director of the Center for Criminal Justice and Public Safety, University of Massachusetts, Boston; Nathaniel A. Whitmal, '85, Department of Electrical Engineering and Computer Science, MIT; and Dr. Michael Lipsky, professor in Political Science, MIT. An open discussion followed and follow-up comments were made by the panel members. This panel discussion format was not continued in future programs for several reasons, including cost. However, it clearly was one of our most intellectually provocative activities that year.[22]

Shirley Ann Jackson (1986)

Shirley Ann Jackson, the first African-American woman to receive a Ph.D. at MIT, and one of the first women to receive a Ph.D. in physics, was chosen to be our 12th annual Martin Luther King, Jr. speaker. In 1986, she was a theoretical physicist at Bell Laboratories in New Jersey. She was the first MIT graduate to be a keynote speaker for this now traditional annual event. A graduate of Roosevelt High School in Washington, DC, as class valedictorian, she received her S.B. and Ph.D. in physics from MIT.

A personal note here is in order. I met Dr. Jackson on my first visit to MIT during an interview for the position of Assistant Dean of the Graduate School. She and a few other African-American graduate students served on the selection committee for the newly created position. I later discovered that she and these other students were the force behind the effort to hire an African-American Dean, to which position I was appointed.

She was a founder and first co-chairperson of the MIT Black Students Union, which helped establish several key minority support programs, in addition to increasing the enrollment of African Americans. She was awarded the Karl Taylor Compton Award from MIT as an undergraduate and a Tutoring Award of the Association of MIT Alumni. She also studied at the Theoretical Physics Summer School at the University of Colorado and the International School of Subnuclear Physics in Erice, Sicily.

Dr. Jackson has lectured at Fisk University, the Stanford Linear Accelerator Center, and the NATO Advanced Study Institute. Highly recognized as an achiever both within MIT and in the scientific community, she was named Scientist of the Year by the National Technical Association and received the prestigious Candace Award from the National Coalition of 100 Black Women. She is listed in *American Men and Women of Science, Who's Who Among Black Americans*, and *Outstanding Young Women of America*. She was also included in the CIBA-GEIGY Exceptional Black Scientists Poster Series. In 1986, Dr. Jackson became the first black permanent member of the MIT Corporation, after having served on that body for ten years.

Her speech was unique in that it brought to bear the perspective of an undergraduate student at MIT during the time of King's greatest triumphs. She personalized her comments to this end. Dr. Jackson is currently a Professor of Physics at Rutgers University, New Brunswick, New Jersey, and a Life Member of the MIT Corporation.[23]

Presently, Dr. Jackson has been nominated by President Clinton and is expected to be confirmed as the first African-American Commissioner of the Nuclear Regulatory Commission.

Samuel D. Proctor (1987)

Samuel D. Proctor, the provocative minister of the famous Abyssinian Baptist Church and an established educator at Rutgers University, was the speaker at the 13th celebration. It should be noted that this widely proclaimed African American was the only individual asked to speak at this event twice. This was no accident. By 1987, we had become very accustomed to his exciting presentations. He had been the lecturer for the celebration in 1981 and keynote speaker for both of our national conferences, as indicated earlier in this introduction. Our invitations to him expressed our deep appreciation for his rhetorical ability.

In his presentation on "Introspection, Outreach and Inclusion: Achieving Pluralism at MIT," Dr. Proctor provided the audience with spellbinding memories of his early life growing up in a Southern city during the pre-King era, where black professionals in all walks of life were visible and supportive in a black segregated community. This speech should raise the consciousness level of leaders in higher education.[24]

Elizabeth B. Rawlins (1988)

Elizabeth B. Rawlins, a long-time local educator and associate dean at Simmons College in Boston, Massachusetts, was our main speaker for the 14th annual celebration. Dean Rawlins was well known in the Cambridge community not only because she was one of the few African-American women who had been successful as a college educator and key administrator, but also due to her active participation in the state's educational policy-making body, the Massachusetts Public Higher Education Board of Regents. She served on this governing board as well as on the Education Commission of the States, providing reasonable and wise advice to statewide and national higher educational systems. As a special education advisor to then Massachusetts Governor Michael Dukakis, she provided a critical link between high schools and higher educational institutions.

Perhaps the major distinction that separated this speaker from the others is that she brought to the occasion an unusual perspective as an African-American woman educator who was a product of the Cambridge Public Schools, from kindergarten through high school. Her presentation covered several important issues in King's life and addressed specific changes for African Americans and other people of color in their struggle for equality over the years. Her perspectives on growing up in the North, the influence of King's assassination on her life, the education of blacks at predominantly white colleges and universities—all are key issues that institutions of higher education should consider. Since the time of her presentation, Dean Rawlins has retired from Simmons College, but her legacy remains a part of that institution through the many women whom she has touched in a positive way. We at MIT will also remember her on that day when she stood before a very attentive audience and addressed so very well the theme, "From Dreams to Reality."[25]

Gregory C. Chisholm, S.J. (1989)

Gregory C. Chisholm was the second MIT graduate to be the speaker at the annual celebration honoring Dr. King. At the time, Mr. Chisholm was a Ph.D. candidate in mechanical engineering and simultaneously preparing for the Roman Catholic priesthood as a member of the Society of Jesus. Since he delivered his address in 1989, he completed his Ph.D. and became a priest. This was a unique achievement that no MIT African-American graduate—and few others, if any—had accomplished. A native of Harlem, Gregory Chisholm came to MIT as a member of the 1969 freshman class. He received the S.B. and S.M. degrees in mechanical engineering and served on the staff of Bell Laboratories and with the U.S. Department of Transportation prior to his graduate studies.

In order to appreciate his eloquent presentation, one has only to review his speech as reproduced in this volume. This very tall, impressive engineer and priest kept the crowd spellbound. He provided MIT with a message that students, faculty, and other members of this community could understand. He related his student experience at MIT by talking in the unique manner to which only other "Techies" can fully relate. Yet, he outlined societal strengths and weaknesses that future MIT graduates must help address. His critique of the alienation experienced by his black classmates in one of the first large black freshman classes at MIT is only one reason to read this speech. His most significant appeal to the MIT community was to recognize and act upon the fact that the black community throughout our nation is under siege both from within and outside its boundaries.[26]

Nikki Giovanni (1990)

Nikki Giovanni, a poet, recording artist, and educator, was the keynote speaker for the 16th annual observance. The theme of this celebration was "The Dream and Hope, the Nightmare of Reality: Closing the Gap for our Youth." Ms. Giovanni was an appropriate personality to address issues related to this theme. Her writings and recordings relate to the black experience and to young people, and are recognized nationally. A native of Knoxville, Tennessee, raised in Cincinnati, Ohio, and educated at Fisk University, she was well equipped to present unique insights about the black experience. She had received numerous awards, including honorary doctorates.

After teaching English and writing at various universities, she joined the faculty at Virginia Polytechnic Institute and State University. As the first poet to speak at our observance, she provided the audience with a different flavor from previous speakers, with her creative and poetic analysis of numerous aspects of living in America. She discussed black life: the difficulties of being young and the pain of growing up; the dreams and myths of success in our society; the keys to happiness; advice to black women about relationships with men; pointers for black men; and the need to bring all races of people together. This presentation is an enlightening and intriguing experience.[27]

Benjamin L. Hooks (1991)

Benjamin L. Hooks, the executive director of the National Association for the Advancement of Colored People (NAACP), was the 17th speaker. Dr. Hooks, a Southern Baptist minister and a proverbial orator like King, was the pastor of the Middle Baptist Church in Memphis, Tennessee during Dr. King's fateful visit in April, 1968. Dr. Hooks came to MIT to express and share a living spirit of the times. He too had lived it, and his presentation revealed the level of his involvement.

With the aura of a provocative Southern minister, he gave a magnificent speech that received a standing ovation for several minutes. The speech provided a personal account of the last days of Dr. King in Memphis; it was breathtaking and yet simultaneously dispiriting. A journey from the 1960s to the 1990s was outlined with examples of national accomplishments and failures. As a civil rights leader and a witness to the historical events that so many young people read about, Dr. Hooks delivered a glorious testimony for Dr. King and all of those unknown civil rights participants, both black and white, who sacrificed time and often their lives to advance the struggle.[28]

Margaret A. Burnham (1992)

Margaret A. Burnham, an innovative Boston attorney and a political science lecturer at MIT, was the keynote speaker for the 18th annual celebration in 1992. As an activist in the civil rights movement since her college days at Tougaloo College in Mississippi, a historically black college, she has continued her mission of fighting for economic, social, and racial justice for women and people of color. As a student in the 1960s, the era of major breakthroughs in the civil rights struggle, she played a significant role as a staff member of the Student Nonviolent Coordinating Committee. This national revolutionary student organization played a major role in the freedom marches and subsequently influenced the positive outcome of the civil rights struggle at

21

that time. Therefore, it is not surprising that Attorney Burnham would become the defense lawyer in 1972 for the legendary Angela Davis, a renowned black visionary and revolutionary civil rights leader who was active with the Communist Party and the Black Panther Party during the 1960s.

Beginning in 1977, Attorney Burnham served six years on the bench of the Boston Municipal Court, one of the first black women to hold this position. She was also a former staff attorney with the NAACP Legal Defense Fund. At the time of her presentation at MIT, she had just become a partner in Burnham, Hines, and Dilday of Boston, New England's first law firm headed by African-American women.[29]

William H. Gray III (1993)

William H. Gray III, President and Chief Executive Officer of the United Negro College Fund (UNCF), minister, and a former congressional leader and college teacher, was the speaker for the 19th annual celebration. Elected to the House of Representatives from Philadelphia in 1978, and majority whip in 1989, he played a key legislative role in 1985 and 1986 in implementing economic sanctions against South Africa.

Dr. Gray received a B.A. from Franklin and Marshall College and master's degrees from Drew Theological Seminary and Princeton Theological Seminary. His father, mother, and grandfather were associated with higher education, while his father and grandfather were ministers of the Bright Hope Baptist Church in Philadelphia. He assumed the position of CEO of the UNCF in 1991, where he is overseeing a $250 million capital fundraising campaign for historically black colleges and universities. In 1994, he was appointed presidential Special Advisor on Haiti.

Dr. Gray's cogent speech, "Where Do We Go From Here: Chaos or Community?," is an uplifting call for black people to move towards community—to achieve academic excellence, to be of service to our communities, to exhibit brotherhood and sisterhood, and to persist in our fight for justice. As Dr. Gray observes, it is only then that we will have moved from chaos to community.[30]

Coretta Scott King (1994)

Coretta Scott King, civil rights activist and widow of Martin Luther King, Jr., received her A.B. degree from Antioch College, and her Mus.B. and Mus.D. degrees from New England Conservatory. She has received numerous awards and honors.[31] Mrs. King was the speaker for the 20th Martin Luther King, Jr. celebration, with the theme, "The Movement for Economic and Social Justice: 1994 and Beyond." Her participation was most timely. In her speech, Mrs. King called for a national "revolution of values," and deplored the recent upsurge in anti-Semitism.[32] She states that Dr. King "saw America not as a melting pot, but as a vibrant mosaic of people of all races, religions, and ethnic groups."[33] Mrs. King shared some of the dreams of her husband, and outlined the role of the MLK Center for Nonviolent Social Change, Inc., where until recently she served as President.[34]

•

THE MARTIN LUTHER KING, JR. YOUTH CONFERENCES

During the 16th annual celebration in 1990, a conference was organized by Melvin H. King, MIT Adjunct Professor and Director of MIT's Community Fellows Program in the Department of Urban Studies and Planning. The conference was part of a four-year project whose mandate is to positively affect national youth development. The theme of the conference was "Realizing the Dream: Youth Programs That Work." The conference was designed particularly for individuals who care about what is happening with young people, who wish to learn more about effective programs, and who would like to gather and distribute information about existing programs.

One of the special features was a series of workshops led by youth who demonstrated to adults and agency representatives the kinds of programs that meet their needs. Some of the organizations represented were the Children's Defense League, YouthBuild, the Dorchester Collaborative, Freedom House, Roxbury Youth Works, We Care, Boston University School of Social Work, the Office for Children, Minneapolis Youth Trust, and the Thomas Jefferson Forum. This conference was extremely successful and proved to be an excellent addition to the activities celebrating the life of Dr. King.[35]

Deborah Prothrow-Stith, keynote speaker at the second Community Fellows Youth Conference.

The second Community Fellows Program Youth Conference organized by Professor King, with keynote speaker Dr. Deborah Prothrow-Stith, former Massachusetts Commissioner of Health, and at the time Associate Dean for Government and Community Programs, Harvard University School of Public Health, was held during the 1991 MLK celebration. The theme of the conference was "Realizing the Dream—Teens, Sexuality and Parenthood." Its goal was to promote support for young parents, to share information with teens about sexuality issues, and to propose concrete ways to form an alliance between adults and youth in the struggle to realize "the dream."

Some of the topics addressed included: strategies for working together; general skills and specific information for self-advocacy; and changes in teen sexuality and parenthood since the King era. The program included panelists of young parents from local and national organizations, resulting in a most successful conference.[36]

The Third Annual Martin Luther King, Jr. Youth Conference— "Media, Music, Microchips, and Models: What Kind of Messages Help Youth Realize Their Dreams?"—focused on identifying stereotypical images presented in the media, exploring obstacles to producing videos, and developing strategies for young people of color to create their own images.[37] The topics discussed included information on how to put together positive media music; role models for youth; how youth can look at the media critically; and how we can use media to advance our development and self-esteem. Some of the workshop topics included: "The Power of Billboard Messages"; "Sexy or Sexist: Decoding Music Videos"; "Is the News Fit to Print?"; "Interactive Critique of Boston

Journalism"; and "Venting Vandalism and Violence Through Creative Writing."

Activities included a discussion of the urban sub-culture and how it ties in with the power of billboard messages, issues of sexism, and cultural politics. The visual contents of popular music videos were decoded. The discussion also included a critique of Boston journalism and an expository exercise on what young people think is wrong with the print media. The conference used poetry and creative and journal writing as vehicles for the youth to constructively express their feelings about the inner city.[38]

Melvin H. King, organizer of the Community Fellows Program Youth Conferences.

In 1993, MIT hosted the Fourth Annual Martin Luther King, Jr. Youth Conference—"Revolution: The Untold Story." Workshop topics included the leadership of individuals (young and old) who work or collaborate with youth as they strive to realize their dreams; an examination of the labels and stereotypes society places on individuals; and a session on how to deal with the issue of race while promoting change. Workshops also addressed the effects of domestic violence on victims, young people, and families; what we can do to encourage change and improvement in our communities and schools; how our peers have taken the initiative, and how we can do the same.

Also presented was a model educational video for young people made by a diverse group of eighth graders, documenting their thoughts and concerns about violence in their lives and communities. The video examines war, violence, racism, and growing up with violence and police brutality. These workshop discussions allowed us to exchange our ideas about what we can and want to do—how to create a Revolution.[39]

In 1994, the Fifth Annual Martin Luther King, Jr. Youth Conference—"Realizing the Dream Through Poetry and Hip Hop: Bringing out the Poet in You"—was an important event for our youth because it addressed issues of the King era in the context of the 1990s. The workshop topics included: "Hip Hop 21st Century Educational Program"; "Youth Speak Out on Hip Hop: Continuing the Dream Through Hip Hop"; "Bringing Out the Poet in You"; "Exploring Hip Hop Through Politics and Technology"; "Hip Hop: An Expression of Cries for Social Change"; "Monologues, Poetry and Humor"; and "Hope for Youth Poetry Workshop."[40]

•

THE MLK VISITING SCHOLARS PROGRAM

On December 29, 1988, President Gray appointed an Institute Committee to review our Martin Luther King, Jr. memorial activities. The Committee was chaired by Professor Robert W. Mann. Other members were Mr. Ronald S. Crichlow, Professor Carl W. Garland, Ms. Yvonne L. Gittens, Dr. James E. Hubbard, Jr., Professor Frank S. Jones, Professor Royce N. Flippin, Jr., and Mr. Ephraim Lin.

The charge of the committee was "to review our experience over the past fourteen years with the Martin Luther King, Jr., Memorial Service and the occasional, associated public lectures." In addition, the Committee was directed to "consider how the Institute could, in the future, call community attention to the life, work, and contributions of Dr. King, and it should make recommendations on the nature and frequency of appropriate memorial activities."

The findings, criteria, and recommendations were developed over the spring semester, 1989. Although there were several key findings, it is important here to include the following from the final report:

> Our future MLK Memorials should both celebrate MLK
> and African Americanism while also engaging white
> Americans with subject matter of substance and impact.
> Our events of the past fifteen years have, in fact, accom-
> plished the former, but by-and-large have not achieved
> the latter. While the Committee feels that enlisting a
> nationally prominent speaker who can address one or

Co-chairpersons of the MLK Planning Commitee from 1975 to 1994, from left to right, Isaac M. Colbert, Yvonne L. Gittens, Clarence G. Williams, Michael S. Feld, Leo Osgood, and Royce N. Flippin, Jr.

another of the concerns which Martin Luther King and MIT share, and who can draw a large and responsive audience, we must not in the process abandon aspects of the format which for the past fifteen years have been an essential and uplifting experience for our Afro-Americans. It would appear that at least for the foreseeable future we need to expand the celebration to include aspects of our past celebrations, but add the prominent-speaker event focusing on a joint MLK/MIT topic.

The Committee defined several key factors essential for the success of this endeavor:

To recruit an appropriate person mandates the existence of an appropriate budget for honorarium, travel, and related hospitality and reception expenses. To most effectively develop and transmit the theme chosen by the "Martin Luther King, Jr. Lecturer," his or her presence on campus should not be limited to just the event, but rather

should extend before and after the event by perhaps a
week. We understand that there is at present no specific
budget allocation for the MLK celebration. We recommend the assembly of an appropriate budget estimate and
either a specific annual appropriation or the establishment
of an endowment, the proceeds of which would cover the
annual costs. The solicitation, establishment, and existence of such an endowment fund would insure the
furtherance of our celebrations and enhance the visibility
and evidence of MIT's commitment to share in and
achieve Dr. King's aspirations.[41]

The Committee's recommendation to augment the celebration
to include a "prominent-speaker event focused on a joint MLK/MIT
topic" paved the way for the enactment of the MLK Visiting Scholars
Program.[42] The Martin Luther King, Jr. Planning Committee of 1991
consequently became the first to organize the MLK Visiting Scholars
Program. A subcommittee comprised of Professor Frank S. Jones
(Department of Urban Studies and Planning), Judy Jackson (Associate
Dean of Student Affairs and Director of the Office of Minority Education), Professor Mark S. Wrighton (Head of the Department of Chemistry and shortly thereafter Provost), Yvonne L. Gittens (Associate
Director of Student Financial Aid),
and Dr. Isaac M. Colbert (Associate Dean of the Graduate School)
undertook the major organiza-
tional tasks.

Henry C. McBay, First MLK Visiting Scholar (1991)

The MLK Planning Com-
mittee of 1991 selected Dr. Henry
C. McBay of Atlanta, Georgia, as
the first MLK Visiting Scholar at
MIT. Dr. McBay was a retired
professor of chemistry at
Morehouse College, Dr. King's
alma mater. He was proclaimed
"one of the nation's leading edu-

*Henry C. McBay, First MLK
Visiting Scholar.*

*Mark S. Wrighton (left) congratulates Henry C. McBay at a dinner
honoring the first MLK Visiting Scholar as US Secretary of Human Services
Louis Sullivan and Charles M. Vest look on.*

cators of African Americans" by Provost Mark S. Wrighton, who in
December 1990 introduced this gala symposium and other related
activities to the faculty at MIT.[43] The four-day program consisted of
several activities honoring the contributions of Dr. McBay, particularly
the crucial role that he played "for more than 40 years as an undergraduate teacher in inspiring, helping, and driving 43 Morehouse
students to go on to get Ph.D.s in chemistry."[44] Dr. Kenneth R. Manning,
Professor of the History of Science at MIT, provided a memoir of
McBay's career and a chronology of African Americans in chemistry.

Three scientists, "including MIT's first African-American Ph.D.
in chemistry, Dr. William Knox. Jr., Class of 1929" took part in an open
discussion.[45] In addition, ten papers were presented by Dr. McBay's
students. Dr. McBay visited the local high school, Cambridge Rindge
and Latin High School, which included students enrolled in the Massachusetts Pre-Engineering Program (MASSPEP), a program designed to
encourage minority students to enter scientific and quantitative fields.
The program culminated with an elegant banquet that featured one of
Dr. McBay's prize freshman chemistry students, the Honorable Dr.
Louis Sullivan, U.S. Secretary of Health and Human Services.[46]

Jeffrey P. Howard, Second MLK Visiting Scholar.

Jeffrey P. Howard, Second MLK Visiting Scholar (1992)

In 1992, the MLK Scholar selected by the committee was Dr. Jeffrey P. Howard of the Efficacy Institute in Lexington, Massachusetts. A distinguished psychologist and nationally known educational consultant, Dr. Howard lectured on his philosophical premises and the experiences that he and his staff have had in assisting educational institutions, school systems, and social agencies. Dr. Howard's efforts have centered on creating mechanisms that enable organizations to operate in such a manner that they convince practically every child he or she can learn. The following comments regarding some of Dr. Howard's views were quoted in the Institute's newspaper, *Tech Talk*, at the time of the announcement of his address:

> Dr. Howard's views on what he has called the social construction on intelligence have been widely reported and commented on. William Raspberry, columnist for the Washington Post, for example, wrote recently: "Howard is convinced that no matter what we say, most Americans believe only a small percentage of children are bright enough to become well educated. And since we also have tests that purport to identify this blessed few, we can begin early on to separate the bright sheep from the dim goats. . . . Jeff Howard, of the Efficacy Institute in Lexington, Massachusetts, won't dispute that some children are brighter than others. But he is insistent on his view that virtually all children can learn—and that the reason so many of them don't is that we made them believe they can't.[47]

Although the presence of Dr. Howard on the campus did not have the focus of the first MLK Scholars Program, his message was well received. He outlined programs widely implemented as a result of his research on the social construction of intelligence and motivation, programs that have inspired educators and raised the aspirations of students.[48]

Vincent Harding, Third MLK Visiting Scholar (1993)

The third Visiting MLK Scholar was Dr. Vincent Harding, who has made numerous contributions in civil rights, education, religion, and scholarly writing. Dr. Harding was introduced to the Planning Committee by Professors Willard R. Johnson and Melvin H. King. He had held the position of

Vincent Harding, Third MLK Visiting Scholar.

Chairperson of the Department of History and Sociology, Spelman College, Atlanta, Georgia (1965-1969); Director of a Library Documentation Project at the Martin Luther King, Jr. Memorial Center, Atlanta, Georgia (1965-70); Director of a New Institute of the Black World, Atlanta, Georgia (1969-1974); visiting professor at Temple University (1974-75), the University of Pennsylvania (1976-77), and Swarthmore College (1985-86); and several research positions.

At the time of his visit, he was Professor of Religion and Social Transformation at the Iliff School of Theology of the University of Denver, a post he had held since 1981. He had lectured widely in this country and overseas on history, literature, and contemporary issues. He and his wife, Rosemarie Freeney-Harding, conducted workshops and led retreats on the connections between personal spirituality and social responsibility.

Dr. Harding has not only lectured widely, but is also a prolific writer. His essays, articles, and poetry have been published in books, journals, and newspapers. Two of his books are *The Other American Revolution* (1980) and *There Is A River* (1981), the first of a three-volume history of the black struggle for freedom in the United States. His two visits to the campus in 1993 included a talk at a forum, a discussion with

MIT presidents during the twenty years of MLK celebrations, from left to right, Jerome B. Wiesner, Paul E. Gray, and Charles M. Vest.

the Community Fellows Program participants, interaction with students from Cambridge Rindge and Latin High School, and various seminars on the "Eyes on the Prize," a production of Blackside, Inc., for which Dr. Harding and his wife were senior advisors.[49] His visit was well received on campus, as well as by young scholars from other local universities and colleges who came to hear him.

•

The message conveyed by all of these speakers and lecturers is that we must continue to emphasize the principles by which Dr. Martin Luther King, Jr. lived his life, and to work hard for their implementation. As Coretta Scott King said in her speech on February 11, 1994: "[Dr. King] saw America not as a melting pot, but as a vibrant mosaic of people of all races, religions, and ethnic groups. We need not surrender our group identities, he felt. Instead, we could weave them into a cooperative and mutually supportive framework."[50]

Over the years, educational institutions—and particularly those in higher education—have been in the vanguard of developing the technical, intellectual, and cultural knowledge and experience of our youth. We in the academic world must address societal problems as they relate to changing demographics. In this regard, we at MIT have dedicated ourselves to expanding our recognition of the Martin Luther King, Jr. legacy. This year, with the encouragement of the Martin

Luther King, Jr. Planning Committee and the support of Provost Mark S. Wrighton, MIT has established a Martin Luther King, Jr. Visiting Professor Program. This program will (1) recognize the work of minority scholars, (2) enhance the presence and contributions of minority scholars at MIT, and (3) honor the life and work of the late Martin Luther King, Jr. Selection as Martin Luther King, Jr. Visiting Professor is open to members of any minority group. We, at this institution, will continue to express our commitment to the causes that this great American so bravely espoused.[51]

Notes

1. Ira Peck, *The Life and Words of Martin Luther King, Jr.* (New York: Scholastic Magazine, Inc., 1968), pp. 7-20.

2. Peck, p. 89.

3. Stephen B. Oates, *Let the Trumpet Sound: The Life of Martin Luther King, Jr.* (New York: Harper & Row, Publishers, 1982), p. 494.

4. Peck, pp. 73-91.

5. Address by Margaret A. Burnham, 18th Annual Martin Luther King, Jr. Program, Massachusetts Institute of Technology, January 17, 1992.

6. "Events to Commemorate Martin Luther King Week," MIT *Tech Talk*, January 7, 1976, pp. 1, 8, and MIT News Office Press Release, December 31, 1975.

7. "Martin Luther King Observances," MIT *Tech Talk*, January 12, 1977, p. 1, and MIT News Office Press Release, January 3, 1977.

8. "Jerome H. Holland to speak at King Day Observance," MIT *Tech Talk*, January 11, 1978, pp. 1, 8, and MIT News Office Press Release, January 8, 1978.

9. "King Birthday Observance to be Jan. 12," MIT *Tech Talk*, January 10, 1979, p. 1.

10. "Dr. Martin Luther King to be Honored at MIT with Silent March January 14," MIT Press Release, December 20, 1979, biographical materials, and "King Birthday Observance Next Monday," MIT *Tech Talk*, January 9, 1980.

11. "King Programs to Focus on Progress," MIT *Tech Talk*, January 7, 1981.

12. *Ibid.*

13. "King Observance to be Tomorrow," MIT *Tech Talk*, January 13, 1982, p. 1.

14. "Lectures January 12, 13 to Honor M. L. King," MIT *Tech Talk*, January 5, 1983, p. 1.

15. *Ibid.*

16. "Events to Commemorate King," MIT *Tech Talk*, January 11, 1984, p. 1.

17. *Ibid.*

18. "King Events are Scheduled," MIT *Tech Talk*, January 9, 1985, p. 1.

19. "Panel to Discuss King 'Agenda'," MIT *Tech Talk*, January 16, 1985.

20. *Ibid.*

21. *Ibid.*

22. *Ibid.*

23. "Jackson to Speak at King Day," MIT *Tech Talk*, January 8, 1986, pp. 1, 3.

24. "Proctor to Speak at King Day," MIT *Tech Talk*, January 7, 1987, p. 1.

25. "Simmons Dean to Address King Program," MIT *Tech Talk*, February 10, 1988, pp. 1, 2.

26. "King Observance to be Held Friday," MIT *Tech Talk*, February 8, 1989, p. 1.

27. "Giovanni to Speak; Conference to Follow," MIT *Tech Talk*, January 10, 1990, pp. 1, 4.

28. "NAACP's Hooks to Speak; Morehouse's McBay Feted," MIT *Tech Talk*, December 12, 1990, pp. 1, 5.

29. "King Talk: His Times, Our Times," MIT *Tech Talk*, January 15, 1992, pp. 1, 4.

30. "W. H. Gray to Speak at King Day Celebration," MIT *Tech Talk*, December 9, 1992, pp. 1, 6.

31. *Who's Who Among Black Americans* (Detroit: Gale Research, Inc.), 7th edition, 1992-1993, p. 822.

32. "Revolution of Values Needed," MIT *Tech Talk*, February 16, 1994.

33. Address by Coretta Scott King, 20th Annual Martin Luther King, Jr. Program, Massachusetts Institute of Technology, February 11, 1994.

34. "Coretta Scott King to Speak in February," MIT *Tech Talk*, January 5, 1994, p. 1.

35. "Realizing the Dream: Youth Programs That Work, January 12-14, 1990." Conference materials and "Giovanni to Speak; Conference to Follow," MIT *Tech Talk*, January 10, 1990.

36. Second Annual Martin Luther King, Jr. Youth Conference, "Realizing the Dream: Teens, Sexuality, and Parenthood." Program materials and "NAACP Hooks to Speak; Morehouse's McBay Feted," MIT *Tech Talk*, December 12, 1990.

37. Third Annual Martin Luther King, Jr. Youth Conference, "Media, Music, Microchips and Model: What Kind of Messages Help Youth Realize Their Dreams," January 17-18, 1992. Conference materials and "King Talk: His Times, Our Times," MIT *Tech Talk*, January 15, 1992.

38. *Ibid.*

39. Fourth Annual Martin Luther King, Jr. Youth Conference, "Revolution: The Untold Story," January 15-16, 1993. Conference materials and "W. H. Gray to Speak at King Celebration," MIT *Tech Talk*, December 9, 1992.

40. Fifth Annual Martin Luther King, Jr. Youth Conference, "Realizing the Dream Through Poetry and Hip Hop," January 14-15, 1994. Conference materials and "What's Happening Around Campus This Month: M. L. King Youth Conference," MIT *Tech Talk*, January 12, 1994.

41. Robert W. Mann, "Report to the President: Review of Past Experience With The Martin Luther King, Jr. Memorial Service With Recommendations For Future Action," September 29, 1989, pp. 1-2.

42. *Ibid.*, p. 2.

43. Mark S. Wrighton, letter to the MIT Faculty announcing the First MLK Visiting Scholar at MIT, December 21, 1990.

44. *Ibid.*

45. *Ibid.*

46. MIT *Tech Talk*, December 12, 1990.

47. MIT *Tech Talk*, January 15, 1992, pp. 1-6.

48. *Ibid.*

49. Vincent Harding, "A Brief Biographical Summary, Winter, 1987"; "Harding is Named 3rd MLK Visiting Scholar," MIT *Tech Talk*, January 27, 1993, pp. 1, 7. Prof. Leo Osgood, Memorandum to President Charles M. Vest and Provost Mark S. Wrighton regarding Dr. Vincent G. Harding, 1993 Martin Luther King Visiting Scholar, January 25, 1993.

50. Address by Coretta Scott King, 20th Annual Martin Luther King, Jr. Program, Massachusetts Institute of Technology, February 11, 1994.

51. "Provost Wrighton Announces New MLK Visiting Faculty Program," MIT *Tech Talk*, January 11, 1995, p, 1, 8.

CLARENCE G. WILLIAMS has served as Special Assistant to three MIT presidents. He also serves as Ombudsperson and Adjunct Professor of Urban Studies. Dr. Williams was the first African-American Assistant Dean of the Graduate School, 1972-74, and served as Acting Director of the Office of Minority Education, 1980-1982. Before coming to MIT, he held positions at Hampton University and the University of Connecticut.

Martin Luther King, Jr. receiving the Nobel Peace Prize from Gunnar Jahn, Chairman of the Norwegian Parliament's Nobel Committee, at the presentation in Oslo, Norway, on December 10, 1964. At 35, King was the youngest ever to receive the prize.

Martin Luther King, Jr., What Does He Mean to Me?

Hubert E. Jones

WE HAVE GATHERED THIS AFTERNOON AS AN MIT community in a posture of celebration and recommitment. We have come to celebrate the life and work of Dr. Martin Luther King, Jr. and to recommit ourselves to the struggle for social and economic justice in America. This birthday celebration is our precious time to claim space to reflect on how far we have come, where we are and the distance yet to travel on the road to social justice in our nation. This is our time to consider the contributions that we are prepared to make in the weeks and months ahead. When you gather here next year for the 1976 celebration, you should be able to truly say that the spaces and social circles in which you live your life are in better condition relative to social justice and equality.

The life and work of Dr. King resonate with special meaning for each of us. For me, as a black American, he was the modern day creator of the black consciousness movement. He reminded blacks of our historic contributions to life of the nation with an eloquence beyond belief. He stimulated in us a pride in our blackness and the strength of our collective existence. Dr. King's courageous leadership strengthened our resolve as black people to stand up against racial injustice and brutality and make the forces of darkness give ground. He seared into our consciousness the idea of "going for broke." More than any other black leader of his time, including Malcolm X, Dr. King put black Americans in touch with their blackness with meaning filled with pride.

In March 1963, I first heard Dr. King speak at the Ford Hall Forum in Boston. The Montgomery, Alabama bus boycott was barely a week old. I arrived at Jordan Hall, the site for the lecture, early that evening to be assured of getting a seat. Fortunately, I arrived early because the lines leading into the hall were already long. That night, Jordan Hall was electric with an excited audience eager to see and hear this new emergent black leader from the South. After being introduced by Judge Reuben Laurie, the moderator, Martin Luther King, Jr. moved to the podium and without a note launched into an eloquent, powerful exposition on segregation in America and the non-violent direct action strategies that he advocated for the struggles ahead. His powerful oratory infused with poetic language was stunning. He lifted my pride in my blackness and my spirits to a height never before experienced. It was the night when my commitment to work for social change and justice in America was rekindled and greatly deepened. At that time I was a recently arrived graduate student at Boston University School of Social Work. That speech was an important marker in my journey here in Boston and America.

As I left Jordan Hall and walked along Huntington Avenue to catch the Massachusetts Avenue bus back to Cambridge, I was so filled with pride and enthusiasm, I felt as if my feet were barely touching the ground as I moved along. It was a profound personal experience that I will never forget.

While stimulating pride in our blackness, Dr. King made it clear that we had a humane and moral responsibility to join hands with our white brothers and sisters in the quest for social justice in America. He preached and practiced a philosophy of racial integration and would not give ground when faced with the call for separatism. His speech at the March on Washington in August 1963 eloquently and passionately appealed for a united civil rights movement across color and religious lines.

Lerone Bennett, Jr., of *Ebony* magazine, probably summed up the challenge for black America best in a special issue in August 1979. He said:

> We must rise now to the level of conceiving the black interest as a universal interest. Too many people think blackness means withdrawing and tightening the circle. On the contrary, blackness means expanding and widening the circle, absorbing and integrating instead of being absorbed and integrated. And from that perspective, it is easy to see that a philosophy of liberation requires black people to cast their light not over one thing but over everything. We must rise to the level of black hegemony, the idea that blacks must establish moral and cultural authority over the whole.

More than any black leader since the 1950s, Martin Luther King, Jr. instructed his people in word and deed about widening the circle. It is a precious legacy that we dare not forget.

Dr. King's mission went far beyond breaking down the walls of legal segregation in America. He also addressed the imperative of breaking down the walls of profound isolation that exist between racial, ethnic and religious groups. Race and racial symbols of all kinds are used as a "bogeyman man" to scare people, you and me, to stay away from others different than we are. We have been socialized to feel discomfort, at best, and abject fear, at worst, when in intimate social contact with others from a different racial and ethnic group.

So this afternoon I ask you: "What does Dr. Martin Luther King Jr. mean to you?" To truly understand the real meaning of one's life, beliefs, involvement and actions, consider what you hear at a funeral. Will we know what Dr. King meant to you? If you were able to rise from your coffin and view the people who have come to mourn your passing, would you see a rainbow of diversity or people just like you? When I attend the funerals of white professional colleagues and friends, there are usually only a few other people of color there. Often the deceased was a very progressive person supporting all kinds of important social causes. I sit at these funerals realizing that I now know how the deceased really lived his or her life. It is the people who come to your wedding, Bar Mitzvah, dinner parties and funeral who reveal the close social relationships that you had. I am saddened over and over again to learn from these events about the profound social isolation that really exists. So I ask you to think about what Dr. King means in your life. Are you living your life engaged or disengaged from people with different racial, ethnic and religious identities? On this personal level, can we make a difference if we broaden the circle of our relationships and friendships? Our lives have to be about widening the circle, not narrowing the circle. It will probably not change institutional patterns overnight, but such action can contribute to changing the social fabric in our communities in the dream of Martin Luther King, Jr.

The socialization of our youth must radically change if they are not to become dysfunctional human beings. Is it not tragic and shameful when a young person gets to college and flips out because the assigned roommate is from a different racial or ethnic group? Or when a white person gets his or her first professional job and goes into a panic because the assigned supervisor is black? Our responsibility is to change this condition in our society. Let there be racial integration in America and let it begin with me. Let this be the new song that we sing and live out in our lives.

For those of us in quest of social justice and racial equality in America, we have not yet entered upon the final road. As Bennett has said: "We must be prepared for 5, 10, 20 or even 40 years of struggle." Central to this struggle must be our commitment to change the terms of public debate in the nation. It has been said that he who changes the terms of the debate wins the debate. We must work to change the terms of public debate in our country.

The debate in America can no longer be "welfare" versus "any old job for the poor." The debate must focus on the provision of adequate income and decent jobs to support family. Dr. King's dream and the meaning of his life were equal rights for all people.

The debate in America can no longer construe affirmative action to constitute discrimination against whites. Let's face it: You cannot compensate for years of racial discrimination in employment without painful readjustments.

The debate in America can no longer be prison expansion versus funding for public education and job creation because the lack of the latter will definitely create the need for the former.

The debate in America can no longer focus on conservatives versus liberals, which we are prone to do, because we need to root out the oppressive behavior of both conservatives and liberals.

No, we are not on the final road. But we better be marching on some road in our quest for social justice and equality in America in the meaning of Dr. Martin Luther King, Jr., and not be sitting on the sidelines. In the meaning and dream of Dr. King, and I quote from the black National Anthem: "Facing the rising sun of a new day begun, let us march on 'til victory is won."

HUBERT E. JONES served as a professor in Urban Studies and Planning at MIT, and later was selected as the first African-American Dean of the School of Social Work at Boston University. Since recently retiring from that position, he remains an active leader in his roles as a popular Boston TV commentator, political analyst, and lecturer at the University of Massachusetts, Boston.

Birthplace of Martin Luther King, Jr., at 501 Auburn Avenue, N.E., Atlanta, Georgia.

Reflection of the Dream: Past, Present and Future

Walter J. Leonard

IT WAS THE FIRST DAY OF DECEMBER. The year was 1955. Dwight David Eisenhower was hero-soldier-president of the United States. Richard Milhous Nixon was vice president and the presiding officer over the Senate. Earl Warren, former governor of California, was chief justice of the Supreme Court of the United States. John Fitzgerald Kennedy and Lyndon Baines Johnson were members of the United States Senate. J. Edgar Hoover was the autocratic, self-proclaimed ruler of the F.B.I. Spiro T. Agnew had not yet emerged through the bowels of Baltimore County politics. John Patterson was governor of Alabama. Billy Graham and Norman Vincent Peale were the spiritual advisors to middle America. George Corley Wallace was an Alabama state judge, and Ronald Reagan was a late-show cowboy.

The Dexter Avenue Baptist Church, located just across the square from the Capitol Building of Alabama, had recently called a new pastor: a young preacher, a doctoral student at Boston University, a native of Atlanta, Georgia. His name was Martin Luther King, Jr.

In practically every Southern state, segregation existed by sanction of state law. Racial discrimination prevailed, or was tolerated, throughout the entire country, by the acquiescence and support of the federal government. A divided and unequal system, very much as had been prophesied by the first Justice Harlan in his dissenting opinion in *Plessy v. Ferguson*[1] more than fifty years earlier, made up the educational, economic, political and social landscape of the Old South. Schools were segregated by law in the South and by agreement in the North. Restaurants were off limits to black people. Hotels and motels had no vacancies when a black face appeared. Theaters, housing, waiting rooms, lavatories, drinking fountains, public accommodations, even lines where one bought dog licenses were segregated. Separate but unequal was the order of the day!

On that same December day in 1955, Mrs. Rosa Parks, a black seamstress, tired from a long day, took the first vacant seat on the Cleveland Avenue bus in the downtown section of Montgomery, Alabama. Rosa Parks's refusal to move to the back of the bus sparked that latent, but ever present, flame of self-worth in black people; it accelerated their demand for an end to humiliation, intimidation and brutal attacks on the *Souls of Black Folk*.[2] The Montgomery boycott was born. Martin Luther King, Jr. said that it was a drama of:

> Fifty thousand [black people] who took to heart the
> principles of nonviolence, who learned to fight for their
> rights with the weapon of love, and who, in the process,
> acquired a new estimate of their own human worth. It
> [was] a story of [black] leaders of many faiths and divided
> allegiances, who came together in the bond of a cause they
> knew was right. And of [black] followers, many of them
> beyond middle age, who walked to work and home again
> as much as twelve miles a day for over a year rather than
> submit to the discourtesies and humiliations of segregated
> buses . . . The majority of the [black people] who took part
> in the year-long boycott of Montgomery's buses were poor
> and untutored; but they understood the essence of the
> Montgomery movement. One elderly woman summed it
> up for the rest. When asked after several weeks of
> walking whether she was tired, she answered, "my feets is
> tired, but my soul is at rest."[3]

Such was the milieu into which Martin Luther King, Jr. stepped. Between 1619 and 1955, this country had worked hard at writing one of history's most sordid pages. A nation which dared to call itself the beacon light of hope for the oppressed of the world, which had declared all men equal, which had built an empire on the backs of slaves and indentured servants, which had promised freedom and equal protection for all, had declared that black men had no rights that white people should consider worthy of respect. Martin King faced a nation, founded and governed by a people who had insisted on life, liberty, the pursuit of happiness and freedom for themselves, but who held that such rights did not apply to black people.

Thus in 1955, in Montgomery, Alabama, the national and international ministry of Martin Luther King, Jr. began. It was to last nearly thirteen dangerous, exciting, necessary, tense and turbulent years. It was to permeate and span most of the experience of the second Reconstruction, and it would cause the world to witness the intense racial hatred of the Old South and the pseudo-liberal sickness of an equally destructive hypocrisy of the North.

What sort of man was this who would go forth into this modern Babylon and raise his voice against the forces of evil? What manner of man was Martin Luther King, Jr.?

To those of us who knew him and who saw him often, he was a compassionate, honest, warm, and wise individual. But we were too close and too involved to know and to appreciate the magnitude of his greatness. The domesticity of our concern did not permit us to grasp the international impact of his ministry. He used his gift of speech to its fullest. Words, to him, were to be employed like arrows, like sledge hammers, or like a soothing or curing balm. With words he could give hope to the poor, friendship to the lonely, and help the lost to find their way. He had a profound sense of, and a deep appreciation for, history. His thoughts were panoramic and his vision spanned the whole of human conduct. He had a strength born of humility, sense of purpose, self-definition, and internal balance. He was a man of his times, but bigger than his times. He was of a despised, exploited, oppressed, but proud and determined people.

Let's look at the man and try to follow him through the decisional mid-passages of his ministry. Let's look at the exacting tolls on the byways of his life. Let's listen to him call a nation and its people to live out the American promise and the credo of their religious heritage. Let us hear him speak with a sharpness and a stirring plea— sometimes in anger—but always urging his country to put aside the dogma of racists and segregationists.

I remember a meeting in 1959 when he restated his belief and strong commitment to nonviolence:

> I am convinced that the method of nonviolent resistance is
> the most potent weapon available to oppressed people in
> their struggle for freedom and human dignity. Therefore,
> I have advised all along that we follow a path of
> nonviolence, because if we ever succumb to the tempta-
> tion of using violence in our struggle, unborn generations
> will be the recipients of the long and desolate night of
> bitterness.[4]

He did not view nonviolence as some sort of passive and ineffective supplication, but as a positive force moving into confronta- tions with the status quo and refusing to be beaten by it. He said often that if one passively cooperated with an evil and unjust system, such cooperation would make the oppressed as evil as the oppressor.

> I do not want to give the impression that nonviolence will
> work miracles overnight. Men are not easily moved from
> mental ruts or purged of their prejudice and irrational
> feelings. When the underprivileged demand freedom, the
> privileged first react with bitterness and resistance. Even
> when the demands are couched in nonviolent terms, the
> initial response is the same . . . The nonviolent approach
> does not immediately change the heart of the oppressor. It
> first does something to the hearts and souls of those
> committed to it. It gives them a new self-respect; it calls
> up resources of strength and courage that they did not
> know they had. Finally, it reaches the opponent and so
> stirs his conscience that reconciliation becomes a reality. [5]

Many who followed Martin Luther King, Jr. found it difficult in the days and events of the early 1960s to remain committed to the pledge of nonviolence. At a few of our sessions we said that we had been slapped on two cheeks and kicked on the other two. Conse- quently, we had no more cheeks to turn. On one occasion, Dr. King laughed heartily, and realizing the growing discontent, he replied in his usual modulated and haunting voice that "violence must never come from any of us. If we become victimized with violent acts or intent, the pending daybreak of progress will be transformed into a gloomy midnight of retrogress."[6]

One could say of King what he said of Du Bois:

> Above all he did not content himself with hurling invectives for emotional release and then to retire into smug, passive satisfaction. History had taught him it is not enough for people to be angry – the supreme task is to organize and unite people so that their anger becomes a transforming force.[7]

He journeyed from one end of the United States to the other, leaving his footprints on the swell and sweep of a nation in conflict with itself. Like the Apostle Paul, like Isaiah and John the Baptist, he generated a pulsating and searching quickness in the hearts and minds of those who would listen. He spoke to the country about its most crippling and dangerous disease—racism. In bold, brave and challenging words he told the country:

> It is time for all of us to tell each other the truth about who and what have brought the Negro to the condition of deprivation against which he struggles today. In human relations the truth is hard to come by, because most groups are deceived about themselves. Rationalization and the incessant search for scapegoats are the psychological cataracts that blind us to our individual and collective sins. But the day has passed for bland euphemisms. He who lives with untruth lives in spiritual slavery.[8]

To those who raise the intellectual effluvia of "preferential treatment," "meritocracy," and "reverse discrimination," and who suggest that the black man's plight is his own fault, Martin King said: "it would be neither true nor honest to say that the Negro's status is what it is because he is innately inferior or because he is basically lazy and listless or because he has not sought to lift himself by his own bootstraps."[9] He told a convention of booksellers that such thinking was a "myth," and that "it is of no use to cite comparisons with other races; there is no parallel. No other group of people was brought here in bondage. The [black man] must have help to win his rightful place. And there is no section of the country that can discuss the matter of brotherhood with clean hands."[10]

The nation still has not been able to adjust to the black man's struggle as it moved beyond the call for the elimination of overt cruelty and the arresting of the "lash of brutality." When Martin King, and other black leaders, sounded the call for an eradication of poverty, a cessation of exploitation by the corner grocer and the downtown merchant, demanded entry into doors of opportunity, sought a seat in the halls of power, and argued for a redefinition and a realignment of the class and power relationships in this country—most white Americans, feeling that enough had been done, retreated from the struggle, and many of them joined the oppressor as his new gatekeeper against black entry.

Some who registered outrage against the indecent social treatment of black people found no emotional outlet in our fight for economic and political equality. Indeed, some seemed to characterize this stubborn persistence as ingratitude and looked upon our meager advancement as some sort of unfair competition. Martin King recognized these facts.

> The real cost lies ahead. The stiffening white resistance is
> recognition of that fact. The discount education given
> Negroes will in the future have to be purchased at full
> price if equality education is to be realized. Jobs are
> harder and costlier than voting rolls. The eradication of
> slums housing millions is complex far beyond integrating
> buses and lunch counters . . . Laws are passed in a crisis
> mood after a Birmingham or a Selma, but no substantial
> fervor survives the formal signing of legislation. The
> recording of the law itself is treated as the reality of the
> reform . . . The practical cost of change for the nation up to
> this point has been cheap. The limited reforms have been
> obtained at bargain rates. There are no expenses, and no
> taxes required, for Negroes to share lunch counters,
> libraries, parks, hotels and other facilities with whites.
> Even the psychological adjustment is far from formi-
> dable.[11]

Dr. King described the reason for white America's evasion and schizophrenic behavior concerning race:

> It lies in the "congenital deformity" of racism that has crippled the nation since its inception. . . . No one surveying the moral landscape of our nation can overlook the hideous and pathetic wreckage of commitment twisted and turned to a thousand shapes under the stress of prejudice and irrationality.
>
> This does not imply that all white Americans are racists— far from it. Many white people have, through a deep moral compulsion, fought long and hard for racial justice. . . . However, for the good of America, it is necessary to refute the idea that the dominant ideology in our country even today is freedom and equality while racism is just an occasional departure from the norm on the part of a few bigoted extremists.[12]

King spoke bluntly to the spewers of racist ethos:

> Since racism is based on the dogma "that the hope of civilization depends upon eliminating some races and keeping others pure," its ultimate logic is genocide. Hitler, in his mad and ruthless attempt to exterminate the Jews, carried the logic of racism to its ultimate and tragic conclusions. While America has not literally sought to eliminate the [black man] in this final sense, it has, through the system of segregation, substituted a subtle reduction of life by means of deprivation. . . .
>
> Racism is a philosophy based on a contempt for life. It is the arrogant assertion that one race is the center of value and object of devotion, before which other races must kneel in submission.[13]

It seems that every age, indeed every generation, spawns its share of pseudo-intellectuals, supported by unknown and unseen sources, to parade the erroneous, discredited and malicious racists' views cloaked in a veneer of academic garb. Strangely, these creatures of retrenchment and negativism usually get their largest audiences in the great universities of our country—in fact, many of them hold professorships in these bastions of open-mindedness. But we all know that racism is racism is racism, no matter how you market it or from whence it comes. It matters not that it might come from the White House, the Congress or the state house—its poisonous fangs leave the same, nearly incurable, scar on the body politic.

The King era saw the demise of Jim Crow, but witnessed the rise of the more sophisticated, but equally dangerous and demagogic cousin, J. Crow, Esquire. It watched the academic justifiers—sometimes called scholars—get enormous grants to redefine and restate the pernicious and erroneous theories that suggest an inferiority of the black man. J. Crow, Esquire, speaks with the two faces of Janus. He couches racism in the soft tones of sociology and psychology. He has given us a new dictionary. He employs such phrases, words, shibboleths and obscurants as "reverse discrimination," "cultural deprivation," "family instability," "low testers," "poverty-prone," "special admits," "academic insufficiency," "quotas," "double standards," "dilution of quality," "anti-intellectualism," "inherent incapacity," "dual admissions policies," "slow learners," "slum children," "urban mentality," "educationally disadvantaged," and "unqualified." He has even moved us from communities and neighborhoods and put us in ghettos. It is an unfortunate indictment on the moral fiber of this nation, that so many good people, through the acceptance, misuse and abuse of such terminology, have become pliant tools in the hands of bigots.

Probably one of the most agonizing and crucial experiences of Martin King's life involved the war in Vietnam. Here was an apostle of peace, the only genuine prophet produced in this country, by the Western world. His country—the land of his birth—was engaging in the second most despicable conduct of its existence; slavery and related actions were its first. Throughout his ministry he had spoken out against the evil of violence; and now this nation, in its mad rush to police and convert the world, was using its military might in lockstep with economic exploitation and international racism. How, he asked the American people, could a nation so blessed and endowed with physical and spiritual resources grow so callous and cold toward human life?

In the mid sixties, the United States allocated more than $30 billion—*$30 billion*—annually, to finance the destruction of Vietnam. At that time, the annual budget for the Vietnam War exceeded the yearly income of all of the black citizens of the United States. One author observed: "It is startling to realize that black income could be doubled by diverting the Vietnam war funds into the hands of black America. Without a doubt, however, such a proposal would outrage the sensibility of white America."[14]

Reliable figures indicated that the United States was spending more than $300,000 for each Vietnamese soldier it killed, while it was spending less than $54 annually on each of its citizens whom it had classified as poor. What measure of morality could one find in a nation that sent its black men to die in disproportionate numbers and at the same time destroyed the limited means available to realize some of their aspirations?

How could the country call on King to be nonviolent toward the bigots of this nation, yet damn him when he asked it to cease its reign of terror on the poor and innocent women, children and peasants of a country which had never done anything to the United States?

How could he, as a preacher, a moralist, a human being, a recipient of the Nobel Peace Prize, stand apathetic and silent while his own nation strayed away from its professed reverence for human life?

The reason that Martin King had to die is not a mystery. He had successfully bridged that communication gap which separates struggling people and permits the greedy and the insensitive to rule. His message was about forming pragmatic and workable coalitions. He had shown that everyone has a common interest in many issues. Inflation, unemployment, inequitable taxation, inadequate health care, education, crime, blight and housing are not just black issues. Such matters affect millions of Americans. They are, however, more critical when viewed from a black perspective.

This country killed Martin Luther King, Jr. The federal government, through the F.B.I. and other agencies, encouraged—indeed called for—his death. How else can one consider the queer conduct of J. Edgar Hoover? Given what we now know, J. Edgar Hoover might as well have pulled the trigger.

Some had made the observation, "The killing of Martin Luther King, Jr. was just like Watergate—first there was the conspiracy to commit the crime, then the conspiracy to cover it up."[15] Maybe the country will have the decency to investigate, and to charge and prosecute those who committed these crimes. But when one considers the enormity of this nation's crimes against black people, that between 1619 and 1968 the United States had participated in the killing of millions of black people, one wonders whether it really gives a damn about a black man named Martin Luther King, Jr. If he could be here now, witnessing the disintegration of his government, the greed, the hypocrisy, the human contempt, the rise of Superfly and the flood of drugs, liquor, and handguns and other genocidal instruments into minority neighborhoods of the country, what would he say? Maybe he would repeat a portion of his Nobel Peace Prize acceptance speech:

> I am mindful that debilitating and grinding poverty
> afflicts my people and chains them to the lowest rung of
> the economic ladder . . . I refuse to accept the idea that
> man is mere flotsam and jetsam in the river of life which
> surrounds him. I refuse to accept the view that mankind
> is so tragically bound to the starless midnight of racism
> and war that the bright daybreak of peace and brother-
> hood could never become a reality . . . I refuse to accept
> the cynical notion that nation after nation must spiral
> down a militaristic stairway into the hell of thermonuclear
> destruction. I believe that unarmed truth and uncondi-
> tional love will have the final word in reality. That is why
> right, temporarily defeated, is stronger than evil trium-
> phant. I believe that even amid today's mortar bursts and
> whining bullets there is still hope for a brighter tomorrow.
> I believe that wounded justice, lying prostrate on the
> blood flowing streets of our nation, can be lifted from this
> dust of shame to reign supreme among the children of
> men.
>
> I have the audacity to believe that people everywhere can
> have three meals a day for their bodies, education and
> culture for their minds, and dignity, equality and freedom
> for their spirits. I believe that what self-centered men
> have torn down, other-centered men can build up.
>
> I still believe that one day mankind will bow before the
> altars of God and be crowned triumphant over war and
> bloodshed, and nonviolent redemptive goodwill will
> proclaim the rule of the land.

Then pulling himself up to his full height he would proclaim to the world that we ain't gonna let nobody turn us around. And with faith in ourselves and a relentless pursuit of our God-given rights, we all will be able to join hands and say, "Free at last! Free at last! Thank God Almighty, we're free at last!"

Notes

1. *Plessy v. Ferguson.* 163 U.S. 537 (1896).

2. Title of a book by W. E. B. Du Bois.

3. Martin Luther King, Jr., *Stride Toward Freedom* (New York: Harper & Brothers, 1958), pp. 9-10.

4. Quotes taken from the speaker's personal notes.

5. *Ibid.*

6. *Ibid.*

7. Tribute to Dr. Du Bois by Martin Luther King, Jr., in W. E. B. Du Bois, *Dusk of Dawn* (New York: Schocken Books, 1968), p. vii.

8. Martin Luther King, Jr., *Where Do We Go From Here: Chaos or Community?* (New York: Harper & Row, 1967), p. 67.

9. *Ibid.*

10. June 5, 1967, at the American Bookseller Convention, Washington, DC.

11. *Supra*, note 8.

12. *Ibid.*, pp. 68-69.

13. *Ibid.*, p. 70.

14. Sidney M. Wilhelm, *Who Needs the Negro?* (Cambridge, Mass.: Schenkman Publishing Co., 1970), p. 72.

15. Bernard Fensterwald, as quoted in *The Boston Globe*, January 4, 1976, p. A1, Col. 6.

WALTER J. LEONARD has recently retired as Executive Director of Cities In Schools, Inc., in Alexandria, Va. Previously, he was a Distinguished Senior Fellow at Howard University, President of Fisk University, and Assistant to the President of Harvard University. Dr. Leonard is the recipient of many awards and honors, and is author of numerous published works, including articles in *The Boston Globe* and *The Wall Street Journal.*

Martin Luther King, Jr. meets with Malcolm X on March 26, 1964 at the U.S. Capitol. They shook hands after King announced plans for "direct action" if Southern senators filibustered against the Civil Rights Bill.

The Dream: Education Is Freedom

Muriel S. Snowden

LTHOUGH I NEVER REALLY KNEW MARTIN Luther King, Jr., I was powerfully influenced by him. I was very familiar with the philosophy and techniques of nonviolent direct action. My brother who was–and is–a pacifist of the Ghandian persuasion spent almost four years during World War II (1942-46) in the federal penitentiary in Lewisburg, Pennsylvania. A bona fide, draft-board-recognized conscientious objector, his case came up in our home state of New Jersey before a visiting judge from Florida who made an interesting statement as he pronounced sentence upon Bill Sutherland. He said: "Young man, your education has been your undoing! Four years in the federal pen." Bill was a graduate of Bates College.

In thinking about men like Dr. King and my brother, it is important to understand where they were coming from. They were strong—not weaklings given to turning the other cheek—but individuals with the courage of their convictions of opposition to war and unrestricted use of military force and their unspeakable belief in the settling of international disputes by arbitration rather than sending men out to kill other human beings.

No amount of philosophical conditioning could have prepared me adequately for the tremendous emotional experience of being part of that fantastic March on Washington in 1963, when my husband, my then eighteen-year-old daughter, and I stood with those 250,000 pilgrims in front of the Lincoln Memorial. There was no way to stop the tears which rolled down our faces as Martin Luther King's magnificent voice rang out with the passion of his dream for black and white people in America and climaxed like a clash of cymbals with "Free at last! Free at last! Thank God Almighty, we're free at last!" There is no way to describe that. You had to be there.

There were three other occasions when we had personal contact with him. During the Montgomery bus boycott he came to Boston to raise money, and, even though Freedom House was then only a poor, struggling, fledgling organization, we held a reception for him and presented him with a small purse. Later, my husband Otto joined the group from Boston that flew south to march with him across the bridge at Selma. (We had a kind of bitter joke about that because I stayed at home to march in the St. Patrick's Day Parade in South Boston.) Then, during the period when Harry Belafonte was traveling the country for the benefit of Southern Christian Leadership Conference (SCLC), my husband took a week off to help Dr. King and his assistants pull off one of the most successful affairs of all here in Boston.

Now that his physical presence is gone, these are precious and treasured memories for us. But memories, no matter how warm, how beautiful, are not enough. Paying homage to Dr. King's memory on the dates of his birth and his death is not enough. Establishing a cult around Dr. King, discussion and dialogue about whether he was a man or saint, whether he was great because of the times or whether he influenced the course and history of black people, whether his philosophy and techniques are no longer relevant—that is not enough.

None of this is enough for you and me who have had the opportunity, through a fortuitous set of circumstances, to cultivate our minds. If we are to be the caretakers and the transmitters of the substance of his dreams, we have to remember that Dr. King was concerned about equality of opportunity and quality in all areas of life—of living as well as of making a living.

And that brings me to what I pose as a question to you rather than as a statement. The Dream: Education Is Freedom? As I see it, there is no simplistic answer to that question, which carries within it the need to define both "Education" and "Freedom."

I feel we need to talk about this, but I make no pretense of doing other than to share with you a few of my thoughts, reflections based upon sixty years of being black and female in white America and upon twenty-eight years of struggling, along with my husband, through Freedom House as a base of operations, to try to make some of those things in Dr. King's dream a reality for at least a few people in Boston.

When Patricia Roberts Harris was being questioned by Senator William Proxmire on her qualifications for Secretary of Housing and Urban Development, his questions and her eloquent responses said much about education and freedom: namely, that education must be broadly defined in terms of academic training coupled with one's total life experience. Pat Harris did not mention her academic degrees, she simply reminded the senator and the millions watching the news that all of her educational background had counted for naught in her freedom to live where she chose in the District of Columbia, or to eat where she pleased, and that she had elected to use her knowledge and her education on behalf of the poor, the black, the disinherited, the oppressed. She assured him that, in her new capacity, she would continue to do so. I would be willing to wager that there is not one black person in this country, "educated" or not, who, if honest, could not echo Pat Harris's experiences. The important thing is that her head is wrapped tightly enough to remember *who* she is and *whence* she comes. On the other side of that coin, however, is the inescapable fact that without her formal training she would never have even arrived at the point of being a viable candidate for a cabinet post in the U.S. government. (Remember Dr. King's epitaph in his own words, "Don't tell them about the Nobel prize; don't tell them about the honorary degrees–just say that I tried to help somebody!")

Education in the formal sense is not in and of itself freedom. It is only one of the paths that may lead us toward it. For the past three years in particular, educational equity for black and other minority children has been the number one concern for us at Freedom House, and our involvement in shaking up the system has been part of that process. Despite all that you may have heard to the contrary, those of us actively waging this battle are not fighting for black children to share in an inadequate educational system. Our objective is to bring about changes in that system so that it does what public school education is supposed to do, at least theoretically: to provide the masses of people with the basic tools of survival in a technological society—economically, psychologically, physically, and emotionally. We work on many levels to try to bring this within reach of the black children in Boston whose only entrée is through the public school system. It must become responsive to their needs, their hopes, their aspirations. For an excellent analysis of our basic posture, I refer you to an article by Dr. Alvin Poussaint and Dr. Toye Brown Lewis entitled, "School Desegregation: A Synonym for Racial Equality" (University of Chicago, *School Review*, May 1976).

In February of 1974 Freedom House established within its structure a full-time educational component known as the Freedom House Institute on Schools and Education. Its purpose was two-fold: (1) to assist black parents and children to understand what desegregation was all about so that they could make informed intelligent decisions about their course of action, and (2) to *insist* that there be black input into the planning, decision, and policy making processes *before* they become an accomplished fact. Freedom House also joined in a coalition, which it anchored, composed of other black-run organizations and agencies, plus black individuals with educational expertise and clout. In 1974 and 1975 all of us together helped to provide community back-up and safety measures for those black parents and their children who were trying to obey a federally mandated court order by riding a bus. Simultaneously, we were grinding out responses, critiques, analyses, and recommendations in regard to the various desegregation plans, university and business pairings with the schools, and literature dealing with the legal rights of black children.

It is really somewhat ironic that we now hear from all sides the cry for "back to basics." Black people have known for years that it was not that our children are "uneducable," but that they were not learning to read and write and count. Somebody in the Boston Public School System had the unmitigated gall to say publicly that there was no such thing as inferior schools: there were only inferior children!

The search for education is a response to the thirst for knowledge, which dates a long, long way back, to the Garden of Eden perhaps. Remember the drama and the pathos of what the slaves and early freedmen went through to acquire a little education and the years of those who tried to prevent it. There is great truth in the slogan of the United Negro College Fund, "A mind is a terrible thing to waste." It was brought home so forcibly to me during these last weeks since November when 247 sixth- and eighth-grade eager youngsters, most of them black, registered for the Freedom House Workshops to help them prepare for the Secondary School Scholastic Aptitude Tests for entry into the so-called Exam Schools, the Latin Schools and Boston Tech.

And that need, that thirst, exists elsewhere. In 1974, I attended the sixth Pan African Congress in Dar-es-Salaam in Tanzania, East Africa. The real highlight of that trip was the chance I had to share in an hour's conversation with another great man, Mwalimu Julius Nyerere, president of Tanzania. "Mwalimu" (teacher) is the title this extraordinary leader prefers. As we sat and talked with him about what he saw as his greatest need, he said very simply: "Help me to educate my people." He meant it in the sense of the words of my Ghanaian sister-in-law who wrote in the preface of her book, *The Roadmarkers*: "We in Ghana must find the ways of moving into the 20th Century without importing the 'junk' of Western Civilization." If you have read *Roots* by Alex Haley, you will understand what is meant about the dignity, the warmth, the strength of the African culture. Let us not barter away our jewels for the ashes of material success as we sit mesmerized by the television tube. I feel the pressure of time and the sure knowledge that I do not have as many years ahead of me as I have behind. So there is undoubtedly some glimpse of my anxiety about the "miles to go before I sleep," and a concern about the future of our people. Basically, I have been talking with you about values of our people.

I came across a magazine article about Prince Philip, in which he responded to a question on values. He thought that people were most concerned about (1) the opportunity to be self-reliant; (2) to feel responsible for the upbringing and development of their children; (3) to feel that their own efforts will enable them to provide for their health and old age; (4) the desire to live in a law-abiding, fair and decent society; and (5) to make useful contributions to their community in one form or another. I think that is an excellent list except that I would place the last one higher up in order of importance.

The true goals of education have to do with a difficult and delicate process of synthesizing and balancing book learning with one's life experiences, in such a way that we achieve the capacity for freedom of choice and for exercising options—and doing this from a position of strength rather than weakness. It also occurs to me that it is very interesting that writers of science fiction are able to come up with exciting and creative technological concepts, but fail absolutely in conceptualizing new ways for human beings to relate to one another.

In that process, we who are black must remain part of the psychological community of black people. As long as there is oppression here at home, in Southern Rhodesia, in Namibia, in South Africa, or wherever, it unites us, whatever our status or position or achievements. We must know that the battle for equality and quality in education, as well as in jobs and housing, individual growth and development, is far from won. It is still one of freedom from want, from fear, from ignorance, from hunger, from disease. It may be nice for our egos to believe that we "made it" on our own, but nothing is further from the truth. We have ridden on the backs and the sacrifices of so many people. Our history is full of them and we must not forget.

I am unhappy with the story in Sunday's *New York Times* on "A Black Middle Class in Dixie," in which a thirty-seven-year-old black mother asked her young daughters if they remembered the Civil Rights Movement: the marches, the demonstrations, the protest. They grinned sheepishly and shook their heads, meaning "No." I feel that such ignorance is unforgivable. In any event, we who are here today are at the top of the list of those who owe heavy debts to those who have gone before. We have dues to pay and IOUs to redeem, and money is not the only currency in which we must pay them. Some of us need to seek out the facts of our past and our present, tell the story, pass it along, and hopefully, add our own part to it.

Finally, as we pay tribute today to Dr. Martin Luther King, Jr., I am reminded of the words of the poet, David McCord, on the death of a friend: "Many trees have fallen from my landscape, but this one had radiance." The radiance of Dr. King is still here in this, the ninth year since he died. It glows, it dims, but it never fades. And those of us who are committed to the substance of his dream, draw our own warmth, our hope, our inspiration from it.

Martin Luther King, Jr. drew his own strength and power from a deep spiritual wellspring, and this refrain from a hymn keeps running through my mind: "Lord, God of Hosts, be with us yet—lest we forget, lest we forget."

MURIEL S. SNOWDEN was active in the Civil Rights Movement for all of her adult life. She is best remembered for her work in the Boston area, where she was co-founder and co-director of Freedom House of Roxbury, Massachusetts.

Martin Luther King, Jr. at a news conference in December 1964.

Keeping the Dream Alive

Jerome H. Holland

I HAD THE PLEASURE OF KNOWING DR. KING AND MEMbers of his family. Dr. King's mother was an alumna of Hampton Institute and I was fortunate to serve as President of Hampton Institute when she returned for her reunion accompanied by her husband, Dr. Martin Luther King, Sr.

Dr. King was a man of destiny. His mission in life was to serve people. In our society, the normal method of evaluating a citizen's contribution to his fellow citizens requires a long period of time for the historical researchers to undertake a study and present their interpretations. Fortunately, in the case of Martin Luther King, Jr. this long time span is not necessary, as his contributions to American life were so dramatic and meaningful that they were immediately recognized. Thus, our nation today is the beneficiary of the efforts of this outstanding leader, who brought to millions of neglected and ignored citizens a hope for living, and who challenged the moral conscience of this nation. On August 23, 1963, at the March on Washington, Dr. King said of his dream for the future:

> I say to you today, my friends, that in spite of the difficulties and frustrations of the moment, I still have a dream. It is a dream deeply rooted in the American Dream. I have a dream that one day this nation will rise up and live out the

true meaning of its creed. We hold this truth to be self-
evident: that all men are created equal.

Dr. King encompassed a very challenging social design in his
search for a true meaning of brotherhood. He was a pragmatist; yet a
dreamer, whose philosophy of life was understood and recognized by
humanity. His dream challenged citizens to overcome their negativism
toward those who differed ethnically and under the frame of reference
of religion to make brotherhood and equality a meaningful reality. In
1963, when Dr. King addressed the nation through television and radio
and the hundreds of thousands of people who participated in the March
on Washington, he outlined his dream for this nation. This statement
is now accepted as one of the finest addresses ever delivered to a public
audience, and the March on Washington has been often referred to as
democracy's finest hour. To be able to achieve such accomplishments
is the mark of a truly great man.

Dr. King epitomized the Civil Rights Movement. From the
Montgomery bus boycott to the struggle for integrated education, to the
destruction of the racial barriers in public services, to the fight for
voters' rights, to the movement for better housing in urban areas, to the
rights of the workers for a decent wage, Dr. King played the role of the
pivotal leader. And being a true leader, he also recognized that
cooperation with others was necessary, and, at times, this necessitated
that he act as a follower. Thus, in a divided context, some fragmentation
of leadership became a part of the movement. This complete understanding by Dr. King of the role of individuals in a mass movement,
provided the Civil Rights Movement with a *modus operandi*, which
ensured its success in destroying legal and traditional barriers of
human dignity.

With the unfortunate passing of Dr. King, the Civil Rights
Movement lost its pivotal leader. As a consequence, the leadership
became somewhat more fragmented. Some observers have stated that
the movement, due to its changing patterns, needed to have a more
diversified type of leadership. This observation is subject to question
and debate. Editorials were also written at this time predicting the
demise and doom of the Civil Rights Movement. Such editorials were
challenged by the late Whitney M. Young, executive director of the

National Urban League. Roy Wilkins, the venerable head of the NAACP for many years, contested this interpretation. Other local and national leaders joined this chorus of protest regarding this prophecy of doom. Several of the present-day leaders, such as Vernon Jordan, Jesse Jackson of People United to Save Humanity, and Benjamin Hooks, executive director of the NAACP, maintain that, on the contemporary scene, the Civil Rights Movement is very much alive, although its focus and implementation differ from a decade ago.

The emphasis is now being placed on solidifying those gains made possible through the efforts of Martin Luther King. One must have employment to travel in dignity. One must have education and training to compete successfully for the employment opportunities and vocational promotions that are available. One must be resourceful in exercising the long denied voting rights. One must be aware and cognizant of the subtle nuances depriving people of securing decent housing, and *ad infinitum*. Thus, the dream of Dr. King is not yet completely a reality, and a major effort must be made to keep the dream alive.

There have been many statements made as to how this dream can be kept alive. Several of these include the following:

Marshall Plan Effort

The late Whitney M. Young stated that this nation should commit itself to a Marshall Plan effort on behalf of raising the standards of living of the black people in this nation. Dr. Young stated that if this nation had the physical, material and moral resources to rebuild Europe after a devastating military conflict, surely it must have the resources and desire to undertake such an assignment at home. Unfortunately, this has not been done. There are many people who believe that this type of effort is necessary to keep the dream of Dr. King alive.

Education and Training

The education and training of the people were of primary importance to Dr. King. In the urban areas where a majority of the black population live, the availability of educational resources is very questionable. Perhaps a massive nationwide effort, with the leadership

Clarence G. Williams, Jerome H. Holland, and Jerome B. Wiesner lead the MLK procession in January 1978. Following them are Paul E. Gray and Walter A. Rosenblith.

coming from the black church leaders and others, may reverse the tide, and bring some effective order to a rather chaotic condition. Such a program may help to keep the dream alive.

Attacking Problems of Social Discrimination

Dr. King stressed community cooperation and cohesiveness in attacking the problems of crime, social disorganization, health, and related matters. Brotherhood and amity were principles he continuously emphasized. Presently, the comprehensiveness of social disorganization in the inner city is at an all-time high. While Dr. King believed in a community effort, his philosophy encompassed the nation. Thus, perhaps the only meaningful approach to alleviating these social problems may be through a combination of local, state and national political leaders, buttressed by local, state and national social welfare organizations. The dream can be kept alive if progress can be made along this line.

Political Participation

Dr. King was acutely aware of the importance of the political process in improving community problems. He urged participation and the wise and select use of the ballot. While the trend in black voter participation has been improving, there is a lethargy on the part of many citizens in the black community to exercise this right and use their votes in an intelligent manner. Voter education must be oriented toward the local community as part of a national program. The dream may be kept alive providing several national organizations direct their efforts along this line.

Brotherhood

Dr. King was committed to the religious principle of brotherhood, which is encompassed in the philosophy of the major religious groups. Through brotherhood he could visualize the dream of black and white children attending school, playing together, and developing healthy social attitudes toward each other. America is a church-going nation, but is the concept of brotherhood a meaningful part of religious programs? Sectarianism, racism, and denominationalism often serve as deterrents to implementing meaningful religious principles. The dream may be kept alive through a massive national effort on a continuous basis and not for one day of one month or even an entire month.

Dr. King was committed to excellence. His commitment was demonstrated through his personal educational program which included three earned degrees. It was Dr. King's belief that he had to be well trained in order to serve and minister to the needs of his parishioners. Thus, it is important for young people to recognize the necessity of being adequately prepared for their mission in life. Dr. King demonstrated that the individual has the potential to assist in making meaningful socioeconomic changes of far-reaching significance. It is important for the individual to accept the challenge of keeping the dream alive.

I like to think that possibly we are on the first rung of this dream, as I think that there is a new day ahead for the black college graduate. One must believe, like Dr. King, that goals and objectives can be reached. It is in this context that I would like to discuss future options for the black college graduate, which were not a part of the contemporary scene during Dr. King's life.

For many years, the minority citizens who graduated from any institution of higher education were confronted with a society that placed rather serious restrictions on their levels of aspirations, especially as related to their participation in the economic and political life of this nation. This pattern of discrimination left some very deep sociological and psychological scars on the minority community and the minority citizen, especially the black citizen. The struggle for equality of opportunity was a concern to many people and groups over the years, and there remain pockets of resistance which must be continuously challenged.

The black college graduates at present have far broader and more interesting horizons than prior graduates. Yes, you have the option of selecting a career of your choice. With options open for participating in business and industry, you must move aggressively toward fulfilling your hopes and aspirations. Unless you take advantage of these opportunities, the work of your brothers, sisters and friends of past generations will have been in vain, and the legacy you are establishing for future graduates and other people will be quite dismal and meaningless.

The option to have some control of our community, which was not the case in the past, is now becoming a reality. Constructive and substantive changes in improving the welfare of the citizens in the minority community and in the larger community often come through political action. Within the past few years, a somewhat new orientation toward political action is appearing on the horizon. It is nationwide in scope and involves the political leadership complex in both urban and rural areas. The increasing number of black citizens holding elected offices is a very dramatic departure from past experiences. It is heartening to note that such positive political changes are often biracial in nature, and do not represent a polarization of ethnic groups. It would have been impossible for Maynard Jackson to be elected mayor of Atlanta, or Tom Bradley of Los Angeles, or Coleman A. Young of Detroit, without the support of all segments of the population. When Dr. Wilson Riles was elected superintendent of schools in the state of California, he had statewide support.

It is at present rather difficult to keep track of the number of elected black officials. It is reported that in the state of Michigan there are more black elected officials than in any other state, and the state of Georgia is second. There have also been significant political break-throughs in other states such as Tennessee, Texas and Louisiana. In some of these states it would have been well nigh impossible to even dream of such a change in the 1940s and 1950s. Thus, the horizons look promising, and the black college graduates are expected to take up this option and play a significant role. While this increase is commendable, it should be viewed as only the beginning. There are exciting and dramatic opportunities through the political process to set new stan-dards for improving community life.

There has been concern for many years that, within the minor-ity community, control of the economic, business, and commercial phases was not in the hands of the residents. This type of absentee control is being challenged because of the negative effect it has within the community. There is no need in this brief presentation to explore the reasons for this outside control. It is a fact of life which continues, although it is being challenged rather aggressively today, and changes are forthcoming.

Black entrepreneurship, which is a more modern definition of *Negro business,* is being aggressively pushed. (While black businesses have always existed, their numbers have been limited and they have often operated in a very restrictive atmosphere.) Black entrepreneurship is now being supported by government agencies on the federal, state and local levels. Private organizations, including philanthropic foundations, are assisting with this program. The business community looks favorably on this development; literally scores of large corporations are participating. They are making special provisions for supporting or subsidizing these entrepreneurs, and are offering special business and industrial training. This new direction is most welcomed as there are many, many opportunities available in this context of entrepreneurship.

There is now also the opportunity to expand one's career horizons internationally. Minority youth for many years were circumscribed to spend their adulthood within limited geographical boundaries. Such restrictions served as impediments in challenging the creative and intellectual capacity of these young people. Presently, unlike the graduates of the predominantly Negro colleges of several years ago, the members of the student body have, as a part of their environment, the wider horizons of the international community. Many opportunities are now available internationally in government service, in business and industry, in social welfare programs, and in private groups and agencies. Since this option has become a part of the experience of black youth only in recent years, it has been, in some instances, completely overlooked. This option must become a part of the career planning program for minority youth.

The late Martin Luther King, Jr. provided this nation with a heritage of dealing with social problems with principles based on religion and equality of opportunity. These principles are encompassed in the political and constitutional statements governing this nation. Thus, one may wonder why the lack of success in making such principles a reality remained dormant for such a long period of time. A century had passed between the issuance of the Emancipation Proclamation and the March on Washington, a century where involuntary servitude was replaced by racism, lack of equal opportunity, and second-class citizenship. These negative conditions continued to be prevalent in spite of some progressive efforts made to eradicate certain elements of racial discrimination and intolerance.

Gunnar Myrdal quite aptly defined the problem with the American social system as the *American Dilemma*. The professed philosophy of this nation (democracy and equality of opportunity) was being compromised by the actual practices accorded the black citizen. For Martin Luther King, Jr. to have been able to crystallize the voices and spirit of this nation behind the principles he espoused may be a testimony to the depth of understanding that he had of the social processes aligned with mass movements. I agree with many citizens who believe that our destiny as a nation may be governed to a considerable degree by how effective we are in keeping the dream alive.

JEROME H. HOLLAND is remembered as a distinguished educator, administrator, and humanitarian. Before his death in 1985, he held the positions of Ambassador to Sweden, President of Hampton Institute (now Hampton University), and President of Delaware State College. He was also a Director of the New York Stock Exchange and served on the governing boards of many national and international organizations.

March 17, 1963—Five-year-old Martin Luther King III having his tie straightened by his father. Coretta Scott King is seated to Dr. King's left, with son Dexter Scott, 2, on her lap, and Yolande Denise, 7, behind her.

The Dream: When Will We Overcome?

Melvin G. Brown

THE CONGREGATION OF THE UNION BAPTIST Church in Cambridge, where I serve as pastor, recently celebrated its one hundredth anniversary. I have been informed by several of the parishioners there that, while studying for his Ph.D. at Boston University's School of Theology, Martin Luther King, Jr. preached on a number of occasions at Union Baptist Church, and that he conducted his first revival meeting for this historic black congregation. There was even talk of a move to call him as pastor of this church.

But destiny had a more urgent calling and task for this brilliant son of the South and emerging champion for the cause of the black masses. And so it was, in 1954, Dr. King and his wife Coretta accepted the pastorate of a black Baptist church, Dexter Avenue, in Montgomery, Alabama, in what Lerone Bennett, Jr., in his book *Confrontation: Black and White*, referred to as "the Cradle of the Confederacy." Indeed, it was there in a hostile, racist and discriminatory environment in the state of Alabama that destiny systematically and effectively set the stage for the unfolding drama of the upsurge of the Civil Rights Movement, with Martin Luther King, Jr. as the articulate and moral spokesperson.

But just how did destiny go about the awesome and difficult task of accomplishing such a feat? Dr. M. K. Alexander, chairperson of the Humanities and Philosophy Department at the University of Ar-

January 1979—Leading the silent march at MIT in honor of Martin Luther King, Jr. are, from left to right, Clarence G. Williams, Melvin G. Brown, Josephine M. Bartie, and Paul E. Gray.

kansas Pine Bluff campus, described it in his literary study on this matter, *Martin Luther King: Martyr for Freedom.*

> It all happened because of the aching feet of a Negro lady. In the early evening of Thursday, December 1, 1955, a Montgomery City Lines bus rolled through Court Square and headed for its next stop; aboard were twenty-four Negroes, seated from the rear toward the front, and twelve whites, seated from front to back. At the Empire Theater stop, six whites boarded the bus. The driver, as usual, walked back and ordered the Negroes in the foremost seats to get up and stand so that the whites could sit. Three Negroes obeyed, but Mrs. Rosa Parks, a seamstress who had once been a local secretary for the National Association for the Advancement of Colored People, did not budge. There was no planning behind it. She refused to obey the driver's order only because she was tired. Indeed she symbolized the fatigue of a people who have been "sore" tired for 350 years.

As a result of Rosa Parks's bold action, she was arrested, booked, fingerprinted, and incarcerated. E. D. Nixon, a former president of that state's NAACP, after bailing Mrs. Parks out of jail, interpreted her plight as a "perfect symbol and test case" for launching a mass black boycott as a protest strategy against the many injustices which were confronting them at that time. A meeting was called and various civic and religious leaders of the black community gathered to discuss the feasibility of such a move. After much debate on the matter, it was agreed that a boycott of the Montgomery City Lines, Inc. was in order.

Three hundred and eighty-two days later the bus boycott was over and the victory was won, but the mass black protest movement had just begun. For Dr. Martin Luther King, Jr., the Montgomery Improvement Association and later the Southern Christian Leadership Conference were very much aware of the other crucial needs and concerns that plagued the black community. Among these needs and concerns were justice in the courts, voter registration education, equality in the public school system, equity in employment, fairness in housing, and humaneness in social relations.

In an attempt to achieve these goals and objectives, Dr. King utilized the love ethic of Jesus' sermon on the Mount and Gandhi's nonviolent techniques. Hence, Dr. King and his followers marched and sang, sat down and prayed, and boycotted and planned. The struggle was by no means easy and without conflict. Dr. King and his followers were spat upon, but they kept on marching. They were beaten with bully clubs, but they kept on marching. They were watered down with fire hoses, but they kept on marching. They were bombarded with tear gas, but they kept on marching. They were attacked by vicious police dogs, but they kept on marching. They were jailed, but they kept on marching. Some even lost their lives, but others kept on marching. The reasons they kept on marching in the face of such stiff opposition were the effective leadership of Martin Luther King, Jr., their desire to be totally free, and their belief in the comforting lyrics of that eschatological civil rights anthem, "We Shall Overcome."

Nevertheless, as the last half of the twentieth century continues to wind down at a very rapid rate, and as we gather here today in this auditorium, over a decade after the assassination of Dr. King, to pay homage to him, we as a black people still have not overcome. In the words of that modern-day prophet, Martin Luther King, Jr., as constantly reiterated by Benjamin Hooks, Executive Director of the NAACP, "We have some dark and difficult days ahead." That brings us to the rhetorical and pragmatic question of the hour: "When Will We Overcome?" But before I attempt to answer this question, allow me a few minutes to outline some of the areas in which we have not overcome.

- We have *not* yet overcome in the courts. The recent decision handed down by the U.S. Supreme Court, in the case of *Bakke vs the University of California at Davis Medical School*, dealt a devastating blow to the small gains made by blacks and other minorities in this country, as a result of the tireless efforts of Dr. King and the Civil Rights Movement. Furthermore, this decision threatens to reverse the gains made in the percentage of blacks and other minorities in the professional schools and other institutions of higher education. And we were already two to three hundred years behind in this country before we ever really got started. Also, the travesty of justice in the cases involving the Wilmington Ten, Charlotte Three, and the Boston case involving the black students from Pennsylvania who were viciously attacked on the sacred grounds of Bunker Hill, makes a mockery of the American judiciary. Yes, racism even invades the courthouse.

- We have not overcome in voter registration education. Sure, we have registered to vote in impressive numbers across the country, but, to a great degree, we have not yet learned how to treasure our votes. As an oppressed people, we cannot afford to go around with our chests stuck out saying, "I am a Democrat or I am a Republican," just for the sake of being identified with a political party. Rather, we must, very seriously, begin to hold both of these parties and their candidates accountable to our basic needs and concerns. If the Democratic Party does not respond positively to our needs and concerns, then we shouldn't throw away our votes on its candidates, and, likewise, the Republican Party and its candidates. It should not matter whether the candidates are black or white, if they don't have our best interests at heart, then we shouldn't vote for them. While I am on this note, I would like to admonish you with the following. Don't forget what happened to Senator Edward Brooke, our only black Senator in the U.S. Senate, during the last election. Don't forget the bigwig Democratic politicians who worked overtime to help bring about his defeat. Don't forget the present Democratic President, don't forget the present Democratic Speaker of the U.S. House of Representatives, and by all means, don't forget the present senior Democratic Senator from Massachusetts. And the best way that we can show our remembrance of these individuals is by *not* supporting them in the next election. Here the black ministers can play a very important role by stressing this matter to our individual congregations. For I believe that if Martin Luther King, Jr., were alive today, he would urge us to do so.

- We have not overcome in the area of employment. I know that the following statement sounds like a worn-out phrase, but, in most cases, we are still the last hired and the first fired, if we are hired at all. We continue to receive inadequate wages for our labors. Job discrimination runs rampant. In the recently published Boston Herald American's 1979 edition of *The World Almanac and Book of Facts*, the following unemployment statistics among both blacks and whites were posted. As of May 1978: a) total white unemployment rate was set at 5.2 percent; b) total black unemployment rate was set at 12.3 percent. The discrepancy between these two figures becomes appalling when we consider the fact that the white population in this country, according to the Census Bureau, is much larger than the black population.

  The unemployment figures for black and white youth are even worse: a) white youth—13.8 percent; b) black youth—38.4 percent. Dr. King observed in his classic work, *Where Do We Go from Here: Chaos or Community?*: "In a booming economy Negro youth are afflicted with unemployment as though in an economic crisis. They are the explosive outsiders of the American expansion." And the most recent unemployment statistics which were released somewhere around Labor Day 1978, make it very clear that this awful situation has not changed for the better but rather has grown worse.

- Finally, we have not overcome in the critical area of housing. We still have not acquired enough decent housing for our families, and we, as yet, cannot live in some parts of this country, even if we do have the money to do so. Unnecessary harassment and racist behavior continue to plague a number of black families in some neighborhoods, especially in greater Boston.

When will we overcome? We should overcome not merely when this nation rises up and lives out the true meaning of the Declaration of Independence and the Constitution of the United States of America with its Bill of Rights and all of its other amendments, but we shall overcome when this nation incorporates into the human framework of its existence the social and theological challenge of the Old Testament prophet Amos: "Let justice run down as waters and righteousness as a mighty stream."

We shall overcome when justice runs down in the White House and righteousness in the State House. We shall overcome when justice runs down in the U.S. Supreme Court and righteousness in the lower courts. We shall overcome when justice runs down in the national job market and righteousness in the local employment lines. We shall overcome when justice runs down in H. E. W. and righteousness in the local school systems. We shall overcome when justice runs down in the national housing industry and righteousness in the local urban and suburban communities. Until these immediate goals and objectives have been realized, the struggle must not end; the struggle must go on. For then, and only then, will the profound dream of Dr. Martin Luther King, Jr. become a reality.

MELVIN G. BROWN is pastor of the Greater New Hope Baptist Church in Washington, DC. He was formerly Senior Minister at the Union Baptist Church in Cambridge, Massachusetts.

Martin Luther King, Jr. leading the March on Washington in August 1963.

Do You Remember?

Anthony C. Campbell

I DON'T FIND ANYTHING ABOUT THE LIFE OF Martin Luther King, Jr. that was not joyous and full of hope. Even after these years, his life rings with a clarion call to do something. You all act like you are spectators, and I can't let you get away with thinking that this is the show and you are the audience. Quite the contrary. You are on the stage of history, and God is the audience. I think you better do something, even if it is difficult.

It says in the first book of Kings, the 19th Chapter, that "Ahab told Jezebel all that Elijah had done, and withal how he had slain the prophets with the sword. Then Jezebel sent a messenger unto Elijah, saying, 'So let the gods do *to me*, and more also . . .' " If you are Elijah, I am Jezebel. It tells us further that Elijah arose, ate and went into a cave and lodged there. And later, he departed from the cave and found Elisha plowing in a field and gave him his coat. If you are Elijah, I am Jezebel. Let's go into the cave and let's come out of the cave.

I don't have to go back ten years to realize that we are still in a situation where Jezebel is calling our Elijah. A few years ago, someone walked across City Hall Plaza and got beaten up with an American flag. Just a few months ago, a black couple was chased across the Boston Common—not down in Jackson, Mississippi, and not some uncivilized place in Iran—by some of our children and some of our friends. Elijah had words sent to him by Jezebel that he might be a prophet, but she was sleeping with the King. That his name might be God is good, but she spoke for royal and civil authority that he might have risen to the heights of spiritual awareness and perform miracles and dazzle people with his energies, but in fact she still had to be dealt with.

All of us have had the experience where we have been challenged by mindless, numbing authority to deny us what we thought we wanted to do. But, whenever God is going to speak through history, whenever He is going to change history, whenever He is going to move a situation, He gives you the disappointments to strengthen you.

It's an absurdity, it's a paradox, it's a strange occurrence, but I know of no changes that ever occurred in history without difficulty. And whenever God is going to line up those difficulties and lay them out, and put one in front of the other, He doesn't go to a group, He doesn't go to a committee, He finds one person. When the world was flooded with wickedness, Noah was found. When a new religion was called forth to chastise the animalism, He found Abraham. People were struggling, and He found Moses. He bypassed generations of slavery and found Martin Luther King, Jr.

Here the man of humankind called forth Martin Luther King, Jr. and made him say to a people ready to run into the cave, "There is another way to do it." The tendency in adversity is to run into the cave. The tendency is to want to say, "Where might I find security and where might I find safety in this world that is about to become unglued. When Martin Luther King, Jr. raised the issue that we ought not be in Vietnam, the President of the United States said, "You may be Martin, but I'm your President." Middle-class black folk said, "I think Martin ought to be cool. He has a mezzo antic complex. I can't go with him on this issue. It sounds communistic to me." As quiet as it is kept, he was on the verge of being abandoned. That reminds me that every time I see a white person over 30 years old, I am told that he was in Woodstock. There were 14 million people at Woodstock. I have never seen a self-respecting black over forty years old who would deny that he was in Selma, that he was in the March on Washington, or that he was in Chicago.

I saw those little thin clouds on the newsreel, and I didn't see their faces, but we all act as if we were there as full participants in the

Leading the silent march in the 1980 celebration of Martin Luther King, Jr. are, from left to right, Kenneth R. Wadleigh, Anthony C. Campbell, Joseph E. Washington, and Clarence G. Williams.

struggle. We put Martin out there on the front line by himself, and we went into a cave of despair and longing and agony and wrote prose that even now comes down to us as if it's poetry. I hear all manner of folks, racists included, talking about having a dream.

There is a mighty wind in that cave and the scripture says it was not God, and after the wind, it was an earthquake, and the scripture says that God wasn't in the earthquake. And after the earthquake, there was fire, and the scripture says God wasn't in the fire. And after the fire, there was silence, and the scripture says God was in the silence. A mighty wind has swept America and it will never be the same again. A mighty fire called the Ayatollah has burned us up with anger and his passion and desire for revenge. We sit in a cave—us, churches, and us churchmen.

Churches are strong on doctrine but light on deeds, much on creed but light on conduct, much on belief but light on behavior, much on principle but light on practice. We won't get out there and work because the cave is comfortable. We won't free ourselves from the shackles of our authority. We won't put our cross down, and just wear a T-shirt, because we still want to have it, so that we are recognized as being what we are. You are the new clergy: the engineers, technicians. Yet the fastest growing churches in our city are churches made up of highly trained, highly educated, highly literate folk trying to find something. What you have found out, as quiet as it's kept, is that a slide rule or a calculator is nothing to warm up to. You can't live by it. You can make a living, even when you cannot make a life.

Some of us went into being liberated. Too many of us have tried anything. We have tried PCP, LSD, angel dust, cocaine, and smoke. We tried TA (transactional analysis), TM (transcendental meditation), TV (the boob tube), TF (touchy feeling), TC (take compose), TJ (take Jesus). We have even tried TB, which is turn back. Now, I'm seeing people talking about nostalgia. Nostalgia and astrology bother me. They are an escape from reality.

As quiet as it's kept, the past wasn't better. In fact, I lived through it, and there were no happy days back there. I remember the times when I took fear in my heart to take a bus from Atlanta to Easley, South Carolina. We stopped in Tacoma, Georgia. We got out. They marched us around to the back window. When I asked for a glass of water, they gave me a Mason jar and a spout sticking out of the wall. That wasn't a hundred years ago, that was twenty years ago. We tried it all, and we finally came back to the notion that we are still in a cave. Because we don't leave the cave until we have a program.

I went through that period with black studies and black power, and I watched so many of us go to the Ford Foundation, trying to get a grant to finance a revolution. I watched all of us be strong on rhetoric, but light on bookkeeping, and without a single piece of understanding about the tax laws. Ron Karenga got his Ph.D. Quiet as it is kept, Howard Zinn never forgot when pay day was. We followed these uncertain trumpets and radicals, so much so, that Eldridge Cleaver got Jesus, Rap Brown is working in a bar, Stokely Carmichael is in Africa, and we are still here in America, having to deal. Our communities, like Roxbury, still consume more TV, more liquor, and more clothes than all of Lagos, Nigeria. We still graduate more people from the Boston Public Schools and the MCI Concord than we do from MIT. More black people and Hispanic people walk the corridors of jails and mental institutions than walk the halls of higher education.

We destroyed the seedbeds of black intellectualism. It wasn't Harvard University, it was Howard. Look around at the faculties of these great universities. If it wasn't for the entry-level opportunities of the great black universities, which still graduate the great bulk of the doctors and the lawyers, you would not have black manpower in the white universities.

In all of your getting, get some understanding. Folks on the block would say, "dig yourselves." Black power without a connection to balance power, skill power without a connection to economic power; truth power is unconnected power, and unconnected power is sterile. Black studies is no substitute for physics, or chemistry, or math, or accounting, or for the control of the delivery system of goods and services that come into our community. We need black physicists. We need black philosophers. We need black politicians, and we need black poets. We need black engineers and black writers and black businesses. We need a black awareness which says that the moment has come for us to seize the initiative and join this great world community.

We sit here in the cave contemplating. You've got to leave the cave. You have got to come out. The story is very simple. There is no past without a future, there is no future without a past. You cannot move forward without telling your children where you come from. The rainbow of colors as I look around this room is astonishing. And we are the picture of the future. It's time to come out of the cave. It's time to recognize that we have to tell our children where we have come from, and have to pass on to them our history. Not in the oral tradition, not with the drum; we have to sit down and write it out, so it stands.

It bothered me a few days ago when black law students petitioned the Maryland bar to drop the requirement of the bar exam. I got scared to death, imagining that I could be lying on the operating table and the man is about to operate, when he says, "Oh, yeah, they waived the exam for me because I was a minority student." When I go up before the Supreme Court, represented by that man, I don't want to think to myself that he may be one who was led under the wire to compensate for all the guilt of those white folks. They are not doing you any favor when they do that trick. They are simply assuring that you can't compete. Take every exam they have and beat them with it. Martin Luther King, Jr. came out of a black school. So did Ralph Bunche. The only thing that makes a man inferior is when he refuses to compete. When I see people getting out of college who can't write, can't fill out an application, can't even spell *application* without going to a dictionary, I know we are still in the cave.

The only purpose of religion, the only purpose of books, the only purpose of poetry, the only purpose of any of these things is that edification of the life and soul keeps us from freezing out here in this world. You get together and talk about black and minority concerns because it is cold at MIT, isn't it? We huddle together at our tables, and have our affairs, and have our fraternities and sororities at white schools because it is cold in those schools. We move out to the suburbs to get the image that we want to have, and get that platform on which we can profile, and get that split level, air conditioned view of the world. Then we find out that our children are growing up needing therapy because we gave up the church, needing psychoanalysis because we gave up the barber shop (which everybody knows is a source of all wisdom). We gave up the corner where we can hang out and be recognized as human beings in exchange for the shopping mall where our kids buy a "fix" and a "joint." We are out there freezing to death. If you want to honor Martin, you have got to realize where the source of his warmth came from. You may disagree with everything else I have said, but Martin *was* a product of the black church, a product of the richness of hymn singing, and the richness of its life. Martin kept from freezing to death out here because he had something to keep him warm.

A man came to the church to take care of an icy sidewalk. He put down a little sand, stood back from it for a minute, and put down some salt. Then he went over to the truck and got a little bag, and he just sprinkled a little bit of it on the ice. I was paying him to remove the snow, and it didn't look like he was doing a lot of work. So I said, "What you doing, man?" He said, "The sand will give it some grip until the salt can melt the ice, and the other stuff I put down is halite. That's just to lower the freezing temperature, so that when it gets cold tonight, it won't freeze again."

A little ice is called racism. A little salt is called intellectualism, it melts it for you if you apply it. But the spiritual, the God-given and the God-inspired gospel, keeps you from freezing overnight as you come out of the cave. It keeps you from freezing as you work toward a Ph.D. It keeps you from freezing as you go up the career ladder, and it keeps you from freezing as you find out that, with all of it, you are still one of those sons of King.

ANTHONY C. CAMPBELL is Professor of Preaching, and Preacher in Residence at Boston University. He was Senior Minister at the Eliot Congregational Church in Roxbury, Massachusetts, at the time he gave his MIT address.

Martin Luther King, Jr. on NBC's "Meet the Press" in August 1967.

King: What Progress Since the Dream?

LeRoy Attles
Samuel D. Proctor

LeRoy Attles

THE ULTIMATE TEST HAD NOT COME. The March from Selma to Montgomery had not taken place. Little did I know that the March on Washington was a form of preparation for what was now to come. Dr. King had called the community leaders and others across the country to join him on the last leg of the march, from Selma to Montgomery, Alabama.

That day remains vivid in my memory. Even today, I can remember the hatred in the eyes and on the faces of those persons who stood on the side making cat calls, saying "Nigger go home. Nigger lovers go home. Go home, we don't want you here. Go home, we can run our own state. Go home, we don't need you here." I will admit that my body was there, but my spirit was crying out to be elsewhere, anywhere that was safe. Montgomery, Alabama, as you all know, was the stronghold of the Confederacy.

I remember how we locked arm in arm and marched down the main thoroughfare, up to the capitol building. I remember so vividly that I saw the Confederate flag waving, and I thought, "Lord, where am I now?" It was a very difficult time. It was hot and fevers were raging. And we walked up to that capitol and made our protest. There was no indication that anybody was going to turn around, and all ministers from all denominations and persons from all walks of life were locked arm in arm as we walked down that street. I happened to be at the end, and there were persons spitting on us, as we proceeded from that place. I say to you that those were some very difficult and frightening days.

In those days, it was the spirit that when you saw another brother, there was no hesitation to speak. As a friend of mine and I disembarked from an aircraft in Jackson, we walked into the terminal, and there were two brothers who came up to us. One was Charles Evers, whose brother Medgar was one of the first to fall in the struggle. He asked if we had any place to stay that night. We told him no, that we were on our way to western Mississippi to see about a Student Nonviolent Coordinating Committee (SNCC) program that our churches were supporting. So it happened that we had dinner that night with Charles, and he helped us to find lodging. I remember very vividly driving down the highway, and Charles was trying to determine which motels had not been broken down (meaning those places where black people could now stay). I don't profess to having any bravery at that time, but we finally stopped at a motel, and Charles said, "Well, we haven't broken this one down. Why don't you fellows go in there?" Well, we had to make some calls, and put some things in order at this particular motel, but it was cleared, and we spent the night there.

The next day, we rented a car and went out to western Mississippi. Mississippi was a very difficult state. That night, when the SNCC workers were looking for a place for us to stay, we had to hide our car, rustle off to a side road, and down beside a creek before we finally got lodgings. We knocked on the door very quietly. A lady came to the door and said, "This is where you ministers will be staying tonight." It wasn't a time when you used your turned back collar, because it seemed at that time that ministers were on the hit list. It was better to camouflage yourself and be natural and normal. Sometime during that night, the townspeople became concerned for our lives, because those in authority knew we were there. Someone tapped on the door about 3 o'clock that morning, and we put on our clothes and left that town. This is the way it was, as we attempted to serve in that state. The hope that was generated in Washington two years before had made it possible to tolerate. The dream was in process. The dream that proposed to make America one nation under God was unfolding right before our eyes. What was the dream? What was Washington about?

I can recall my alarm clock going off at 2 A.M. I shut off the alarm and lay still, thinking about my pending trip to Washington. I got up, dressed, and made preparations to leave. About forty-five minutes after the alarm rang, I was looking in on my nine-month-old daughter, kissing my wife good-bye. I always knew that my wife suffered a profound sense of ambivalence from my involvement in the Civil Rights Movement. It was a risk that all civil rights workers faced. There was no question that something could happen at anytime. I met one neighbor, Ray, from across the street and another neighbor, Steve, across the hall. We got into my car and we drove to Washington, DC. We estimated a four-hour drive from New Jersey, which would put us there about 7 A.M.

When we drove into Washington, about seven o'clock, the streets were deserted, except for the security forces and a few marchers. We stopped at a coffee shop, and the three of us ate breakfast and speculated on what kind of a day we thought it would be. It must have been 8:30 A.M. or so when we finished breakfast and started to make our way towards the Lincoln Memorial, all the time listening to a pocket radio we had brought along. As we walked around in the Washington monument area, the atmosphere seemed to change with a special kind of excitement. Later on that morning, the news commentator reported that the buses were bumper to bumper moving through the Baltimore-Washington tunnel.

The mood had intensified. The atmosphere had taken on a new kind of lightness that generated a feeling I will never forget—a feeling that I hadn't felt before or since. The psychological climate was charged with a pervasive feeling of goodwill towards men. Courtesy was at its best. The slightest inadvertent bump was met with an "excuse me," or "pardon me." Special care seemed to have been taken not to offend or to be offensive to anyone. It was the tenor of the social milieu. For the first time in this spot in America, there seemed to be a real chance for brotherhood. The March on Washington was an extremely valuable experience, an unusual experience for all of us who participated. Here, together, were human beings of every hue: Protestant, Catholic, and Jew. There were few unrepresented religious groups, if any.

Barriers had been let down for this day. Organizations of all kinds had come together at that time. Who was there? A. Philip Randolph, Father of the March, President of the Negro American Labor Council, AFL-CIO, and International President of the Brotherhood of Sleeping Car Porters; Roy Wilkins, Executive Secretary of the National Association of the Advancement of Colored People; Whitney M. Young, Jr., Executive Director of the National Urban League; James Farmer, National Director, Congress of Racial Equality, and Executive Director of the National Catholic Conference of Interracial Justice; Rabbi Joachim Prinz, President of the American Jewish Conference; Dr. Eugene Carson Blake, Vice Chairman, Commission on Religion and Race of the National Council of Churches, and Executive Head of the United Presbyterian Church of the United States of America; Walter Reuther, Vice President and Head of the Industrial Union Department, AFL-CIO, President of the United Auto Workers Union; John Lewis, Chairman, Student Nonviolent Coordinating Committee; Bayard Rustin, Deputy Director, March on Washington; and, of course, a most esteemed brother, Martin Luther King, Jr., President, Southern Christian Leadership Conference.

Yes, it was a special day for America. We were all there lodging a protest against racial inequality, and, while there, heard the content of a dream that could make America one people. The Bible informs us that young men shall see visions and old men shall dream dreams. Therefore, there must be something special when a young man like Dr. King dreams a dream.

In the book of Genesis, we read about Joseph, the dreamer. Dreams, when told, got him into all kinds of trouble initially, but

January 1981—Leroy Attles, Paul E. Gray, Priscilla K. Gray, and Clarence G. Williams lead the procession to Kresge Auditorium to celebrate the life of Martin Luther King, Jr.

ultimately came true, and made Joseph and his brothers one. The Pilgrim fathers had dreams that they could come to a land, be free, work and worship God under their own vine and fig tree. So they settled in this country. The very Commonwealth of Massachusetts became a haven for puritans escaping their homelands for the purpose of economic and religious freedom. But unfortunately, their preoccupation with self and wealth made them insensitive to freedom and justice for all. This dream became a nightmare for scores of slaves who were brought thereafter. The puritans forgot that the freedom they sought was the same freedom that all men seek. They forgot that the opportunities they wanted for themselves were the same opportunities that other men wanted. Despite the amnesia of our founding fathers, and the perpetuation of that memory loss to this very day, the dream can still make us one people.

If you recall, the loss of a dream is not an accident. Lillian Smith, in *Killers of a Dream*, tells of persons who consciously and laboriously train the children in the ways of segregation. Dreams must be attended, if they are going to live. Dreams must be worked at, if they are going to be vital. The dream that Martin Luther King, Jr. had for America was not his own, but the dream for all America, because that dream could make us one. The reality of the dream is not easy. Frederick Douglass, in 1857, wrote that:

> All concessions yet made to an august cling have been
> born of earnest struggle. If there is no struggle, there is no
> progress. Those who profess to favor the freedom, and yet
> deprecate agitation are men who want crops without
> plowing up the ground, they want rain without thunder
> and lightening, they want the ocean, without the awful
> roar of the many waters. This struggle may be a moral
> one, or it may be a physical one, or it may be both moral
> and physical, but it must be a struggle. Power concedes
> nothing without a demand. It never did, and it never will.
> Men may not get all that they pay for in this world, but
> they must certainly pay for all they get. If we are to get
> freedom from pressure and wrongs heaped upon us, we
> must pay for their removal. We must do this by labor, by
> suffering, by sacrifice, and if need be, by our lives and the
> lives of others.

King said that he had gone to the nation's capital to cash a check that was in the form of a promissory note to which every American was to fall heir, that all men would be given a guarantee of their inalienable rights of life, liberty, and the pursuit of happiness. But here we sit, a decade plus, with that same note, standing in line at the bank of justice waiting for the doors of justice to open for us. We have already received a statement in the mail saying that the bank of justice didn't pay the note fully, and even levied a service charge for our request of payment with insufficient funds. The question that might be posed to us today is: Do we knock on the door of opportunity for ourselves, or wait for opportunity to knock on our door?

The genius of King was that his whole nonviolent confrontational approach left authorities stymied and confused. The reason was that King was espousing the rights and privileges that they were supposed to represent. The United States government could not argue in clear conscience that there was something wrong with people seeking life, liberty, and the pursuit of happiness. This was an unusual kind of revolution. It did not address itself to the overthrow of the government, rather it addressed itself to perfecting the present government. Here was a revolution that did not ask for any special privileges for any particular group of people. Rather, it sought the same rights that the majority of people were already guaranteed. Here was a revolution that was asking not what the country could do for its people, but what its people could do for the country. Here was a revolution that was trying to use right to gain its ends, and not using any might. Here was a man who was guided by a vision that was large enough to incorporate our presence.

Martin Luther King, Jr. said, "There is no time to engage in the luxury of cooling off or to take the tranquilizing drug of gradualism." During those long, hot summers that we recall so vividly, much of our time in the clergy ranks was spent in rallies, trying to impress upon employers and persons in government the need for all persons to be free. There was a time when ministers would speak from their pulpits on racial issues. There was a particular effort to cause Tasty Cake to hire minorities. Our leader said at the time, "We are going to cause Tasty Cake to succumb. Now, I want the ministers to go back to their pulpits. I want you to talk about the gospel for twenty minutes. I want you to talk about Tasty Cake for ten minutes." And so it was, we went back to our pulpits, and we spoke about Tasty Cake. Then we came back that same week for another rally. And Tasty Cake had not yielded. We went before them and they said, "We will not hire any black people." So the call in the rallies said, "Well, let us talk about the gospel for fifteen minutes, and let us talk about Tasty Cake for fifteen minutes." So we went back to the Tasty Cake authorities, and they stood their ground. At our rally that night, the call was, "We want you to talk about Tasty Cake twenty minutes, and preach the gospel for ten minutes." Yet Tasty Cake still maintained their ground. That very week, the call was, "We want you to talk about Tasty Cake twenty-five minutes and just mention the gospel." It was then that Tasty Cake succumbed, because the stores were stacked up with Tasty Cakes. And the last thing we heard at that time was that they were in the street looking for people to hire.

The boycott was certainly very effective. And it was a means of obtaining our objectives. King said in 1963 that this was the beginning of the end—the end of prejudice, the end of injustice, the end of racism. It was the end, and the beginning of equality. I don't know about you, but today as we think about the dream, we don't hear the enthusiastic cries of justice and equality ringing through the land. There is no longer the heart pounding, panting breath. We see a change in strategy on how to integrate the public schools. The new strategy is business as usual before the marches. We see the clear manipulation of equal opportunity employment laws, where a firm, for example, will hire a black woman over forty and claim credit for three minorities. You see cases like the Bakke case, which seems to threaten affirmative action laws.

Now we see a new phenomenon. Where are those who, in effect, say we need no Martin King to prick our conscience, to remind us that America is the home of the brave and the free. We can do it ourselves if we are righter than right. We will do it in the name of the Lord. We will wash our own dirty linen at home. What happened to the whirlwind of revolt that was shaping the foundation of our nation until a brighter day of justice emerged?

What progress since the dream for those who sat in, for those who stood in, for those who walked in, for those who had their bodies on the line, for those who lost their lives, for those who spent hours and hours in strategy sessions, for those who jeopardized jobs and other possessions for the cause, for those who sacrificed all they had for the cause, for those who were touched with the cattle prods, for those who were bitten by dogs, for those who were clubbed, for those who were knocked down by water hoses, for those who gave so much and received so little? Could all this have been done in vain?

We read in American history that a president who was elected in 1860 was gunned down with an assassin's bullet. We saw in 1963 a president gunned down by an assassin's bullet. We read about Reconstruction in the 1860s and early seventies, and somehow, in a real sense, we see the civil rights struggle as a Reconstruction period. There are very serious questions to be asked. Is history repeating itself? In the seventies, when the Klan started to ride, it brought a crashing end to the justice and the freedom that was gained by the Reconstruction period. Is it now, that we see the Klan riding again? Does history repeat itself? Frederick Douglass again speaks to us from the period after the Civil War, by saying "whether the tremendous effort was heroically fought and so notoriously ended shall pass into history a miserable failure barred by any permanent results. A scandalous and shocking waste of blood and treasure." In a letter written to the National Association of Colored People in New Orleans, April 7, 1872, Charles Sumner shares with us some very valuable and pertinent information along the same line:

> It is absurd for anyone to say he accepts the situation and then denies the equal rights of the colored man. If the situation is accepted in good faith, it must be entirely, including not merely the abolition of slavery and the establishment of suffrage, but also those other rights which are still denied or abridged. There must be complete equality before the law so that in all institutions, agencies or conveniences, created or regulated by law, there can be no discrimination on account of color, but a black man should be treated as a white man in maintaining their rights. It will be proper for the convention to invoke the Declaration of Independence so that its principles and promises shall become a living reality never to be questioned in any way and recognized always as a guide of conduct, and a governing rule and interpretation of the national Constitution being in a nature of a Bill of Right preceding the Constitution. It is not enough to proclaim liberty throughout the land unto the inhabitants thereof. Equality must be proclaimed also. And since both are promised by the Declaration ... both must be placed under the safeguard of national law. There can be but one liberty, and one equality. The same in Boston and New Orleans. The same everywhere throughout the country.... It only remains that I should say stand firm. The politicians will then know that you are in earnest, and will no longer be trifled with. Victory will follow soon. And the good cause secured forever.

As we gather on this day to commemorate the life of the Reverend Dr. Martin Luther King, Jr., the question, "What progress since the dream?" is still valid. Are the minorities the last to be hired and the first to be fired? Do we have to have some supernatural skills to gain certain spots throughout industry and the university? Do we have to demonstrate some unusual talent to be selected to serve? What progress since the dream? I think it is a question that all of us could ask ourselves, understanding that if there has been no progress, there has been no struggle. We need to remember that the Reverend Martin Luther King's dream can be our dream, but only if we put legs on it, only if we put lips on it, only if we put our bodies in the way, only if we commit ourselves to a dream. For if we do that, Dr. King's dream can truly make us one, a nation under God, dedicated to liberty and justice for all.

 LeROY ATTLES is Senior Minister of the St. Paul African Methodist Episcopal Church in Cambridge, Massachusetts. Dr. Attles has served as Chairman of the Board of Examiners for the New England Conference of the A.M.E. Church, Vice Chairman of the Board of Christian Education for the First Episcopal District, and on many community boards and committees in the Boston and Cambridge area.

Samuel D. Proctor

ARTIN LUTHER KING, JR.'S LIFE WAS SO
deeply involved in social ethics. In order to lead you into a discussion
of the dream and what has happened since, let me talk about King as the
right man, at the right place, and at the right time. It is not easy for
anyone who is close to a person like King to make an assessment of him
that's fair.

A singer can hardly be measured by his or her contemporaries.
We can never have it both ways on the one hand, to enjoy the personal
warmth and the clear resonance of a human voice, and then to feel the
vibration of a motion and the touch of the hand or to observe every
arching of the eyebrow; and, on the other hand, to see the same person
painted on the canvass of time, and evaluated by the sages and scholars,
scrutinized by the psycho-historians, and tested by the vestiges of the
passing years. We are just too enwrapped by the presence and our
involvement in the moment. At a distance, we see these persons with
an informed kind of vision, and we assess them with a trained eye.
Nevertheless, let me try to comment on King as a friend and as a
colleague close up, and as a participant in the long pursuit of his dream
for the past twelve years since his untimely death.

It is a very special privilege for all of us, because he embodied
so much of what we ought to be celebrating, cherishing, reflecting upon
constantly as citizens in a free society that holds the promise of matur-
ing into a genuine, humanized community someday. The only way to
remember King is to see him in the context of the struggle that possessed
him. For all of his life he was possessed, and he was engaged. He laid
down his life in Memphis in April 1968 for the cause of justice,
compassion, and human dignity. This ought to be the reason for
remembering him, to be inspired to renew our commitment to these
very ideals. I suppose that this year, we come upon his birthday with
a keener awareness and with a poignancy that goes far beyond the

perfunctory remembrance of the revered deceased. The cause of justice and human dignity is current, relevant, and urgent.

The nation is now reassessing its priorities and important matters are being hidden today under some broad flat labels like conservatism, and the new right, and the moral majority. We need so much, especially in an academic community, where the truth ought to be dealt with with great care—we need so much to call things by their right names, and to see the new political reality in the light of the shaft, the beam that the great spirits such as King have cast upon our day and time. He was the right man, in the right place, at the right time.

In retrospection of the right man, King came out of the best of what I call the Morehouse tradition; and, perhaps better than any other school, Morehouse reflected the aspiration of black people for three generations before King was born. He was an incarnation of the aspiration of Morehouse men. He had a kind of hypnotic transcendence of the ignorance and poverty of the Georgia clay hills that Morehouse stood for. He was transfigured into a new view of what a black person could be, a kind of Morehouse intoxication. He was the right man. He was a Morehouse man who believed what the old white teachers, in general, brought to the freedmen of the South during the Reconstruction from Brown University, Oberlin, Dartmouth, and Andover Newton. Small effort, but ever so productive in sending people to teach religion, philosophy, and ethics in the black colleges founded during the days of Reconstruction.

These teachers came to guarantee that the free black person would be properly inducted into the cultural ethos of the Anglo-Saxon community in America. Whether this was good for free black people or not, is not the question. The teachers also came South to guarantee that black souls were saved, whatever that meant in that day. They wanted them to be saved for the proclamation of the Christian gospel.

Virginia Union, founded in the mid 1860s, started in a jail for former slaves. No one would sell real estate for a black college. The whipping posts were turned into lecterns, and the cells into classrooms, and the whole yard where they rounded up the slaves and beat them, was turned into an assembly area.

This is one of the chapters in American history that should be revived. We've forgotten that this was not an office of economic opportunity. There was no government or program requiring this. The Freedmen's Bureau set up some money for it, but this was a missionary activity of the Protestant denominations to establish these schools. These schools were founded at a time when black people had no friends, and no public-school education. And many of these schools had to function as elementary schools and colleges. They called them universities, but they were everything. At Morehouse, one could go there at age nine and stay through the bachelor of arts degree.

I would call this the period of *disintegration* for black people. Disintegration means that for the first time they were separated from the *integer*, from the plantation society, where they were a part of the whole. They were present, close by making the beds, cooking the biscuits, brewing the whiskey, nursing the babies, chopping the cotton, and planting the tobacco—taking all of the tedium out of life. They were so close by that—like it or not—they absorbed that Anglo-Saxon Protestant culture. They learned to sing the hymns and to use the language. And incidentally, when I hear people talking about black English—this English was first poor-white English of the South. It's rural talk. It's the talk that black people learned when they had to be close to uneducated white people, who supervised them. Some of the preaching that we hear in some of the ghetto churches seems like something we invented. If you go across the deep South and keep your radio turned on, you can hear that kind of preaching from poor white people—all through the Ozarks, and the Appalachian region. Black people absorbed the culture of the rural South, lock, stock and barrel.

And suddenly with the Emancipation, they were taken from that environment and pushed up to one end of the county, or pushed across town or the railroad tracks—a time of great *disintegration*, with no money, no friend, no power, and no land—to acculturate themselves to the larger society. So after this period of disintegration, they scattered to Boston, Kansas City, Buffalo, and Toronto, wherever they could find freedom.

Then they went into a period of what I call *acculturation*, trying to survive, and almost begging the larger society to accept them. Some

of the college programs from this period, 1885 to 1905, imitated everything that was done at the larger universities. They had people right off
the cotton fields learning Greek, Hebrew and Latin. And they were
singing all of the great arias from the Italian operas, and the chants from
the Gregorian church. They were going through all the motions of
saying, "Look, we are human, can't you see?" It was a period of extreme
innocence when black people were saying you stripped us of our
African culture. And in the midst of this period of acculturation, two of
the great minds parted ways.

Booker T. Washington thought that the best way to acculturate
was to get some money, to learn how not only to build a brick house but
to make the bricks, not only how to paint a fence or a wall but how to
make the paint. He took the Hampton Institute illustration and carried
it even further at Tuskegee Institute. His idea of political and social
equality, however desirable, was started at the wrong time and place.
He said "You are too poor to be reciting poetry, talking about the opera,
or pushing people to vote." And Washington was taken to be one of the
biggest Uncle Toms of the day. Monroe Trotter and W. E. B. Du Bois and
others just hated him because he accommodated himself so easily to
that which white people found comfortable.

Other schools were teaching people how to study philosophy
and rhetoric. Washington said, "Put that down for the moment and
learn how to do something with your hands and get some money, and
some land and some property, and then start learning poetry and the
symphony." One wonders today, while driving through Harlem
seeing so many young black people unemployed and without skills, if
we didn't put down all of Washington too fast.

At that speech in Atlanta in April 1895, where he compromised
and practically said to the whole white community:

> We are not going to push it on you, we are not going to
> bother you about political and social equality, but let
> down your buckets where you are among your black
> friends. We are the best friends you have. Let down your
> buckets where you are. You don't know these other white
> people who have just come. [The Irish and Italians] have
> another religion—Catholicism. They don't know you, you

don't know them. But you know us, let down your bucket among us.

He was pleading for economic cooperation. Then he said to the black people, and he overstated the case:

> The white man of the South is your best friend. You plowed the fields with him, etc. You let down your buckets where you are, and don't go running up North where there are people you don't know.

He was trying to say to the South, come on, get together on economic things first, and put the other things aside.

And incidentally, while he was speaking, there was a big, fancy, passenger coach right behind him with all of the wheel work and all of the leather work, and the velvet. The whole thing was built by Tuskegee students. Washington stood there to show it off at this exposition—what Tuskegee students could do. You know in those days, when you went to an exposition like that, you would advertise your products. It was a big thing to be asked to make a speech at a fair like that. So here was the cotton exposition of the South, and everybody was supposed to show what he could produce. Washington brought this coach to show what Tuskegee boys could do. He was saying to these fellows who were studying philosophy and theology: "You started at the wrong place. If you want to acculturate, if you want a permanent place in American society, get some money, and some property first."

Now Du Bois, on the other hand, said: "You know that is so well and good, but what you are really doing is asking us to settle for menial labor. You are discouraging intellectual inquiry. We have a talented tenth here who ought to be trained to take the highest places in this society." Du Bois argued that the Morehouse kind of experience ought to prevail. Both men were trying to prepare black people to obtain a substantial and a continuing participatory role in this society. Unfortunately, after all of their talking and exposing all of this to the whole wide, wide world, it even got to England. At home, Washington was turned down, and Du Bois was turned down. The country wasn't ready for either of them. The period of *alienation* that followed this Washington-Du Bois debate was something awful.

When the Civil Rights Bill was thrown out in 1883 and the Plessy-Ferguson decision turned against us in 1896, the Reconstruction closed down with the Hayes-Tilden election and alienation came descending upon us. Segregation laws, a whole library of segregation laws were written around the turn of the century—1903, 1904, and 1905.

The State of Virginia, as late as 1905, invented segregation laws. After this period of *alienation* settled down amongst us, a period of *litigation* followed. In 1935 when we began to have the lawsuits regarding equalization of teachers' pay in Virginia, persons who sued were thrown out of their jobs. These lawsuits began the process by which the NAACP and Charles Houston and others won 39 cases in a row. Then came the 1954 decision that was the culmination.

Now Martin Luther King, Jr. came on the scene, just at the time that Dwight Eisenhower had asked to engage in this process with all deliberate speed. The Supreme Court gave him his language. I call this a process of *reintegration*. King was not asking us to go to the Bahamas. He was not asking us to go to Africa. He was not asking us to go to a separate part of the United States. He was asking us to come back *into the center of the society* and become a part of the *integer* again—not as a slave, but standing tall in the full height of our dignity and having equal participation with justice. Where did he get all of this idea from? I call it the Morehouse tradition that he incarnated.

When Henry L. Morehouse was raising money for that school, he made a remark that many of us will long remember. He said:

> I believe in the thorough humanity of the black man,
> capable of culture, capable of high attainment with
> sufficient time and under proper circumstances, not a
> being fore-ordained to be a hewer of wood and a drawer
> of water for the white race, predestined to irrevocable
> inferiority, but a being whose mind and soul can expand
> indefinitely, to comprehend the great things of God and to
> take a place of usefulness and honor in the world's
> activities.

That was the Morehouse spirit. King was its embodiment. King believed that the sufficient time had come, and he had the mind and soul that had expanded indefinitely. He was the right man.

The magnitude of the King movement cannot take place unless you do have the right man. The moment can come. The situation can be right, but if there is not somebody around who incarnates the ideals that ought to be brought to the fore, that moment in history will be passed. The fact that King was the right man made so much that was wonderful come to pass.

Now, consider that he was in the right place, Montgomery. Alabama State College was there. A large college established by the state, controlled by the state, where everybody had careful instructions on what to teach, what to say, and who could appear as a public speaker. It was a pitiful way in which black intellectuals had to earn a livelihood working in such places at that time, where there was no academic freedom whatsoever. This College was only one of such schools; they were all over the South. The President was almost always caught in some kind of dilemma. On the one hand, he was trying to keep the place open for young black children; on the other hand, he was embarrassed and called an infernal Uncle Tom by everybody who had to watch him. Who would want to be caught like that?

I visited a college in Mississippi that had a brand new campus. My student escort and I came upon a large tomb right in the middle of the campus. I said, "Who's buried there?" He said, "That Uncle Tom son-of-a-bitch who used to be President." I said, "What did you say? That is not a respectful way to refer to your deceased and revered president." He said, "That's what he was and that's who's there." Then later on I said, "You have a beautiful campus." And he said, "We surely do." And I said, "How far does your land go?" He said, "You see that creek way over there, it goes right over to that creek." "How far in this direction?" "It goes way over to the cluster of trees way back over there." "How far over there?' "It goes all the way over to the highway. We got all the land that we need for expansion for a long time. We are still building." I said, "Son, who in the world got all of this land and these buildings for you to have this wonderful campus here?" He said, "That Uncle Tom son-of-a-bitch." Well, now you can get on either side of that issue that you want to. That was the issue in Montgomery, when King went there. It was the right place. He was right there where black folks were caught in this dichotomy—this compromise, this contradiction, the whole range of contradictions and compromises.

In Montgomery, a black person could work for a white family and have the run of the house, be in charge of everything, preparing the medicine, bathing the baby, and cooking. Marie Annabelle had a chance to poison the whole crowd, but trusting white people knew full well that she would do nothing to hurt the family. She walked around that place as she was in charge, and her limitations only came when she left the house, and stepped out onto the sidewalk, and joined the "real" society again. But in that house, she could order people around, and tell them what they were going to eat, and what they were going to wear, and how things were going to be—all of these strange, strange contradictions.

When I was Director of the Peace Corps in Africa in 1962-63, I had to come home suddenly. Sargent Shriver sent a cable saying, "Come back right away and assume the position of Associate Director." My boys said to me, "You know, if we are going home, daddy, the main thing we have to get is an automobile." I said, "You are right, we don't want to go and shop for one; we want one waiting for us, don't we?" They said, "That's right, daddy." So I went down to the cable office and I said to my Nigerian friend, "I am here to send a cable to order an automobile." He said, "Where is your money?" "I don't need money." "You are going to buy a car without money?" I said, "You just don't know how Southern white folk relate to Southern black folk. I can buy a car without money. Selling me a car is no difficulty for them. There are other things they won't let me do. But they will sell me a car without money." He said, "What's the cable?" I said, "Send this to Mr. Paul H. Pusey, Lincoln Mercury Dealer, Broad Street, Richmond, Virginia.

> Dear Mr. Pusey, please have a 1963 light blue Ford Galaxy delivered to me at Pan Am Flight 151 with two snow tires mounted in the trunk, licensed and insured in my name. Use my mother-in-law's address. I'll see you when I get there."

One of my preacher friends met me at the Kennedy Airport. He said, "Sam, do you need a ride? Do you want to borrow my car?" "No, I don't need your car." "You have a car?" "Oh, yes." "Where is it?" "I don't know yet. But I know one thing, that white man has that car here to meet this flight." I had no doubt in my mind that the car would be there. No response needed, no nothing. That's the strange thing about that relationship. Old times, strange relationships. The man from Fort Lee Motors came up to me and said, "Are you Proctor?" "Yes." "We have a light blue Galaxy four-door, air conditioned . . ." I said, "I know you do. There is no doubt in my mind that you have one for me. And what else do you have? You have two snow tires mounted in the trunk." He said, "How do you know?" I said, "That's what I told him I wanted." Now, you would never understand this unless you lived in a place like Montgomery, Alabama, where you had no rights, but where you had a certain level of interpersonal trust, and that had to substitute for civil rights. Did you hear me? And you knew clearly what those limitations were all the time.

There was the Dexter Avenue Baptist Church, where the "big shots" came and sang out of hymn books and didn't shout and scream in church. They had always had highly educated ministers, men trained in the best schools, and they always said: "We don't want an ignorant preacher around here splitting verbs. We want somebody who can talk about God without splitting infinitives as well." They looked all around the country to find one, and here was young Mike King with a Crozer Seminary degree, and a doctor's degree from Boston University in "personalism." Well, that's exactly what they wanted. They didn't want too much religion. They wanted a Ph.D. preacher to lecture to them about some polite aspect of God. Where did all of the faculty from Alabama State College belong? At the Dexter Avenue Baptist Church. And where do you think the administration of the College went to church? At the Dexter Avenue Baptist Church. And why do you think the whole faculty belonged there? Because the administration belonged to Dexter Avenue Baptist Church. I am telling you what it was like in Montgomery when King came along.

King talked with me about the Dexter Avenue Baptist Church. He said, "Sam, you know, I have got thirteen Ph.D.'s in my congregation." I said, "That's fine, how many Christians have you got in your congregation?" He said, "My music director has a doctorate in music education. You know one thing, I have always wanted to be a preacher like Mordecai Johnson and Howard Thurman and Benjamin Mays. I always wanted to be an intellectual Baptist preacher."

King did not go to Montgomery to start a bus boycott. He did not go to Alabama to march against Sheriff Clark or Bull Connor. He went down there in his Hart Shaffner and Marx suit, and his Florsheim shoes, middle-class to the core, to be an intellectual Ph.D. Baptist preacher, and to talk like Howard Thurman every Sunday morning. Bull Connor, Sheriff Clark, Governor George Wallace, and that bus driver were waiting for him down there. That's the strange thing about that relationship. An old preacher said, "Man proposes, but God disposes."

Now you see, you have an excellent laboratory for the testing of the black cause in Montgomery, Alabama. I have tried to explain to you how we missed the point, if we think in simplistic terms that all of these black folks were sitting there being ground down and uncomfortable and too dumb to do anything about it. White people had fixed that thing so that they could be comfortable and that the circumstance was livable. Just a little bit of love and a little bit of tenderness caused people to accommodate themselves to the situation. Then Wallace came in and made big noises about it all over. So when King went, Alabama was exactly a testing for the black case in America. Geography has always meant so much with historical outcomes.

Look at what geography did. Martin Luther King, Jr. did not start his movement in New York City to be diluted by big city politics. He did not start it in Chicago or Los Angeles, but in the worst place of all, where Bull Connor used to brag that he had the most segregated city in the whole United States. So he was the right man, and he was in the right place. All of these people represented the logical extremities of the notion that black people had a fixed and subordinate place in America. And King was there, a blushing rose in this desert of negation and rejection. He was like a kind of grand mutation. You see, the social genetics had taken a strange twist and what was needed now was a kind of host vector to keep this new gene alive. Alabama had the exact chemistry needed to be the host vector for this strange mutation we know as Martin Luther King, Jr. Think of the right time.

The country settled for the safe, stable and protective prosaic presidency of General Dwight Eisenhower. A caretaker administration of eight years had kept America well manicured. They were building up the suburbs. Social change was monitored for what was called all deliberate speed. Talk about benign neglect, we had eight years of it at that time.

But all deliberate speed had no place in such a world. Justice deferred is justice denied. The whole world was groaning for a new order. Africans trained at Lincoln University, MIT, Harvard, and Yale, with deep Yoruba marks on their faces, spoke plainly of independence, decolonialism, and a new day. The NAACP had won 39 cases. It was the right time. Any time is the right time to stop oppression and to honor human dignity. Any time is the right time to correct old abuses. And any time is the right time for reconciliations and the movement toward genuine community.

And the moment came. A bus driver had no more sense than to ask Rosa Parks to move. He could not have chosen a "wronger" person to ask to move. Rosa Parks didn't chew chewing gum, didn't use profanity, didn't wear lipstick, combed her hair back in a neat bun. She sewed for rich people on the edge of the city, was active in the church, active in the NAACP, soft spoken but hard as a rock on what she thought. She was a person of dignity.

In those days, the buses filled up from the front with white people and from the back with black people. Rosa Parks sat just a little too near the front. All the people got on and when the bus got to town, there she was sitting too close to the front. Had that bus driver known— I don't know where that fellow is today—but had he known that this was the right time, he would have gone on to lunch somewhere and left the bus, and let that lady sit there. But he didn't know—it was the right time. He went there and asked Rosa Parks to move. And she said, "Not today. I am just too tired." It's the right time. Everything is prepared and the moment has come. Now suppose Rosa Parks had jumped up and called him a bunch of bad names, referring to his ancestry, and whipped out a knife and chased him off the bus. There wouldn't have been any movement, and you wouldn't be at MIT today. The man didn't know what to do with her except to call the police: "This strange person sitting here, soft spoken, looking up in my face saying, 'I want to break the law today.' " And King was in town.

I often heard him tell the story about what happened that night. He hadn't been in town but a little more than a year. His credit hadn't been ruined. People still thought well of him. His daddy was an important person. People knew about him. His family had money. They weren't going to keep him in jail too long. So when they asked who is going to be the leader for this bus boycott, they went all around the room. One man said, "I have a mortgage at the bank. Don't ask me to lead the boycott." Another man said, "My wife just got a job teaching school, don't ask me to lead the boycott." They checked out every candidate, and God in his infinite providence left King sitting right there with no excuse whatsoever. "You came down here to be an intellectual Baptist preacher, but we have a new job for you right now. You propose, but God disposes. We want to organize a bus boycott."

King told me, "You don't know what it feels like to have a state trooper to follow you all day long with his car 18 inches off your back bumper, or a state trooper follow you less than a yard off your tail lights from Montgomery to Tuskegee—two or three of them sitting in there—along the long stretches of a lonesome road." But you see he was the right man, at the right place, at the right time. And here we are today telling this story over and over again.

It belongs in the record of the redemption of mankind, like Moses leading his people out of Egypt; like the exiles in Babylon trying to sing Zion's songs; like Gandhi, his goat and his stick defying the British Empire; like Washington at Valley Forge. We have to tell it every time we can to let people know that this young man came to the right place, at the right time with the right equipment. He led us in prayer and marching and singing and testifying until the walls came tumbling down.

Now comes the hard part for you and me. Segregation is legally over with, but integration is a difficult goal to attain. If we don't give up, and if we are able to pull this off, black people with courage and white people with goodwill, do you realize what a unique thing this is going to be in the world? No people anywhere who constitute a ten percent minority distinguished by racial differences, hair texture and facial expressions, are distinguished by these 315 years sojourn, 250 years of it in physical bondage. No people anywhere at all stayed around on the same piece of real estate to move toward the center of the new society with equality and with justice. It hasn't happened anywhere.

I wonder if people in fine universities ever stop to think of themselves, not as moving from day to day with small chores to be accomplished, but caught up in a great moment of history. The black people in America moving toward the center of the society would be something brand new. The outcasts of India were not situated as we were; they all belonged to the same basic racial stock of many other people in India. They had been there together for 2,500 years. We were dragged here and enslaved. The Maoris of New Zealand were there on those two islands for 1,000 years before the Anglo-Saxons arrived. Theodosius brought the Goths into the Roman Empire in the fourth century. But they were all Caucasians together.

We don't have a situation that parallels what we have facing us today right here in America. And if black folk can keep their courage, and if white people can enlarge their vision and together create a great community, this is going to be something greater than Alexander's March to the East, greater than the Rome of Augustus Caesar, greater than the Athens of Pericles, and greater than the French under Napoleon. Something wonderful awaits us, if we can maintain our courage, and if we can find the goodwill, the bases for a new community here in America.

SAMUEL D. PROCTOR is Senior Minister Emeritus at the Abyssinian Baptist Church in New York City. Previously he was President of Virginia Union University (his *alma mater*), President of North Carolina A&T State University, Associate Director of the Peace Corps, and Professor at Rutgers University.

Martin Luther King, Jr.'s funeral procession through the streets of Atlanta drew a huge crowd of mourners on April 9, 1968.

The Legacy of Martin Luther King, Jr. and the New Movement for Justice

Charles S. Brown

THE REFERENCE TO THE NEW MOVEMENT FOR JUSTICE in the title of this address is more a call for development and a summons to action than a description of a currently existing phenomenon. That such a movement is needed can hardly be doubted by any conscientious person. All one has to do is look at the headlines or listen to the leading news items on radio or television. Consider Saturday's *New York Times* headline: "U.S. Drops Rule on Tax Penalty For College Bias." Here, the Secretary of the Treasury personally decided, in direct opposition to Justice Department arguments before the Supreme Court in September of 1981, to reinstate the tax exemption of Bob Jones University and to grant tax-exempt status to the Goldsboro, North Carolina Christian Schools, despite the racially discriminatory policies mandated at both schools. In the words of Tom Wicker, drawn from a comment by Representative Charles Rangel, this amounts to "subsidizing racism."

In effect, the action restores tax exemption to more than one hundred private schools and other organizations that practice segregation. It also opens the door to the formation of new segregated schools. All of these schools will be excused from paying federal income taxes. Moreover, those who make monetary contributions to them will be able to take a federal tax deduction. The revenues lost will show up as an increased budget deficit, chargeable to U.S. taxpayers. Given this combination of factors, I think Tom Wicker is quite right in saying that, in this decision, the Reagan administration "has moved from a lack of interest in fighting racial discrimination to active promotion of it."

This is not the only situation in which the Reagan administration action or inaction may be interpreted as hostile to federal policies for the elimination of racial discrimination in American public life. As Wicker further points out:

- The Reagan administration has said it will no longer seek or enforce busing orders for school desegregation.

- The Justice Department, misnamed in this case, will seek reversal of a Supreme Court decision approving a voluntary affirmative action program.

- President Reagan wants to take the teeth out of the ten year extension of the Voting Rights Act already passed by the House.

- Neither the President nor the Justice Department has offered opposition to a pending Senate bill that would strip the Supreme Court of its constitutionally mandated jurisdiction in school segregation cases.

Or consider this headline: "New Layoffs Push U.S. Jobless Rate to 8.9% from 8.4%." Four hundred sixty thousand workers were laid off in December, causing the total number of unemployed workers to climb to almost 9.5 million. Adult male unemployment rose to a post-World War II high of 8 percent. Unemployment among blacks rose to 16.1 percent, two-thirds of the record Depression rate of 24.9 percent for all Americans. The unemployment rate in the auto industry jumped from 15.6 percent to 21.7 percent, even closer to the Depression figure, in an industry with perhaps the largest number of organized black workers.

These jobless workers, and their 1.2 million counterparts called "discouraged" job-seekers, face reduced unemployment benefits, limited access to food stamps, lack of school lunch programs, and a general reduction in the level of public services. One can hardly look on these as rewards for their part in the effort to "put America back to work again." The President may have assured them and us that these "tragic conditions are temporary and necessary to turn the situation around," but one may wonder how many of these workers will become part of the permanently displaced group, constituting a "floor" of 6 or 7 percent unemployed in a so-called full employment economy.

Consider further this inside story: "NOW Asks High Court to Reverse Idaho Judge's Equal Rights Ruling." The article begins: "With the Reagan administration's legal position still in doubt, the National Organization for Women filed its brief with the Supreme Court today requesting a speedy reversal of a lower court's decision on the ratification of the proposed federal equal rights amendment." NOW was joined by some forty organizations and individuals calling for an expedited review to prevent derailment of ratification of the amendment before the June 30, 1982 deadline set by Congress. Unsurprisingly, the suit will be opposed by the Justice Department, which favors appeal but not expedited review.

To these must be added the "assault on the poor" contained in the much-publicized budget cuts that have been a clear priority of the administration. The budget cuts already in place have taken away approximately $4 billion in food from people of low and marginal incomes in the current budget year, $2.5 billion of this amount from reductions in food stamps and $1.5 billion in child nutrition programs. The effect of these cuts will be a sharp increase in the incidence of malnutrition, hunger, and sheer starvation among American citizens. Moreover, these cuts eliminate programs that were aimed at solving these problems.

In 1967 a team of six nationally known pediatricians, familiar with the signs of starvation and malnutrition in the poorer nations of the world, examined several thousand poor children in Mississippi. They were shocked to discover conditions among these American children that were similar to those which they had witnessed in the poor nations of Asia and Africa. They reported their findings in testimony before a Senate subcommittee.

In sum, we saw children who are hungry and who are sick—children for whom hunger is a daily fact of life and sickness, in many forms, an inevitability. We do not want to quibble over words, but malnutrition is not quite what we found; the boys and girls we saw are visibly and predictably losing their health, their energy, their spirits. They are suffering from hunger and disease and directly or indirectly they are dying from them—which is exactly what 'starvation' means.

In a nation moved to compassion during the sixties by the activity of the Civil Rights Movement, that testimony prompted the creation of a Senate Select Committee on Nutrition and Human Needs, along with other actions to establish mechanisms for addressing the problems. From these efforts came an enlargement of the food stamp program, the distribution of surplus foods to institutions (schools, hospitals and child care centers), the establishment of meal programs in neighborhood Senior Citizens Centers, subsidization of school lunches and the establishment of breakfast programs in target areas. In addition, they also led to the very important Special Supplemental Program for Women, Infants and Children that has supplied highly nutritious foods to high-risk pregnant and nursing women and their very young children.

The latter program has had a direct impact in reducing the infant mortality rate. Along with day care and public school breakfast and lunch programs, it has helped to arrest the deterioration of the nervous system resulting from starvation and malnutrition, that has made so many poor children losers before they started school. At the other end of the age scale, evidence shows that malnutrition accelerates the onset of senility and endemic physical illness. Thus, a follow-up national study in 1977 found far fewer grossly malnourished people in the United States than there had been ten years before. Ironically, this was probably part of the data used by Presidential adviser Martin Anderson in his insistence that very few Americans are really poor, and fewer still "truly needy."

If this is so, it is because the visible ravages of poverty have been ameliorated by the very programs that are being targeted by Reagan budget cuts. One thing is certain, the outcome of these cuts will be an increase in infant mortality rates, more sickness and disease among vulnerable segments of the population, and deepening alienation among the working poor of the nation.

In the long run, it is neither wise nor just to require the most vulnerable people in our society to make great sacrifices and take great risks for the sake of the well-being of the economy, while people who are already better off are afforded greater protection. But this is exactly what the Reagan administration's policy is doing.

Let us be clear and honest about something. The basic issue regarding the federal budget is not the size of the budget deficit. If this were so, the recent projections of a $109.1 billion deficit would be unthinkable and intolerable. Leave aside the fact that the anticipated deficit is more than twice that projected in the Carter budget for fiscal 1982, which included all the social spending cut in the revised Reagan budget and more than 50 percent of the Reagan budget's increase in military spending. It is also more than twice the average of $48.5 billion deficits during the four years of Carter's administration. What matters is who benefits from the deficit and who bears its costs.

Here the evidence is clear. The source of the dramatic increase in the size of the deficit is not social spending, but the additional increase in military spending in the Reagan budget, and, more significantly, the revenues lost as a result of the generous tax cut awarded upper-income individuals and corporations. How is the size of the deficit to be addressed? It will be addressed by even deeper cuts in social spending and increases in excise taxes that disproportionately penalize middle- and lower-income citizens. In other words, deficit spending is all right as long as it benefits the wealthier segment. The gospel of "Reaganomics" is good news for the rich and bad news for the poor.

How different this gospel is from the good news celebrated in Mary's song, "The Magnificat." She rejoices that, in the promised birth of her son, God has "filled the hungry with good things" and sent the rich away empty-handed; that is, with no more than they had. But the impact of the Reagan budget on food programs for the poor has been described by one writer under the title: "Season's Greetings From the White House . . . And A Hungry New Year!"

I am well aware of the logic of supply-side economic theory, at least on the popular level. I know that the distribution of benefits and costs in this way is supposed to encourage capital accumulation and stimulate investment which will produce jobs and a general prosperity that will benefit everyone. I hope so! Because, in the meantime, babies will be dying, and children, unemployed young adults, and poor elderly people will go hungry—and be otherwise exposed to the vicissitudes of life. This is worse than tragic.

By what right do we require of them this extraordinary sacrifice, other than the conventional wisdom that it has always been so? ("The poor you have with you always.") How can we repay them for the suffering they endure so that those who are already well off may feel more secure, assured that the government "safety net" protecting their resources will not break? Will the recovery be worth the cost in lives and misery that it requires? Is this really the only way recovery can be achieved? And, most important of all, will the general prosperity expected to follow this season of suffering distribute sufficient benefits to the bottom segment of the economy to assure that they are included among those protected by the safety net of public policy?

I know that to the practical minded in our midst, the thrust of my analysis and questions raises apparently uneconomic considerations to the level of economic concerns. But I am bold in doing so because the one whom we honor here today was always clear about the fact that practical policymakers must not be allowed the luxury of ignoring the claims of justice. Martin Luther King, Jr. was frequently heard to say, "Justice delayed is justice denied."

There is a moral issue at stake. We are not just moving backward in a society oriented toward progress, but we are moving against our charter principles of equality and the right to life, as well as liberty and the pursuit of happiness. Seen through the analysis presented above, the economic policies of the present administration fall far short of the Pledge of Allegiance's promise of "liberty and justice for all." And here, justice means more than the right to a fair trial in the case of criminal charges. It includes the constitutional guarantee of the "equal protection of the laws" including, and in this case especially, public policy.

Martin Luther King, Jr.'s spirit cries out for justice in this situation. And the challenge comes to us individually and collectively to do our part to see to it that economic justice for the poor, the excluded and vulnerable people in our society, is not neglected in the rush to the prosperity promised by supply-side economics. We must be prepared to be part of a new movement, a movement that will generate and maintain sufficient momentum to get this nation back on the track of justice.

We don't have to start from scratch. Some elements of the old coalition are still active in the struggle: the NAACP, the National Urban League, SCLC, OIC, PUSH. Numerous other organizations—religious and civic, black and white, Protestant and Catholic, Christian, Jewish, and Muslim—are also active participants in the struggle. To these must be added old and new political groups, especially organizations of black elected officials, mass political movements, party organizations, and labor and philanthropic organizations. For example, on the political front, we must remember that it took black Republicans in the Reagan administration to communicate to the President the apparent racism in the tax-exemption action of the Treasury and Justice departments.

Obviously, such a collage of organizations does not constitute a movement, and these organizations have conflicting and competitive, as well as convergent, claims. Moreover, conflict over leadership and jurisdictional rights, along with competing survival needs, frequently makes more than occasional collaboration impossible. Nevertheless, their existence and diverse constituencies indicate that there is a place for everyone who is willing to work on issues of justice in our nation.

Now we must turn our attention to the question of the legacy of Martin Luther King, Jr. and the question of how this legacy can contribute to the integrity and effectiveness of a new movement. For this we shall turn to an autobiographical statement by Martin Luther King, Jr., in which he expressed his personal aspirations in this regard:

If any of you are around when I have to meet my day, I don't want a long funeral. And if you get somebody to deliver the eulogy, tell them not to talk too long. Every now and then I wonder what I want them to say. Tell them not to mention that I have a Nobel Peace Prize, that isn't important. Tell them not to mention that I have three or four hundred other awards, that's not important. Tell them not to mention where I went to school. I'd like somebody to mention that day, that Martin Luther King, Jr. tried to give his life serving others. I'd like for somebody to say that day, that Martin Luther King, Jr. tried to love somebody. I want you to say that day, that I tried to be right on the war question. I want you to be able to say that day, that I did try to feed the hungry. And I want you to be able to say that day, that I did try, in my life, to clothe those who were naked. I want you to say, on that day, that I did try, in my life, to visit those who were in prison. I want you to say that I tried to love and serve humanity.

Yes, if you want to say that I was a drum major, say that I was a drum major for justice; say that I was a drum major for peace; I was a drum major for righteousness. And all of the other shallow things will not matter. I won't have any money to leave behind. I won't have the fine and luxurious things of life to leave behind. But I just want to leave a committed life behind.

In this memorial service it is important that we come neither to bury King nor to praise him. Rather we must come appropriately to draw inspiration from the life and leadership of one whose vision and commitments remain untested in the common life of America. This vision and these commitments are necessary to motivate and sustain the new movement for justice that is needed in America today.

True to his word, Martin Luther King, Jr. left a committed life behind, a life committed to the struggle for justice. He saw America as a covenant people whose bonding was fundamentally established in the Declaration of Independence: "We hold these truths to be self-evident: that all [human beings] are created equal; that they are endowed, by their Creator, with certain inalienable rights; that among these are life, liberty and the pursuit of happiness." And he believed

Charles S. Brown, Paul E. Gray, Priscilla K. Gray, and Clarence G. Williams leading the march during the MLK Celebration in January 1982.

that even if the founding fathers had not intended to include the black people being held in bondage at that time and their descendants, America cannot be true to this vision of itself until its common life includes them.

Prophetically, Alexis de Tocqueville, in his penetrating analysis of *Democracy in America*, wrote: "If ever America undergoes great revolutions, they will be brought about by the presence of the black race on the soil of the United States; that is to say, they will owe their origin not to the equality, but to the inequality of condition."

Along with Rosa Parks, E. D. Nixon, Daisy Bates, Medgar Evers, Fannie Lou Hamer, Malcolm X and countless others, well-known and unknown, Martin Luther King, Jr. was a participant in this critical effort to make the promise and the dream of true democracy and freedom a reality in America. And in seeking to accomplish this end, he was committed to the dignity of every human being. Not just of black people, and of those he regarded as his peers and his friends, but even of those who would count themselves his enemies. He dared to love his enemies; not because he was a coward or because he believed their claims to superiority and to prior rights, but because he believed that they had a dignity as human beings worthy of his respect, despite the error of their ways. And, even more than this, he dared to take a stand for the dignity of the people at the bottom of the economic structure of our society.

No more eloquent testimony to this can be found than the fact that he died working in the cause of predominantly black garbage workers in Memphis, Tennessee. He was there because he believed they had a dignity worthy of the respect of their employers and fellow citizens, despite their station in life. He was on his way to Washington to lobby for the nation to deliver on the Declaration's promise of an inalienable right to life for poor and excluded Americans.

In his final sermon in Memphis, the night before his assassination, Martin Luther King, Jr. described the situation in terms of the parable of the Good Samaritan. He pointed out that the reason the priest and the Levite passed by the man they encountered, the man who had been beaten, robbed and lay wounded on the road, is because they asked the wrong question: "If I help this man, what will happen to me?" The Good Samaritan stopped to help the man because he asked the right question: "If I don't help this man, what will happen to him?"

Martin Luther King, Jr. died because he refused to "pass by on the other side"—to be so busy getting ready to go to Washington that he didn't take time to stop off in Memphis, answering one more Macedonian call. And this is the question we must ask ourselves, as we consider those who must bear the costs of President Reagan's "jellybean" budget. If we don't help alleviate their suffering and seek to get the nation back on track, what will happen to them?

King operated in terms of a profound understanding of the intrinsic relationship between peace and justice. He understood, like de Tocqueville, that there could be no peace in America as long as injustice and inequality were allowed to prevail. He worked for justice for the oppressed and most excluded segments of society so that peace might truly be realized.

On the other hand, he understood that the means by which justice would be achieved were critically important if the end of peace was to be attained. He knew that a partial justice, achieved for some at the expense of others, would only accomplish a short-term peace. Thus, he insisted that the way of peace and nonviolence, which recognizes the dignity and just claims of all involved and pursues love as the more excellent way to work together, was the only means for achieving a just and peaceful world.

In the dream articulated in his memorable March on Washington address, in the vision of the "world house" presented in *Where Do We Go From Here: Chaos or Community?*, and in the effort to build an inclusive coalition to undertake the Poor People's Campaign, Martin Luther King, Jr. presents us with a vision of the oneness of humanity. The chapter entitled "The World House" in his last book draws its inspiration from notes found among the personal effects of a famous author. These notes sketched the scenario for a proposed novel and read: "a widely separated family inherits a house in which they must live together." King goes on to describe the earth, this planet upon which we live, as a world house that we must learn to inhabit together. All of us are answerable to the claim of human solidarity.

If we are to be part of the new movement for justice, we too must be unswervingly committed to the cause of human solidarity, like Martin Luther King, Jr. in his solidarity with the garbage workers in Memphis and with America's neglected and excluded poor. He didn't have to do it. He chose to do it. He was born privileged, as the son, grandson, and great-grandson of preachers. He grew up buttressed by the shelter and support of a substantial church. He earned the Ph.D. degree at an early age and, throughout the period of his labors in the movement of the fifties and sixties, he received many offers of positions in colleges, universities, and distinguished pulpits. Nevertheless, he chose to cast his lot with the poor and to give his life working in the cause of justice.

We, too, must choose in his spirit and in the spirit of Eugene V. Debs's confession of faith: "I believe that one cannot be fully Christian except as one enters in fact or in imagination into the privations, sufferings, and misery of the economically dispossessed; therefore, I will identify my own interests in life with those of the dispossessed until justice shall have been won."

Finally, the legacy of Martin Luther King, Jr. to us is an abiding faith in the possibilities of America and the promises of a just God. Despite the forces around and sometimes inside him conspiring to provoke alienation and despair, Martin Luther King, Jr. loved America and gave his life to help the nation be true to its covenant of freedom and equality. He believed that we ought to be claimed by the possibilities in our ideals, rather than be mired down in the limitations imposed by circumstances. Thus, in the March on Washington address, he expressed his fervent hope—his dream—that "one day this nation will rise up and live out its creed." We dare not give up on this commitment to the possibilities of our common life, no matter how difficult it seems to overcome the obstacles in ourselves, in others, and in our circumstances.

Most important of all, however, we cannot be motivated and sustained in our participation in the new movement for justice, without an abiding faith in a just God. This is the faith we need to "hew out of the mountain" of our despair "a stone of hope." It is the faith that has sustained slaves and their descendants in their long pilgrimage in America. It is the faith that kept people walking in the turbulent, dangerous and exciting days in Montgomery. It is the faith that kept so many going when it seemed there was no reason to go on at all. It is the faith that fueled the Civil Rights Movement of the sixties and prompted not only the significant gains described earlier in this address, but also imparted a spark of dignity that was ignited by the movement, and caused a mass of black people to "straighten their backs up." Martin Luther King, Jr. frequently pointed out: "Nobody can ride your back unless it's bent."

This faith can get us started and keep us moving even in these days when the tide seems to be turning against us. It can motivate and sustain us as we seek to get involved in a new movement for justice in America.

It's all right to be tired. We're tired of injustice. We're tired of war. We're tired of the oppression which destroys the life of the poor and the weak, and undermines the peace of our society. It's important for us to be tired of some things. But we should not get weary.

As Reverend James Cleveland's updated version of an old Negro spiritual says, "I don't feel no ways tired; I've come too far from where I started from. Nobody told me the road would be easy. I just don't believe He brought me this far to leave me."

We didn't come this far because those who enslaved us wanted us to make it. We didn't get this far just because of our own efforts and the help of our friends. We got this far because, despite our obstacles and in addition to our efforts, God is just and works with those who work for justice.

And God didn't bring us this far to leave us.

CHARLES S. BROWN was a tenured Associate Professor of Practical Theology at Yale University's Divinity School before accepting the pastorate of the Bethel Baptist Church in Dayton, Ohio, where he is today. Dr. Brown is a graduate of Morehouse College and Boston University's School of Theology, the recipient of several prestigious academic awards and grants, and has served on the boards of numerous organizations.

Martin Luther King, Jr. addressing marchers in August 1963.

Rekindling the Spirit of Martin Luther King, Jr. in a Time of Retrenchment

Price M. Cobbs, MLK Lecturer
A. Leon Higginbotham, Jr.

Price M. Cobbs

I THINK THAT IF ANY OF US TOOK EVEN A CURSORY look at national policies and practices over the past several years, whatever our political or social orientation, we would have to acknowledge that, indeed, there has been a retrenchment, if not a calculated retreat, from the ideals of Martin Luther King, Jr. Further, I think any reader of daily newspapers, any viewer of television, weekly periodicals, or any reader of that organ of national policy, *Reader's Digest*, could not escape the conclusion that the ideals of Martin Luther King, Jr. have been tarnished by a national administration, and by policies that have stated that the civil rights gains of the sixties, including affirmative action, are the things that have most contributed to the present plight of black Americans. Those comments were also made at a meeting recently of our President and Republicans, most of whom were black. As I read it, these comments are indicative of a mind-set that clearly shows that there has been a retrenchment.

What are some of the determinants of the retrenchment? Over the past decade, there has been a gradual abandonment of wanting to look outside of ourselves. Many of you have read books of the "me" decade, the culture of narcissism, a culture that essentially began to look inward. An unhealthy part of that inward-looking trend is that people are no longer interested in helping others, and helping others was at the heart of the ideals of Martin Luther King. I sometimes hear people talk about the social work mentality or the bleeding heart mentality, as if the ideals of wanting to reach out, of wanting to go beyond yourself to help others have been tarnished. That is an indication of a retrenchment. There continues to be an indifference, and at times an outright hostility, to even looking at the idea that racism and sexism remain alive and well in this country.

I think another indication is that there is a growing psychological tiredness, tinged with irritation and laced with anger, in hearing anything about the demands of black Americans, about the poor, the disenfranchised, or the downtrodden. That contributes to a retrenchment. I think the retrenchment is manifest in the many articles and books and comments about reverse discrimination, and the sheer intellectual dishonesty in statements about white males being the new victims of discrimination. This is not to denigrate an individual who feels that way. But I think we are involved in intellectual dishonesty and hypocrisy, if we claim that white males, as a category, are the new victims of discrimination in this country.

The retrenchment is further hastened and highlighted by a sluggish economy, economic conditions which disproportionately affect the have-nots and allow the conventional wisdom to prevail that says that we can no longer throw money at problems, as if significant sums of money were spent over decades in a focused way to undo centuries of this country's fundamental contradiction of a democratic society. One of the key legacies of Dr. King was his eloquent statements about his patriotism and love of this country. Out of that patriotism he recognized some of the fundamental contradictions in a democratic society that need to be addressed.

In my view, retrenchment means that this country has gone from benign neglect to a hostile indifference to any policy that might positively impact the lives of black Americans. I think that many blacks have contributed to this retrenchment. I do not think that the retrenchment is exclusively a white phenomenon. I see too many blacks who are essentially unhooked from the history, who know little about the tears that were shed, the blood that was spilled achieving integration, in getting a few students into schools like MIT. We cannot point the finger and say that it is white America that has retrenched. I think any number of black Americans have retrenched from understanding the ideals of Martin Luther King, Jr.

For many of us who were active in the sixties, and who viewed Dr. King as a towering hero and an historical role model, it almost comes as a rueful surprise that so few people are aware of any but the briefest aspects of his life. We've constantly focused on the future, the building of a country, the frontiers. Anything that goes beyond a five- or ten-year time frame becomes almost ancient history.

As we look at the ideals that we want to rekindle about Dr. King's life, we can think of some of the things that were going on, and why many people related to them. I think there were those who were stirred by his words. Dr. King had a way with words. And there were those who were stirred by the enduring strength of his compassion. He came out of the black Baptist tradition, and the best of that tradition was to hook up intellect with compassion, and to know how to stir people with a message. That was one of the major things that attracted people to this very charismatic figure. I think there were others who were attracted by the magnificence of his concepts, and the brilliance of his insights. He was a theological scholar who was number one in his class at his seminary. He was considered by his professors to be one of the four or five most brilliant students that they had seen in their careers. The brilliance of his insight was another thing that attracted people to him. I think that some were lured by the fire and the idealism which he brought to his work. I think one of the key legacies of Dr. King was that he spoke so eloquently of his patriotism, his love of country, and then, out of that patriotism, talked about some of the fundamental contradictions that we had to address in a democratic society.

As described in the excellent recent biography, *Let the Trumpet Sound*, by Stephen B. Oates, Dr. King was born on a cold and cloudy Saturday, January 15, 1929, in Atlanta, Georgia. The doctor feared him stillborn and had to spank him several times before he cried. He was the second of three children of Reverend Martin Luther and Alberta King. His grandfather, Reverend Adam Daniel Williams, had been a minister. In all biographies, critical and adoring, he is described as a precocious and intelligent child who pondered weighty issues and who spoke on advanced ideas that were always far beyond his years and experience. We must remember that Dr. King was born in 1929, in rigidly segregated Atlanta. He was a child of the black middle class. His father was a prominent minister of that city. I remember talking with my therapist, as part of my training, about the difficulty in describing the experience of being at the front end of a segregated bus. I clearly think that Dr. King experienced "the front end of a segregated bus." His was a loving family, an intact family, a family that knew that they were going to survive the Depression. But he also was in a rigidly segregated city with an intelligence and a curiosity that would have allowed him to see the incongruities, the contradictions. He experienced firsthand what it was like to grow up sitting in that segregated bus. And I think at some point deep in his unconscious, he must have dedicated himself to doing something about it.

He attended Young Elementary School and David T. Howard Elementary School, entered Booker T. Washington High School at the age of thirteen, graduated at the age of fifteen. King entered Morehouse College the same year and encountered the legendary Dr. Benjamin Mays, who has impacted the lives of so many Americans, black and white. Prior to that time, Dr. King had felt some pressure to get to the ministry, coming from a religious family, but as with so many bright, curious people, he felt too many contradictions. His encounters and discussions with Dr. Benjamin Mays influenced him.

At the age of seventeen, Dr. King made a decision to become a Baptist minister. After leaving Morehouse College, he went to Crozer Seminary in Chester, Pennsylvania. When he went to Crozer, his intellect truly became focused. He earned an A in every course that he took. It was here that he began a serious quest for a philosophical method to eliminate social evils. He read all the great philosophers (Rousseau, Bentham, Mill and Locke, and some of the writings of the great black theologians, Howard Thurman, and various other people).

Finally, he came across some books by Walter Rauschenbusch that were very critical of the social system, and from there Dr. King began to fuse what he called a Christian activism. He also began to think of passivism. Passivism had some tradition in this country, with Quakers and various individuals, but passivism was a movement whose currents had pretty much passed by the black community. Historically, the black community's passivism was reactive. "I must be passive because I know if I am too active, white folks will get me." As Dr. King began to come in contact with passivism, with the life and teachings of Mahatma Gandhi, he began thinking of what Gandhi called soul force. He began looking at something called the power of love and truth as a vehicle for social change. Probably the most important intellectual and emotional influence on his life was the life of Gandhi and how someone could fuse his own deprivations into a social movement to liberate a people. Dr. King graduated from Crozer at the top of his class and went on to Boston University School of Theology. In all of this, he was acknowledged as a first-rate scholar who fused the ideals and currents of the time into a world view of liberation.

He completed his work at Boston University in 1954 and accepted the pastorate of the Dexter Avenue Baptist Church in Montgomery, Alabama. He preached his first sermon there on a Sunday in May of 1954. It is ironic that Dr. King preached that sermon during the same month that the United States Supreme Court, under Chief Justice Earl Warren, handed down the history-making *Brown vs. Board of Education* decision.

Then, in December 1955, in Montgomery, a boycott of buses began after Mrs. Rosa Parks refused to move to the colored section of the bus. Dr. King accepted the presidency of the Montgomery Improvement Association. It was from there, historically and psychologically, that Dr. King became first many things to black America, then many things to all of America, and then finally, many things to the world. Dr. King was an advocate, an orator, a field general, an historian, a fundraiser, a symbol, a scholar.

As Dr. King left Atlanta, moving on to the national and eventually to the world stage, he took an admonition of one of the great observers of America, Alexis de Tocqueville. When de Tocqueville came to America in the 1850s as an observer from France, he addressed what he called the basic problem of the evolution of the democratic society: how to make America a more just society. In many ways, Dr. King hooked into that tradition as a patriot looking for a way to make his country a more just society.

In talking about rekindling the ideals of Martin Luther King, Jr., we need to continue to ask ourselves: What has changed? What has changed within me? What thoughts have I wrestled with? What dues have I paid to extrude things in myself? And therefore, where do I see the world change, not the visible external changes? We see more jobs and we see more positions. We see more affluence in certain people. When Dr. William H. Grier and I wrote *Black Rage* from the context of the early to mid 1960s in psychological dimension, so much time had passed and so little had changed. How much have we really began to cut into the basic paradigm of black presumed inferiority, white presumed superiority? As I look at the historical view of the sixties, I think of the meaning of Dr. King's life. It is clear that blacks were hungry for leadership that would allow us to move on.

Blacks in the sixties wanted to coalesce and begin to believe in a cause. We wanted something to bring us out of our apathy. Dr. King provided us with that opportunity. Then as now, it was so much of a search, an illusive search, for the end to racism, for an end to something that you know continues to victimize you and also makes you continue to victimize yourself. Many blacks were tired and angry, and the rage was beginning to build—rage and people searching for some type of comfort. Yet, for all the social ferment, for all the changes, the passage of civil rights laws, the erection finally of a government superstructure that came down as advocates rather than resisters, what happened and probably what was most important for me—in terms of Dr. King's life—was psychological.

Erik Erikson, that great psychoanalyst, defined in the 1950s a basic quest for identity that is inherent in all people. Who am I? What's my meaning? What are the elements of my identity? And I think Dr. King began that positive process for black Americans. But until that time, as Afro-Americans, we had been, and continue to be, very ambivalent about that basic part of our identity which is black. We have psychologically paid the price of living in a land where to be black is almost always equated to being made to feel inferior. Dr. King got us to look at that part of our identity and begin to think of the positive. He helped us address that part of our identity by helping us to see the morality of our cause, and ultimately, the morality and humanist residing within ourselves. I think it is no coincidence that "black is beautiful," which is now a cliché, became a forceful statement during the time of Dr. King. He performed one of the major tasks of leadership.

Norton Long has written that one task of leadership is the transformation of the doubts of followers into the psychological grounds of cooperative action. A leader helps us resolve doubts and move to action, and this is what Dr. King did. In the parlance of managerial science, Dr. King's troops were ragtag. The people who were marching, who were sitting-in, were a very ragtag band of people. Dr. King's leadership helped us dispel doubts, helped us to move beyond ourselves, to work on our own behalf. He reached in and tapped what Carl Jung called our "collective unconscious," and in the process made us redefine ourselves as the tippers of American thought and action, rather than victims for American thoughts and actions.

Through the currents of American history, there runs a theme of what defines America. And whatever else defines America, what goes on with those fragile bonds between black and white helps to define this country. We must never forget that what defines our country is how we manage ourselves multiculturally, how well we understand difference, how well we value the difference. As we look at some of the meanings for whites in a psycho-social way, Dr. King evoked a fear in many whites. He was, after all, aiming to reshape the social order and redefine the American national character. He made America confront an unspeakable evil, and that is psychologically difficult. He threatened America's view of itself as the democracy where all people are created equal. There were whites who responded to the theological part, to the social part, to the justice part, and who joined with Dr. King and followed his leadership.

The Selma March on March 25, 1965 was the most democratic scene I had ever experienced in this country. It was just an exhilarating day that people were laughing and crying for once the words of "We shall overcome" were changed to "We have overcome." There was euphoria, there was exuberance. It was a multicultural day. It was really a sense that there were no more mountains to climb. And then I think that we were too unaware in our naiveté of exactly what had been tapped. I think all of that cross-current unleashed an unyielding hostility that led to his assassination on April 4, 1968.

I think something told us that summer that the old order was changing. If we are rekindling those ideas, we need to continue to focus on that change. All of us need to move past our ambivalence about being American. I don't think we can change America if we are ambivalent about it—black, white, blue or green. I don't think you can change MIT if you are ambivalent about being an MIT student or faculty member. At some point, if one wants to change something, one almost has to look for total immersion. Then you unleash the energy and the excitement necessary for change. Dr. King defined himself and his world, and made others respond to that definition. That is an ideal to which we all must aspire. We must continue to define what Dr. King started, and what others contributed to: What does it mean to be a black American? We spent much of the sixties trying to define what the black part of that meant. In the eighties we must look at what the American part means.

Some of my friends, who were part of the turmoil of the sixties, moved back to Africa thinking that there they would be accepted as black. They have moved back here now. In Africa they were Americans, and they were rejected just like any other American. We have to come to grips with reality, define ourselves and redefine ourselves, and expand that definition in ways that are comfortable, that broaden our vision rather than limit it. As we rekindle those ideals, in all of this, maybe, just maybe, sometime in our life we can say, "Free at Last! Free At Last! Thank God Almighty, I'm free at last!"

PRICE M. COBBS is a business executive and psychiatrist. He is currently President and CEO of Pacific Management Systems, a human resources consulting firm, and a Fellow of the American Psychiatric Association. Dr. Cobbs is co-author of *Black Rage* (1986) and *The Jesus Bag* (1971).

Martin Luther King, Jr. attempts to register at the Hotel Alberta in Selma, Alabama in January 1965. To his right are F. L. Shuttleworth and Ralph Abernathy.

Martin Luther King, Jr. and Ralph Abernathy being placed under arrest by police chief Virgil Stuart, when they asked to be served at a motel restaurant in St. Augustine, Florida, on June 11, 1964.

A. Leon Higginbotham, Jr.

ABRAHAM LINCOLN, IN 1855, SAID OF THE FOURTH of July, "When we were political slaves of King George, and wanted to be free, we called the maxim that all men are created equal a self-evident truth. But now, when we have grown fat and have lost all dread of being slaves ourselves, we become so greedy to be masters that we call the same maxim a self-evident lie...The Fourth of July is not quite dwindled away, it is still a great day for burning firecrackers." That's what our Fourth of July appears to be most of all these days, with seldom any pause for reflection, and almost never any reaffirmation of our desire for certain national goals. This could be one of the great tragedies on Martin Luther King's birthday, that we could become so insensitive that, as Abraham Lincoln said on the Fourth of July, it will become a day which is almost a self-evident lie.

How can we rekindle the spirit of Martin Luther King, Jr.? It appears that one way of doing this, particularly at universities, is to recognize what a heroic figure he was. I submit to you that if the high court of history had to evaluate him, they would put him at a level reserved for only a few highly revered leaders, such as George Washington, Thomas Jefferson, Abraham Lincoln, Franklin Roosevelt, and John Fitzgerald Kennedy. Yet I submit to you, that the high court should probably place Martin Luther King one level higher. For King did not have soldiers armed with rifles, as did George Washington. He did not write at ease from his study, as did Jefferson. One of King's most elegant expressions was a letter written from a Birmingham jail. He did not have the massive resources of the federal government as did Presidents Roosevelt, Kennedy, and Johnson. Yet, despite the shortage of staff, despite his inability to command governments, or armies, Martin Luther King was able to inspire, to prod, and to encourage Americans to move from a valley of despair toward, as he would phrase it, a mountain top of hope. Through the moral strength and eloquence of his arguments, he caused state governments to surrender their positions of nullification, and to repudiate their pledge of segregation forever. He motivated presidents, senators and congressmen, faculty and students. He won the Nobel Peace Prize, though in an official capacity he had little to do with foreign affairs. He was a legend and prophet of our time, not merely for blacks, not merely for America, but for the entire world.

What is the danger when someone has left such an extraordinary legacy? The danger is that he or she will be forgotten or underestimated. Many Americans will never know of the Montgomery bus boycott, or of the bombing of the children in Birmingham, or the march in Selma, or the August 1963 March on Washington, or the slaying and burial of three civil rights workers in Philadelphia, Mississippi. And maybe some will not even know of King's assassination on April 4, 1968. Yet these events, for blacks and for all Americans, are as sacred as our Valley Forge. King's walk from Selma to Montgomery was as significant as George Washington's advance across the Delaware. King's speech at the March on Washington was as moving as Lincoln's at Gettysburg. King's "Letter from a Birmingham Jail" was as profound as anything that Thomas Jefferson wrote. The danger is that the current generation may perceive him solely as a dreamer. That would be the most tragic distortion of all, because King was both a dreamer and an activist. His greatest contributions went far beyond pure eloquence, of which he had such an abundance. It was the movements which he organized, the marches he led, the battles he fought which became the compelling forces to transform our nation.

I would like to spend a few minutes with you probing an intellectual concept. I am thinking in terms of a comparison. Thomas Jefferson is ranked as one of our leading philosophers and statesmen. Why would you rank Thomas Jefferson so highly? What would you say was his most important writing? Some might say it was the Declaration of Independence. Others might say it was the Declaration of the Causes and Necessity of Taking up Arms. Others might say it was his extraordinary inaugural address. If you want to compare Thomas Jefferson with Martin Luther King, let me submit to you what at least one person, Sandy, would say was Thomas Jefferson's most important writing. Jefferson wrote this advertisement, which appeared in the *Virginia Gazette:*

> Runaway from the subscriber in Albemarle, a mulatto
> slave called Sandy, about thirty-five years of age. His
> stature is rather low, inclining to corpulence . . . slave to
> me in Albemarle shall have forty shillings reward if taken
> up within the county, four pounds if elsewhere within the
> colony, and ten pounds if in any other colony.

Thus Thomas Jefferson, by this very advertisement, was repudiating the equality of men which he had lauded as a self-evident truth in the Declaration of Independence.

How can one put Jefferson and Martin Luther King in the same context? I would have to go back to a place that may not be recognized by a department of astronomy, some lofty galaxy where all God's children would one day meet. I ask you, for the purposes of this lecture, to give me your imagination. Assume, for a moment, that there is a heaven, and that you have the opportunity to eavesdrop on a conversation between Thomas Jefferson and Martin Luther King. Martin Luther King has just read this advertisement for Sandy, and he starts to talk to Thomas Jefferson.

> Mr. Jefferson, now that we are here in heaven, where there
> is no reward for evasiveness and where immoral conduct
> will not be tolerated, please tell me, why did you have
> slaves? On what moral principle could you justify that
> advertisement for Sandy? And on what moral precept
> could you justify your ownership of hundreds of other
> slaves? Mr. Jefferson, how could you defend the institu-
> tion of slavery with all of its pernicious consequences?
> How could you condone a system in which individuals
> were subjected to lifetime servitude, knowing that their
> children and their children's children would suffer the
> same thing. In fact, Mr. Jefferson, since you were the
> leader of our country, let me read to you another adver-
> tisement which was typical of thousands appearing in
> your newspapers throughout the nation. How could a
> society which had pledged to the justice of the Declaration
> of Independence tolerate such?
>
> **Negroes for sale. A Negro woman twenty-four years of
> age and her two children, one eight and the other three
> years old. Said Negroes will be sold separately or
> together as desired. The woman is a good seamstress.**

**She will be sold low for cash, or exchanged for groceries.
For terms, apply to Matthew Bliss and Company.**

Mr. Jefferson, how could you have created a society where a woman, who had harmed no one, could have the child which she had brought into this world taken away from her, and sold just the way you sold your tobacco and your cotton? On what concept do you explain the type of society which you had? Mr. Jefferson, since we have such equality here in heaven, do you mind if I call you Tom? Now, Tom, how is it that individuals, who were as philosophical and as profound as you, men as brave as George Washington, and as eloquent as Patrick Henry, could treat an entire group of people with such special harshness and cruelty, solely because of their skins?

And I would imagine Martin Luther King concluding, perhaps after pausing for some tea:

Tom, I did not intend for my comments to be construed as a diatribe against you, but since, as a leader, our school children give you so much credit for so many of the significant accomplishments of our country, you must share part of the blame. For, as a nation, we failed to be as humane as we should have been. I have been talking nonstop. What is your answer?

And I would imagine that Thomas Jefferson, as a thoughtful lawyer, might first try to answer King's question by relying on precedent and quoting from scholarly treatises:

Martin, your questions disturb me. As I see all of the cruelty which was perpetuated for two centuries, and one-half century after our Declaration of Independence, it is not justifiable. You may recall that when I wrote my notes on Virginia, I included this line when looking at the issue of slavery. "I tremble for my country when I reflect that God is just, that his justice cannot sleep forever."

I have used this fictional dialogue as an example to reveal what can occur at any time in a nation, just as what happened in 1776 shows most dramatically. Leaders who are supposed to be good people may protect the rights of 80 percent of the people, while perpetuating a system that is oppressive and obstructive to the other 20 percent. That is what occurred in our revolutionary period—justice for most whites and gross injustice for all blacks.

As for that 20 percent of our society who were forgotten in those days, the same thing is happening in the 1980s. It is essential today, more so than ever before, that Americans understand the breadth and the importance of Martin Luther King's concerns—concerns which dealt with the failures that Thomas Jefferson was not able to, or did not, cope with. Although in speech after speech King made reference to the ugly villain of racism, never forget that he focused on jobs, housing, education, health care, poverty and hunger. Does this nation want to implement Dr. King's dream? We do not carry forward Martin Luther King's dream if we applaud him while simultaneously cutting out food stamps for the truly poor. We do not carry forward Dr. Martin Luther King's dream if we leave our cities so destitute of funds that the aged cannot get housing, and deprived children cannot get adequate sustenance or quality education. We do not carry forth Martin Luther King's dream if we adopt tax policies which tolerate, or even encourage, racism and hatred. We do not carry forward Martin Luther King's dream if the poor feel alienated and perceive those in power as insensitive to the plight of the weak and the dispossessed.

To bridge the gap from Thomas Jefferson's unfinished tasks to Martin Luther King's dream means increasingly that all of us must focus on the functioning of the economic mechanisms in our society. We must enter the dialogue as to how national resources are used, and how national, state, and local budgets are allocated. We must study with care how much is spent on defense to fight enemies abroad, and how much is spent to deter poverty, disease, and despair—crippling enemies at home. We do not carry forward Martin Luther King's dream if we applaud his dream and remain silent while diatribes on race are espoused all around us. Just as we make judgments on events surrounding Jefferson and his contemporaries 200 years ago, so our generation will someday be evaluated. Questions will be asked of the 1980s which will not apply solely to race. They will probe deeply the options for the weak, the poor and the dispossessed. What values and priorities will be identified? What will be the blind spots and the gaps? Will it be the irony that, in a nation of higher educational achievement, millions of children receive an inadequate public-school education? Will it be the contradiction that segregation was proclaimed illegal in

1954, but, twenty-nine years later, still exists *de facto*? Will it be the fact that a nation which landed a man safely on the moon, and often sent space shuttles into orbit, could not create viable jobs for millions of its citizens who seek a better life? Will it be the paradox that a nation with the highest standard of living still had twenty-five million persons living below the poverty level? And the high court of history will ask questions about MIT.

MIT stands almost alone as a symbol of the highest excellence in science in America and in the world. It is impressive to note that five current members of your faculty are Nobel laureates in physiology, medicine, economics and physics. But please remember that we meet here today to honor a person who did not earn his Nobel laureate for any discoveries in the laboratories of academia; he earned his for the human values he pursued, for the human values he advocated, and for the nonviolent confrontations he led, in order to bring more justice in America. And thus, notwithstanding the technological excellence achieved on this great MIT campus, we must always remember that technological excellence will never be and has never been, per se, the equivalent of human values. In pursuing his goal, Martin Luther King was not aided by MIT's radiation laboratories' extraordinary break-throughs in the development of microwave radar. His fundamental social justice concerns were not solved in any of your laboratories or advanced by any of your computers.

Dr. King recognized that education and technological excellence were important, but that did not mean they would be translated into social justice. Martin Luther King said, "I have a dream that one day the State of Alabama whose governor's lips are presently dripping with the words of interposition and nullification will be transformed into a situation where little black boys and black girls will be able to join hands with little white boys and white girls and walk together as sisters and brothers." Who was it who helped blacks and whites in Alabama to later walk together in greater harmony? And who made it possible for blacks and whites to compete almost as if they were brothers even on the football fields at the University of Alabama?

Certainly, it was not MIT's efforts to harness thermonuclear fusion in your Alcator project. It was the March on Washington, the civil rights protests, the civil rights litigation, King's confrontation with Governor George Wallace, and the political and financial efforts of millions that made such a critical difference.

We must not forget that King's great contribution was not a contribution which merely helped blacks; it helped all minorities. Perhaps women have been helped more than any other group by the 1964 Civil Rights Act. If you doubt it, look over the data. The March on Washington and the ultimate passage of the 1964 Civil Rights Act transmitted a warning signal, telling America to provide more social justice in our land. And these higher new levels which these statutes made possible were unaffected by even the Herculean efforts at the Lincoln Laboratories in developing the distance early warning system, the semiautomatic ground environment projects, and your experimental satellites which have been thrust into outer space. I admire your mastery of devices to determine the physical properties of molecules, such as viscosity, thermo-conductivity and diffusion coefficients. Your leadership in these technologies must continue, but we must never forget that, despite your increasing mastery of science, the weak and the poor in this country can end up as excluded from the current American mainstream, as slaves were excluded from the benefits of Thomas Jefferson's egalitarian teachings of the Declaration of Independence. Thus, if we wish to develop the proper coefficients of true social justice in America, we must have fusion, a fusion of Martin Luther King's dream with MIT's symbolic superior technology.

Last week the distinguished President of Tufts, Dr. Jean Mayer, said, "Several economic calculations show that there is a growing number of people who cannot literally afford what nutritionists consider to be a minimum diet. Of all the foolish ways to save money, not to feed people, particularly at a time when we have food surpluses coming out of our ears nationally seems to be one of the most shortsighted." If Dr. Mayer is correct, and I believe he is, and if we are in a period of retrenchment, which I think we are, what would Dr. King say to us today, if he could speak? What would he say to the scholars, the faculty, the administrators, and the students of MIT, and to our nation? He would want us to understand what I think many don't. In his view, integration alone was never enough. He was not interested in integrated hunger, he was not interested in integrated poverty, he was not interested in integrated unemployment, and he was not interested in integrated crime.

What would he ask you? I think he would ask, thinking of Dr. Mayer's remarks: "What is the value of superior technology, if we can produce big agriculture surpluses and still the poor needlessly starve or suffer malnutrition?" I think that he would ask you, "What is the worth of superior technology, as we expand the number of people who desperately want to work and cannot get jobs?" I think that he would ask you, "What is the value of superior technology, if children can't get quality education in elementary school, in junior high school and in high school?" He would ask you to reflect on the last sermon he preached in Ebenezer Baptist Church:

> If any of you are around when I have to meet my day, I
> don't want a long funeral. And if you get somebody to
> deliver the eulogy, tell them not to talk too long. . . . Tell
> them not to mention that I have a Nobel Peace Prize, that
> isn't important. Tell them not to mention that I have three
> or four hundred awards, that's not important. Tell him
> not to mention where I went to school.

> I'd like somebody to mention that day, that Martin Luther
> King, Jr., tried to give his life serving others. I'd like for
> somebody to say that day, that Martin Luther King, Jr.,
> tried to love somebody. I want you to say that day, that I
> tried to be right on the war question. I want you to be able
> to say that day, that I did try to feed the hungry. And I
> want you to be able to say that day, that I did try, in my
> life, to clothe those who were naked. I want you to say, on
> that day, that I did try, in my life, to visit those who were
> in prison. I want you to say that I tried to love and serve
> humanity.

These are the critical issues on which we must focus, if we truly want to rekindle the spirit that Martin Luther King symbolized. He would want us to focus on love, peace, hunger, and jobs, rather than simply honoring him today. He would want us to improve the standards of justice in our courts, our legislature, our city halls, our state houses, and the White House. He would want us to recognize that verbal platitudes on justice and equality are at best deceptions and at worst venal, if we are not committed to—and don't ensure—justice and equality for all.

How will we in our generation, as individuals and in our institutions, respond to the retrenchment? Will we have the courage to seek the truth, to speak out against those practices that fall short of our ideals? Will history be able to say of us that because of our values and priorities, the poor, the disadvantaged, and the weak were needlessly harmed, denigrated and ignored? Or will historians be able to say that, because of our priorities and values, we understood and strove as valiantly as we could to achieve the kind of world Martin Luther King envisioned when he said, "I have the audacity to believe that people everywhere can have three meals a day for their bodies, education and culture for their minds, and dignity, equality and freedom for their spirit."

A. LEON HIGGINBOTHAM, JR. is Chief Judge Emeritus (Retired) of the United States Court of Appeals, and the Public Service Professor of Jurisprudence, Kennedy School of Government, Harvard University. In 1962, when President Kennedy appointed him to the Federal Trade Commission, Judge Higginbotham became the first African American to become a member at the commission level of a federal regulatory agency.

The Legacy of Martin Luther King, Jr.: The Path to Human Dignity and Freedom

John R. Bryant
Helen G. Edmonds, MLK Lecturer

John R. Bryant

I DID NOT COME TO SHAKE THE BONES OF MARTIN King. It is always so very easy for Americans to celebrate the dead, and so difficult to respond to the challenges of the living. Instead of spending a lot of time talking about Martin, I want to spend the time I have talking about us.

If I were to take a text, and every black preacher, whenever he speaks, has to take a text (you don't have to say anything about it, but you do have to take one), I will take Luke 10:30 which is the story of the good Samaritan. And I want you to hold that in your mind as our foundation piece. I want us to think about the question: Who is going to take the weight?

The story is told, whether it is legend or not I do not know, that two young brothers found themselves orphaned, and that they, of their own accord, decided to make their way to Boystown. They didn't have train fare, they didn't have bus fare, so they decided to hitchhike. And when the rides ran out, they walked. Late one night, they made their way to the front steps of Boystown, and the Father who was the headmaster opened the door. He could see from the way they looked that they had come a great distance. The elder brother, because his younger brother had long since become tired, had carried his younger brother the last couple miles on his back. Upon seeing this, the Father said to the oldest boy, "Put him down. That boy is going to break your back." And the elder brother responded, "He ain't heavy. He's my brother."

Jesus challenged us in the same way nearly two thousand years ago. He told the story trying to communicate that we—who are ethical people—must be neighbors. We must be driven by love and respect for each other to bear each other's load. He told the story of the Good Samaritan.

The Word says that when a certain man was going down the road from Jerusalem to Jericho, he fell among thieves who robbed him. The scripture does not say the man's name. It simply refers to him as a certain man. It seems as if the man had no identity. A certain man, an unidentified man, a regular man on the road between Jerusalem and Jericho was fallen upon by thieves who robbed him, beat him, and left him for dead. They stripped him of his clothing that he needed to protect himself from the chill of the morning and the blistering sun in the day. Then they robbed him, beat him, and left him for dead. A certain man on a distant road.

Then the Word says that a priest came by. He—who represented ethics and morality—looked and walked on. He left the stripped, beaten, robbed man on the road. After he left, a Levite came by—one who represents law and justice—and he looked and saw the stripped, beaten and robbed man, and he walked on. There are probably many good reasons why both walked on, why neither decided to take the weight. It was a dangerous road, twelve miles between Jerusalem and Jericho that was infamous for being a place where desperadoes hung out. If they had stopped, the same thing could have happened to them. They could have stopped, but they had a different agenda, and to stop would have meant to reorder their priorities completely. They could have stopped, but if they stopped, they could have become liturgically unclean, and they were on their way to a clean place to do a clean thing, to be amongst clean people.

Who's going to take the weight? Maybe that road is too far from us. Let me try to bring it closer, to a certain man and a certain woman. Certain men and women fell on the road called the Middle Passage. I really don't know their names: coon, boy, girl, uncle, auntie, nigger. They were fallen upon by robbers, set upon, held down, captured by thieves who stripped them, stripped them of their inalienable rights— life, liberty and the pursuit of happiness. Stripped them of their culture, told them they were a no people from nowhere. Stripped them of their language, stripped them of their drums, stripped them of their identity, their pride. Stripped them, and then beat them with slavery, with oppression, with segregation, and lynched and tarred and feathered them. Beat them until that which was once called beautiful, even to their own eyes, looked ugly. Beat them until they became dizzy and confused from the blows to their heads, until they even thought that the thieves were right and they were wrong. Beat them, robbed them, and left them for dead. Left them to become spooks by the door, to become Ellison's invisible man and invisible woman. Left them out of business, out of government, out of academia. Left them on that terrible bloody dangerous road. Left them for dead.

Who's going to take the weight? Patriots looked and kept walking. Justice, too often, looked and kept walking. Liberals stopped long enough to say, "Isn't it a shame?" and too many of them kept walking. Reformers stopped long enough to say, "One day things are going to be better around here," and kept walking. Academia stopped long enough to hold a debate, a research study, a dialogue.

God always has somebody who will take the weight. Sometimes God has had to use those who had been beaten up themselves to help others who had been more severely beaten. Frederick Douglass said, "I'll take the weight." Lincoln said, "I'll take the weight." Harriet and Sojourner said, "We'll take the weight." Nat Turner said, "I'll take the weight." John Brown said, "I'll take the weight." Marcus Garvey and Malcolm X, and John Kennedy, all said, "We'll take the weight." And the thieves on the road made each one of them pay.

We are here because a black boy from the red clays of Georgia had the mitigated gall to declare, "I'll take the weight." He had a Ph.D. from Boston University. He was just as acceptable as his classmates. He could have "tripped on out" under his degrees. Martin King could have escaped from his people, from the blood and the dirt. He could have gone on down to Alabama and taken a comfortable pulpit and there resided. He could have taken a chair over at Florida A&M and just taken it easy, stayed out of the movement, out of the involvement, been safe and secure. But Martin King said, "I am going to take the weight. I'll let them call me Martin Luther Coon."

That's what happened to me on a street corner in Boston, Massachusetts the morning Martin died. I thought I was out in heaven. I thought this was supposed to be the liberal seat. On the morning he died, I thought my heart would break. As I stood on the corner of Commonwealth Avenue in my grief, a car full of young men rode by and said, "We are glad they killed the coon."

Now black brothers and sisters, I've come here to remind you who you are. Ph.D., engineer, researcher, don't ever forget you are a certain man in America, a certain woman on the road. Ph.D., yes, split-level home, yes, income, yes, but don't forget, in America you are a certain man, a certain woman. Have they beaten you up so badly that you don't know you have taken a severe whipping? Maybe it's too far from here. You say, "Reverend, it is 1984, nobody calls me that. I'm not a certain man or a certain woman. I'm Dr. So and So. I'm senior research assistant. So I have identity." Do you change, or have your titles been changed? Are you now minority students? Are you now nonwhite? Do you have identity? A certain man and a certain woman, not necessarily on the roads of Georgia, Mississippi, Alabama, or Louisiana, but on the roads of Massachusetts Avenue and Boylston and Newbury and Commonwealth Streets. A certain man and a certain woman stripped.

We have been stripped economically. The U.S. jobless rate is down from 8.7 to 8.2 percent. Ronald Reagan got on the television and declared an economic recovery, but I heard a certain man from the room cry out, "25 percent of us are unemployed." And I heard certain teenagers cry out from that same room, "50 percent of us are unemployed." We are twenty-seven million in number, but nine million, or 34 percent of us, are in the poverty area because we have been stripped. Blacks earn 33 percent of the white median income, and the average black college graduate makes no more money than the average white high school graduate.

Darrell Poole, with Executive Opportunity Funding Corporation in Washington, DC, writes that the net income of the United States exceeds $3.5 trillion. The assets are put somewhere over thirty times that figure. Of the asset wealth of the United States, the banking, financial and insurance sectors own roughly $2.6 trillion. By comparison, all black financial institutions own $3.4 billion in assets or 0.00013 percent. Even though we spend a minimum $142 billion a year, we have no economy because we have been stripped. We have been stripped, and you want to create a fairy-tale land.

As long as my brothers and sisters are lying on the road, pleading economically, we are in major trouble. We have waited. My God, we waited. If we were dressed right, and if we could look right and wear our hair right, if we could fry it right, color ourselves right, walk right, talk right, and eat right, maybe we could make the difference. We waited and we waited to be recognized in a market for expenditures other than liquor, soda, and cars. We waited for the entrance of principal business partnership where we are the major owners. We waited through the sixties and seventies for economic opportunity, and got recession after recession. We waited through the depression of the early eighties for our share of the recovery, but instead of the trickle down, we are being trickled upon. We waited through twenty-five years of urban renewal redlining, redistricting, for the 1980s regentrification programs, where unfriendly banks took our deposit and simply gave them to white investors, who took the money and took our houses and built condominiums that we ourselves could not buy back.

We waited too long. Here we are in 1984. And I don't know any black person in America who is proportionately sharing in this recovery. Instead, we have a combined percent of American asset wealth that begins with three zeros to the right of the decimal point. We waited, we waited, and we waited. But, we have been stripped.

We have been wounded politically. Less than 2 percent of all elected officials in this nation are black. And our heads are so dizzy, and we are so confused and so full of despair that on the east coast alone, there are more than four million black unregistered voters who have given up on the electoral process altogether. I am told that in this area they threw a great tea party because they did not believe in taxation without representation. Yet blacks are told they are racists if they vote for another black.

Wounded and left for dead. Left by Ronald Reagan's White House, who calls news conference after news conference to convince us that we haven't been beaten up after all. Left by the Civil Rights Commission, which has decided that instead of dealing with the problem, they will study how we say ouch. We have been left by the food committee who's trying to decide whether we are really hungry, because they cannot properly analyze the sound of our hunger pains. Left by so many liberals and left by so many academic centers, which have cut scholarships and professorships and cut out programs and centers. We have been robbed, and stripped, and wounded, and left unemployed, and disenfranchised, and cut out, and cut off.

Who's going to bear the weight? Who's going to take the risk? The legacy that Martin Luther King has left with us is a legacy of pride. And whoever stops on the road must believe that God can use them to do some good. I don't care what your talents are, what your gifts are, you got to believe that God can use you. You got to believe that in you there is something that is of worth and that is of value. We, as black people, have bean beaten up for so long, we do not believe that we are able. We believe that somehow other folks' stuff is better than our stuff. We believe their ice is colder than our ice. We believe that their intellect is greater than our intellect. That is not reality. That is a sign that you have been beaten up around the head entirely too much.

How about you? Who's going to take the weight? Yes, it has gone completely out of style. You can't even put it on your resume. Liberal—it'll get you in trouble today. If anything, call yourself a neo-liberal, that means something different. You could get dirty, because you don't even know that those whom you stopped to help will appreciate it. Will you stop? Will you help? With your new degree and your prospect of $30,000 or $40,000 a year, you can escape out of the ghetto back out into the suburbs. Will you stop? If you don't stop, there is a possibility you can be accepted to the cocktail party and to the inner circle. They may find you altogether pleasing and altogether accept-able. Will you stop? Stop. And you may say, "Reverend, the cost might be too great." But if, like Martin King, you are driven by love, you will be able to conclude that "he ain't heavy, he is my brother."

JOHN R. BRYANT is now a Bishop in the A.M.E. Church, a position he has held since 1991. Dr. Bryant has preached on five continents and served as a guest lecturer and minister at more than twenty-five U.S. colleges and universities. He has served as the pastor at St. Paul's A.M.E. Church in Cambridge, Massachusetts, and the Bethel A.M.E. Church in Baltimore, Maryland.

Helen G. Edmonds

O N NOVEMBER 2, 1983, PRESIDENT RONALD REAGAN signed into law a bill that established the third Monday in January, beginning in 1986, as a national holiday commemorating the birthday of Martin Luther King, Jr. This historic event was brought about by a number of events piling one upon another for the last fifteen years, since Dr. King's death. I would like to say a few words about the forces which brought this to bear.

Legislation

The coordinated lobbying efforts of the Congressional Black Caucus, which had sought to have this legislation brought to the floor of the House in each congressional session since King's death, finally found a bit of luck or fortuitous circumstance which permitted the bill to come to the House in 1983. A black woman, Katie B. Hall, a former state senator from Indiana, recently elected to the United States Congress, was made chairman of the Subcommittee on Census and Population, the committee that handles holidays and celebrations. She was able to bring this bill to the floor for a vote.

Civil Rights Organizations

We had civil rights groups throughout the United States clamoring for a national celebration to honor King. Many organizations were involved. You know of the NAACP, the NAACP Legal Defense Fund, and the National Urban League, but there were many more with a civil rights thrust that participated. Even some that wouldn't call themselves civil rights organizations, like the Masonic Order and the Elks, made Martin Luther King a priority. Alexis de Tocqueville observed in the 1830s that he was struck by the fondness of this country for forming associations and interest groups. He further stated that "associations are established to promote public safety, commerce, industry, morality, and religion. There is no end in which the human will despairs of attainment to the combined power of individuals united in a society."

Educational Institutions

The public schools, the colleges, and the universities played significant roles. The public schools petitioned the superintendents and the school boards. Wherever there was a number of black students on a predominantly white university campus, no matter how small the number, the clamor rose to "let us have a celebration for Martin Luther King." And those colleges and universities succeeded. I note that this is the tenth anniversary of MIT's Martin Luther King celebration. I congratulate MIT on its commitment. You march in very good company. No educational institution has escaped this consideration since 1968, since King died, almost like a concerted pounding of a waterfall upon a stone.

Sororities and Fraternities

There are approximately eight such groups with a total of 500,000 Greek-letter graduate members involved in civic programs and activities. This is one of those unwritten chapters in black sociology. When black men graduate from college in the South, and many times up in this area, they are not taken into the Lions Club, the Rotary Club, or the International Kiwanis. These were groups forbidden to black men. The same thing for black women graduates; they didn't go into the League of Women Voters, or the Altruisa Club, or the Zonta Club, they simply went out and formed graduate chapters of their own undergraduate sororities. These chapters promote scholastic achievement, raise money for the poor, and organize for voter registration. At every convention, they went through the ritual of adopting a resolution to create a Martin Luther King holiday.

State and Local Politics

The state and local politicians deserve their mention. Wherever you have at least two or three blacks in a state legislature, you have a component known as a black caucus. These blacks get together to discuss what they are going to do—the men and the women. The black caucus has an agenda, and will bargain with votes to get that agenda passed. I am sure there are many people in the state legislatures who had no thought of giving Martin Luther King a holiday, but seven or eight states had created a birthday event with some high degree of visible symbolism before Reagan signed it into federal law. Part of the impetus came from blacks on city councils and county commissions requesting recognition of King's birthday.

Churches

Churches throughout the nation lent their support. About this time of year, churches would invite someone to share the pulpit to talk about Martin Luther King.

In fact, I know of no institution which was left uncoordinated or untouched in this effort. And in the back of it all stood Mrs. Coretta Scott King, the guardian of his dream, the guardian of his memorial, and an agent of social change. There she was, appearing on television, speaking at Democratic National Conventions in 1972, 1976, and 1980. All of this gave a high degree of visibility to the campaign for a Martin Luther King, Jr. Holiday.

Mr. Reagan said once that he did not think he would sign the bill, and then that talk faded. He wobbled on what he was going to do. Why? Because Americans had witnessed the political coming of age of blacks, and a rare political irony. The King Bill honors a man who, more than any other, paved the way for blacks to become politically empowered enough to put pressure on the President of the United States. For this reason, I classify King as the second Emancipator. The first was Abraham Lincoln, at the conclusion of the Civil War. Martin Luther King was a catalyst for the second Emancipation. The forces of history helped him by converging at a significant moment. It did not matter what Mr. Reagan was saying or doing; he was caught by a moment of history. Any president would have been caught at this particular moment, for the simple reason that blacks were voting throughout this nation and records were being kept. When it was revealed by the Joint Center for Political Studies, Washington, DC, that many of the 456 congressional districts had from 25 to 52 percent black voters, people in Washington did not hesitate to push for the King Bill. They couldn't afford not to, with the election of 1984 just over the horizon. Politicians from districts such as Roxbury, Massachusetts; Bronx, Manhattan, and Brooklyn, New York; Philadelphia and Harrisburg, Pennsylvania; Watts, California; and many Southern cities and towns didn't vote against the King Bill. In Idaho, Montana or Vermont, nobody was looking over your shoulder.

This is what I mean about the forces of history converging at this time to give this affair a high degree of possibility. The *zeitgeist*, or spirit of time, was favorable. History, like a volcano boiling inside, decides every now and then to belch forth its lava and change the landscape. King was the catalyst in creating that *zeitgeist*.

So, my friends, that's the history behind the King holiday. It falls upon the shoulders of historians to place Martin Luther King, Jr. in historical perspective. Briefly, very briefly, I present a set of factors in American history that prepared the scene.

In 1865, the Civil War ended and blacks were made free people. Then we had Reconstruction, that period after the Civil War when four million black people had nothing but the dusty roads beneath their feet and the open canopy of the heavens above them. Yet they were thrown out to make their way in a land where their former masters lived. The forces that had helped Abraham Lincoln fight the wars so successfully gave us the Fourteenth Amendment, with the due process clause making blacks citizens; and the Fifteenth Amendment, which made blacks voters. After that, corporate America, which had helped Lincoln succeed in the Civil War, lost interest in the black question. Corporate America began building the great railroads to the west. It was interested in the development of monopolies, trusts, and selling to the South, so it was not going to put one offending finger on the South.

The Fourteenth Amendment has that rare clause called due process, but nobody worried about it. It said that the state's delegation shall be reduced in Congress by the proportion of people denied the right to vote. So the right to vote, in my view, was never fully utilized in American history. The only time we saw some light of day was in the 1940s, with court cases opening up higher education for blacks. In 1954, the Earl Warren court rendered unanimously that segregation in the public schools was null and void, and that segregation creates a stigma of inferiority.

Well, you know there were critics of that. And what grew out of that court decision was massive resistance in the South to school desegregation. A Southern manifesto was written. But then, in the little town of Montgomery, Alabama, a woman by the name of Rosa Parks decided that she was tired after a day's work and she was not going to move so that a white man could have her seat. Rosa Parks refused to move, and she was arrested. Her arrest motivated the Montgomery bus boycott and the establishment of the Montgomery Improvement Association, with a young minister over at Dexter Avenue Baptist Church, Martin Luther King, Jr., as its leader.

King left us a legacy of leadership. The cause was great; he felt a responsibility toward change, and he was not going to shirk it. He had no idea that he was taking on a problem that would arouse the conscience of all America, and even lead to his death. But a leader cannot shirk his responsibility. So Martin Luther King accepted it and moved forward with it.

He left us the legacy of being trained for a job. Martin Luther King had the Ph.D. degree, the highest academic degree. Martin Luther King could handle the English language. If you don't think he could, read the "I Have A Dream" speech. This was a man who knew the power of words, knew how to handle them carefully. He was trained, he knew his grammar and sentence structure. When they put him in jail in the South, he sat down and wrote letters, just like the Apostle Paul. Paul wrote to the Corinthians. King wrote *Letters From a Birmingham Jail*. This man could handle the language, and that's an indicator, too, of commitment to the cause.

King left us a legacy of brotherhood. He called for people to walk with him in his crusade: Chavez of the Mexican farm organization, Jewish rabbis, Catholic priests and ministers of all denominations, young people, old people, white, black, yellow and brown. King's point of view was that when we create a common bond of friendship, we become a common bond of brotherhood to fight oppression.

Martin Luther King left us a legacy of nonviolence. Though spat upon, though people turned their water hoses on him in Birmingham, and though Bull Connor unleashed the bulldogs against him, he had one point: "You can't fight back. If you fight back, you lose the ranks of call." There were a lot of young people whom he had to drill that into. He had to reaffirm the teachings of Mahatma Gandhi and transpose them to our group. Some of them did not like it. That's why some of them said, "I don't believe this man is going to get off the ground." But that was his way. He believed that nonviolence could "shake the conscience of America, arouse the people of the nation" and the world.

Why did King select Montgomery? The march from Selma to Montgomery precipitated the fall of the Southern theory on racial separation. During the Civil War, when the South left the union, the capital had been located at first in Richmond, Virginia. That was too far North, so it was moved to Montgomery. King wanted to lead that march on the center and guardian of the Confederacy, an age-old symbol of the racial divide.

He had a great impact on civil rights. He was not a Congressman, nor a judge; nor was he the President of the United States. But the atmosphere created by 1963, the great marches and demonstrations, aroused the conscience of America. The oppression had gone on for over a hundred years, and not only in the South. Pastures were not so green in other parts of the U.S., either.

John Kennedy asked for the Civil Rights Act in June of 1963, but couldn't have gotten it through even had he survived the assassin's bullet in November that same year. Lyndon Johnson, the most crafty politician in Washington, knew all of the opposition in the South. He had a little black book. If you were down in South Carolina saying you were going to vote against this Civil Rights Act, Johnson would take out his little black book and say, "Well, you got Fort Sheridan there haven't you? We have been thinking about closing eight or nine forts." He would come into North Carolina and people would say, "We are against the Civil Rights Act. We could never get elected again if we voted for it." He would respond, "How much does Fort Bragg bring into North Carolina?" Lyndon Johnson knew how to twist arms. He had a sense of commitment. I grant you that his foreign policy caused him a downfall in Vietnam, but Lyndon Johnson capped the wells of this nation. He had a vision of a great society. He had a vision for the poor.

And where did King fit into this context? I don't want you to go out thinking that he wrote the Civil Rights Act of 1964, which is our

Magna Carta, or that he wrote the Voting Rights Act. King didn't write those, but the marches for change, the demonstrations for change, and the violence wrought upon him thrust this nation to a point where it had to come to grips. Our founding fathers didn't intend a mass democracy. The government now feels some responsibility for the poor and destitute, even as a new school of political scientists is saying to President Reagan that it is time to cut bait.

And so, in closing, I want to say to you that King leaves us a legacy of nonviolence, a legacy of training and education, a legacy of establishing leadership and being prepared for leadership qualities, a legacy of watching, of standing guard. Some are now telling us that we have to prove the intent of discrimination, that it's not enough to show its effects—a dramatic departure from the policies of past administrations. It is more difficult to prove intent than to show effects. What we need, then, is even more training, if we as a racial group are to compete in the mainstream of America. We've got to stop getting mad and get smarter. We must measure ourselves by competence; we can't just keep saying, "Racism kept me from getting this or that." Young people, you can and must improve your standing in school. You can, and I pray that you do.

When I went to college (that was fifty years ago), I didn't have any money except fifty cents a day to spend: fifteen cents for breakfast and thirty-five cents for dinner. There were some others in the school with me who didn't have any more than that either, like Jesse Owens, Bill Bell, and Jake Gaither. All these great Olympians of 1936 were there in school with me at Ohio State. We used to eat at a place where we paid thirty-five cents for dinner. Now the dinner was always a special, but a special had something on it that you didn't want, like prune whip. Bill Bell, Jake Gaither, Jesse Owens and all the fellows never got enough, so when we girls came along, they would take all the unwanted stuff from our plates. But that didn't worry me; nor did it worry me when somebody went down the line, broke a ten-dollar bill, and ordered T-bone steak or lobster or filet. I had thirty-five cents and I knew what I had to do with it.

I knew why I was at that university. I did not miss a word that the professor said, nor miss a word in a book that he had on the reading list. If the professor laughed in his lecture, I wrote "ha, ha" in my notes. So it never worried me about not having enough money because, I tell you, I was not even interested in the food. My heart was marching to the beat of another drummer, for in that tomorrow when my education would be completed, the choice of the menu would be mine. And that's all I wanted to know. I say that to you young people in your preparation for life, "March to the beat of another drummer."

King was a man who would virtually say the same, although his life was not as hard as that of many. He came from a middle-class family. He was educated, he had the money, and he could have assumed another course in his life. But he assumed the leadership role "to march to the beat of another drummer to bring about a legacy of change." So, with indications in the air that things may be changing, let us take a lesson from his legacy of watchful waiting. Let us be sentinels posted high on the ramparts, watching the social order to ensure that the clock of time will not turn back and rob us of our gains.

HELEN G. EDMONDS taught history at North Carolina Central University, 1941-77. She was Professor of History, Chairman of the Department of History, and Dean of the Graduate School of Arts & Sciences. Dr. Edmonds held six presidential appointments, worked on governmental advisory councils, and held positions in many national organizations.

An Illinois National Guardsman holds back a crowd of jeering people at a civil rights march in Cicero, an all-white community west of Chicago, on September 4, 1966.

Birmingham, Alabama, May 3, 1963—Firemen ignore seated demonstrators on the sidewalk and turn their hoses across the street to disperse a crowd of demonstrators.

The Unfinished Agenda of Martin Luther King, Jr. in the Context of the Eighties

John H. Adams
Julius L. Chambers
Leo Marx
Michael R. Winston

John H. Adams

THE UNITED STATES OF AMERICA IS A STUDY IN irony. In order to understand our nation, it is necessary to piece together a large number of contradictions. This ironic character of our nation was interestingly portrayed by Dr. Reinhold O. Niebuhr in his book, *The Irony of American History*. Dr. Niebuhr notes that when America was a new, poor, ragged, loose-knit collection of thirteen colonies, it had the will, the strength, and moral character to throw off the rule of the British empire. And now that we are the mighty United States, rich and strong in manpower, resources, and technology, America is less able to cope with its problems either at home or abroad. It is incredible that as we sit here, poverty increases, homeless people die within a block of the White House, and the nation polarizes.

Martin Luther King, Jr., by the gift of his eloquence, by his strong sense of that which was right and just, and by his courageous faith made America face these terrible ironies and increased the possibility of changing this nation. His unfinished agenda of equality, justice, and empowerment is unfinished even in the eighties. For American history can surface no other person, who, without benefit of any political position, any economic power, or any official status challenged and began to change the terrible ironies which destroyed the American dream. Martin Luther King would not let us live quietly and comfortably with these terrible ironies of great wealth on one hand, and extreme poverty on the other. He made us face the issues of injustice, of personal, institutional, and systemic racism. He made us face the issue of violence and war. He made us face the issue of hunger and poverty more effectually than it had ever been done before. And because he lived, the definition of what America represents is clearer. His vision of America in the "I Have A Dream" speech contributes to the definition of what America is all about. For example, in the United States the idea of blind justice is extolled and paraded to the rest of the world, while at the same time, and in the same place, the nation is saturated with racism and injustice.

I believe the Montgomery bus boycott was the event during which this awful irony was challenged, under the leadership of Dr. Martin Luther King. When Rosa Parks refused to move to the back of the bus, and was arrested, this catalyst mobilized the community, and a new strategy was born. Martin Luther King emerged as the leader. He rose to national prominence like a meteor, and he stayed there the balance of his life. The public transportation system of Montgomery was simply a symbol of injustice in both the deep South, where the incident occurred, and the far North where we still had to face it. In the successful assault on this system of injustice, all the systems were exposed. The economic system, the judicial system, the political system, the communications system, the cultural system were all put under the search light of Biblical justice and world opinion, and were found wanting. And today, the agenda of Martin Luther King, Jr.—justice—is unfinished. So are the agendas of the hungry, the homeless, and even those of our brothers in South Africa whom Bishop Tutu describes as aliens in their homeland.

In America, the image of the law-abiding and the peace-loving community is the mythology we practice. Yet, we protect our race and class systems by any means necessary. I think it is ironic that it was a victim of oppression, a black person, who set loose in this nation the moral and spiritual power of nonviolent love. The civil rights activists of today, and those of yesterday, do not need to borrow the concept "by any means necessary" from some revolutionary theoretician. All they needed to do was watch Bull Connor in Birmingham who protected the racism of the city by any means necessary—cattle prods, vicious dogs, water hoses—or Jim Clark of Selma, with the unjust jailings. But an idea whose time had come and whose leader was available had hit them. So the life and death of Martin Luther King eloquently tells us that the sources of violence in America are its legacies of racism and economic exclusion which have been protected by our seeming obsession with the military mentality. It is an illusion to believe that law and order will ever precede or produce justice. Justice is love organized to serve the people. And Martin Luther King's life teaches us very clearly that if we let love be institutionalized as justice, law and order will follow as night follows day.

This agenda of a peaceful, law-abiding society is an incomplete one. In America, we brag about the right of our citizens to participate in policy making and in selecting the leadership which will govern them. We call it sacred. Yet, it was necessary for Martin Luther King and his followers to generate massive movements to finally have enacted the Civil Rights and Voting Rights Acts of 1964 and 1965. The repressive discriminatory laws that were put in place and in practice in the Reconstruction era, during the Hayes-Tilden election, were not only statutes of law; they shaped the mores and style of our churches, our universities, and our society. And now with the massive March on

Washington which was reenacted just fifteen months ago, the March from Selma to Montgomery, the Voting Rights March in Mississippi, and the Birmingham jail, the Chicago movement finally convinced a reluctant nation that it must pass new laws to supplant unjust laws. And the struggle goes on to ensure the enforcement of the law.

The struggle goes on to get black people to take full advantage of the new law. The number of black people not registered to vote is appalling—over 3 million on the eastern seaboard alone. But, my brothers and sisters, the forces of justice, injustice, and preference are both relentless and ruthless, and the eighties see us face-to-face with these forces all over again. The Burger court takes back the hope and possibility of justice which the Warren court once suggested. The national administration systematically dismantles civil rights and human rights gains of the last generation. It systematically shrinks the Constitution and redefines the role of government and sabotages affirmative action.

The struggle continues to make America the land of the free and the home of the brave. And now the religious right stampedes the nation with petty morality on single issues, but lacks any sense of moral vision and principle that applies always, and to all people, and to all issues. The America which enjoys a multi-trillion dollar gross national product lives side by side with the other America of poverty and hunger. This affluence on one hand, and depletion on the other, is a terrible irony in our nation, and Martin could not live with it. He could not understand why you could have both Beverly Hills and Watts in Los Angeles. He could not understand why you could have Westchester and Harlem in the same New York. Why you could have the North Shore and the West Side in Chicago. Why you could have Highland Park and East Dallas in the same city in Texas. And why, in the nation's capital, we could have Bethesda and Anacostia in the same community.

Out of this terrible irony of complete affluence on one hand, and complete depletion on the other hand, Martin Luther King envisioned and began what was known as the Poor People's March. Martin Luther King went to Appalachia, to the arid reservations, to the barrios of the southwest, to the urban ghettos, and to the rural countryside of the South. Poor whites, poor blacks, poor Hispanics, poor Native Americans were being brought together to address the common pain of their depletion in an affluent society. The prosperous ought not live insulated and isolated alongside the destitute. And so the hopeful name Resurrection City was planned.

I think it is strange that we can sail the new ocean of space, but cannot house the residents of earth. We build rockets to drown out the sound of angels, and will not feed the hungry. With Martin Luther King's unfinished agenda, we cry out, "Let the poor rise and have their rightful share. Let the hungry be fed at America's table of plenty. Let the powerless be empowered." There is more than enough for everybody to have a share. Perhaps it is only incidental that Martin Luther King was killed while he was helping the garbage workers in Memphis and developing the poor people's campaign. Maybe just incidental. However, organizing the poor of all colors and all kinds to demand economic justice and to challenge the unfair distribution of wealth raises questions America cannot hear and will not answer. Economics has been and still is the area from which most of us, especially minorities, and particularly blacks, have been brutally excluded.

I believe Martin Luther King, Jr.'s unfinished agenda, set in the context of the eighties, puts a spotlight on economic development and economic inclusion of the poor and the minorities for several important reasons. First of all, the economic order must be an object of redemption. At the heart of Martin Luther King's profound faith, and at the heart of the mission of his movement, is the task of redeeming our society. This theology of redemption requires that we not only redeem individuals, but that we redeem institutions. As we respond with Christmas baskets to the needs of the hungry, we must also redeem the structures and systems which created the hungry and oppressed, and which limited the opportunities for individuals to be fully human. When an economic order sets priority which upgrades access and exclusion, and downgrades sharing and inclusion, the theology of redemption in the New Testament, the theology of justice in the Old Testament must speak. When the economic order employs its power to restrict access and equality, the theology of redemption and justice must speak. The economic system must be redeemed and made more just, humane, and equitable. And I stand today to declare at MIT that charity is no substitute for justice.

The central issue of people having the goods and services they need and ought to have is a matter of economics. Getting justice in America is a matter of money. If you can hire the Edward Bennett Williamses of the world, the likelihood of justice is good. But if you've got to use a recent law-school graduate working for legal services, the opportunities of justice are rather remote. Education is a matter of money. (Parenthetically, just ask the question, how much does it cost to go to MIT?) A decent house is a matter of economics.

The inequity of economic positions of blacks in America, indeed in the world, makes this important. This is the place where we have been completely left out. While blacks represent between 10 and 12 percent of the population in the United States, we own and control a small fraction of 1 percent of the gross national product. Thirty-five percent of all black Americans have incomes below the designated poverty line. Black unemployment is consistently twice the national index. The gross earning of the top 100 black businesses is a mere $1.5 million per year, which is only one-third of the income of the black church and only one-fourth of what black folks spend on whiskey every year. Therefore, the unfinished agenda of Martin Luther King, Jr., put into the context of the eighties, would declare with his resounding eloquence that we must address the issues of economic development and the economic exclusion of most citizens, especially minorities, and in particular black Americans.

The America which talks about peace and pretends to hate violence is the same America that was at war, hot or cold, during the entire adult lifetime of Martin Luther King. And it used violence, or the threat of violence, as an instrument of policy. If you do violence by invading Grenada, it is heroism. If you do violence to feed your hungry children, it is crime. But both are violence. In the last SCLC convention Martin addressed, he used the parable of the Prodigal Son to call this nation and the world from what he called the "far country of war and violence." This was the first serious excursion of a black American into the business of making foreign policy. And it was not popular, but it was right. "America," Martin says, "must stop fighting in other people's civil wars when it won't finish the promises of its own Civil War." America is not the policeman of the world. America does have a moral deficit on the issue of violence, because it alone has dropped nuclear weapons on population centers. As Martin warned this nation in those years about the tragic mistake of Vietnam, I hope his words will give us wise counsel about the Middle East and Latin America.

Martin King was deeply aware that humankind has never developed a weapons system that it has not used in some way. And that dark cloud hangs over our head this very moment. The fear of annihilation by nuclear weapons, the fear of massive destruction by the moral madness we call war, the fear of cosmic chaos created by Star Wars, clones, computers and robots will take us over—the fear of a revised creation by advanced genetic engineering and a biomedical technology, while we do not yet have a moral order which transcends and governs the application and use of this new engineering and this new technology. Our enlarged capacity for destruction in the context of the eighties adds urgency to the unfinished agenda of Martin Luther King. There is something very perverse when the most sacred item in a nation's budget, the chief instrument of policy in the nation, is its weapons budget.

Let me cry in this auditorium that there must be a nuclear freeze. What Martin's unfinished agenda says is: there must be nuclear disarmament. There is a better way than war to solve our problems. So let me paraphrase the song and say: Let there be peace on earth, and let it begin at MIT.

Finally, Martin was calling us to examine ourselves deeply, deeper than many of us are capable of doing—to go beyond our race, beyond our nationality, beyond our creed, and live as brothers and sisters. I think he phrased it eloquently when he said, "We will live together as brothers or die separately as fools." Martin Luther King, then, was a prophetic black preacher who could do that much better than all the rest. And it was ironic that this preacher could rap radical, social philosophy in traditional theological jargon. That too was ironic. The strong words of Earl Marlatt's poem, "Far Music," describe Martin:

> They have chanted their hymns
> To Olympus
> And the vales of Arcady;
> They have clothed them in rifted clouds
> And rainbow pageantry;
> But Calvary . . .?

Pagans may pipe of Pan
Of Daphne,
Apollo and Aphrodite,
But I shall sing of God,
The God of Moses,
The God of Prophecy,
The God of Him,
Whose life and death were poems,
Singing, singing,
Down the measures of eternity
The motifs of love
And death
And life that carols on forever . . .
Amen.

Let me conclude this statement of the unfinished agenda of Martin Luther King with the poetic language of his Nobel Peace Prize acceptance speech:

> I have the audacity to believe that people everywhere can have three meals a day for their bodies. Education and culture for their minds, dignity, equality, and freedom for their spirits . . . I believe that what self-centered men have torn down, other centered men can build up again. I still believe that one day mankind will bow before the altars of God and be crowned triumphantly over war and bloodshed, and nonviolent goodwill will be proclaimed the rule of the land. And the lions and the lambs shall lie down together and every man shall sit under his own vine and fig tree and none shall be afraid.

"I still believe," says Martin, even in 1985, "that we shall overcome."

JOHN H. ADAMS is currently a Bishop in the Seventh Episcopal District, Columbia, South Carolina. He served as President of Paul Quinn College and Professor at Payne Theological Seminary, is active on the boards of many national organizations, and is the recipient of the Man of the Year awards of B'nai B'rith Northwest and the National Urban League (Seattle and Northwest area).

Julius L. Chambers

I AM TO ADDRESS THE UNFINISHED AGENDA OF Martin Luther King, Jr., in the context of the 1980s. My reference is the legal and judicial perspective. Having represented Dr. King and his followers in a number of cases in past years, I am not sure he would be particularly interested in my frame of reference. His vision and goals were always the complete liberation of mankind and the elimination of injustices. Laws, which generally inhibited or prevented these objectives, simply had to change. The question, therefore, was not the status of the law but rather the status of the constituents Dr. King tried to serve, and how the law could change to improve that status. Necessarily, therefore, we measure the progress of his mission by the changes in the law and in public support which extended opportunities and freedom to minority Americans.

In the years immediately following *Brown v. Board of Education*, we measured progress largely by the degree of desegregation that had taken place in public schools. To be sure, we observed and began to chip away at racial discrimination in other areas, but our focus was principally on school desegregation and overt and intentional acts of discrimination which were clearly prohibited by *Brown*.

As late as 1971, the Supreme Court supported desegregation in a series of decisions which established the remedial principle that segregated schools had an affirmative duty to dismantle dual systems by whatever means necessary. The court held in *Swann v. Charlotte-Mecklenburg* that not only discrimination or discriminatory practices by school systems, but also their lingering effects, had to be eliminated. Following *Swann*, however, the Court, Congress, the executive branch of government, and public opinion, faced with the consequences of the fullest implementation of *Brown*, began to retreat from its promise. By 1973, in *Milliken*, a case involving the Detroit school system and adjoining suburbs, the Supreme Court set more demanding standards for successful claims for relief, requiring more detailed proof of intentional violations. Chief Justice Warren Burger, who called in *Swann* for the elimination of segregation "root and branch" by whatever means necessary, stated in *Milliken* that courts cannot reach across district boundaries in effecting remedies to desegregate schools unless one demonstrates that intentional discrimination had reached across those boundaries. Justice Thurgood Marshall, dissenting in the Detroit case, wrote that the majority decision was "more a reflection of the perceived public mood that we have gone far enough in enforcing the Constitution's guarantee of equal justice than it is the product of neutral principles of law."

Following the Detroit case, the court narrowed further, in Dayton, Ohio, the definition of what constitutes discriminatory practice. Renewed emphasis on the complete elimination of the vestiges of discrimination was restored in 1977, in a second decision in Dayton and in a decision involving the Columbus schools. But the die had been cast. Unanimous decisions of the Supreme Court would no longer characterize that Court's opinion in school desegregation cases. Courts and some private citizens also began to question whether *Brown* and legislative and constitutional provisions should reach unintentional, racially neutral and structural practices which also limited minority access to equal opportunity.

Gradually, we have accepted the limited reach of *Brown*. One result has been that, under current standards, educational inequities built into the public-school system cannot be adequately attacked through the judicial process. Even school systems that appear integrated on the surface have segregation in classrooms based on tracking and testing. New developments, like magnet schools, tend to select white, middle-class children for high quality programs and to relegate minority children to inferior programs. Compulsory segregation has been eliminated, but black children are still denied equal access to quality education. They are not being equipped to compete fairly in order to assume a responsible role in society.

Coupled with these obstacles and practices are policies of the federal government that reject well established legal remedies that provide system-wide relief. An ominous note was sounded recently when the Justice Department intervened in the Norfolk school case, and argued that the school system which had operated a desegregated system for thirteen years should be allowed to return to neighborhood schools, even though the schools would resegregate in the same way that existed before *Brown*. If the Department's position prevails, it will pose a major threat to implementation of the basic principles established in *Brown*. Many school districts, particularly in the South, will be encouraged to attempt to resegregate their schools.

All of this is taking place in a period when public attitudes are changing. In national debates on public policy, a growing conservative trend underlies efforts to convince people that affirmative action and other programs to help advance the status of historically disadvantaged groups do not work. For example, we anticipate a major push to establish the principle that race may never be used in a remedial program attempting to correct discrimination—whether in housing, in education, in government contracts or in admission to higher education. The principle would govern judicial and administrative remedies and would apply to voluntary and court-ordered plans. The only exception would be where there is proven and intentional discrimination against, as the Justice Department says, an individual victim of discrimination. This approach would effectively eliminate affirmative action in class discrimination suits.

Following the Supreme Court's decision in *Memphis Firefighters*, a case which overruled a lower court decision providing protection for black workers from layoffs, the Justice Department now threatens to re-open and challenge over 350 cases that had long ago been closed. You might remember that, in the *Firefighters* case, black firefighters who were underrepresented in the Memphis fire department had been hired under an affirmative action plan. The court held that affirmative action could not protect those individuals in layoffs. Affirmative action consent decrees that had been resolved and that continued to govern the practices of private employers are now threatened by proposed actions of the Department of Justice.

Since the *Memphis Firefighters* case, the EEOC has been threatened or requested to change its affirmative action guidelines. These guidelines now permit private employers as well as public employers to institute affirmative action programs to correct past practices of discrimination. We faced an example of the government's position recently in a case involving the University of Tennessee. In Tennessee less than 1 percent of blacks are in graduate and professional schools, and we had a consent decree that provided for seventy-five seats or positions to be set aside for minority students, in order to increase that dismal representation. The Department of Justice has challenged those set-asides as reverse discrimination. That case is now proceeding on appeal.

We conclude from recent pronouncements by EEOC that further steps are being taken to challenge the progress that has taken place over the past few years. EEOC now proposes to redefine what constitutes illegal acts of discrimination by imposing a standard of *intent* for what had previously been *effect*.

It is appropriate today that we draw an analogy between the promise of *Brown* and the hope, accomplishments and dream of Dr. Martin Luther King, Jr. As we look back on the progress since *Brown*, we can point to some significant success in school desegregation, particularly in the South. We have to acknowledge, however, that our goal of a society free of racial discrimination has not been achieved; nor can it be said that equal opportunity exists for all Americans. We must also recognize that the resources and support available today do not offer much promise for immediate success in achieving these objectives.

But we can find encouragement in the accomplishments of Dr. King's life, and be nourished by his hopes and dreams. Like many of us, he lived with overt, legally sanctioned, racial discrimination. But his dream went beyond the hope of black and white children being educated together. He anticipated and fought for a society in which equality and justice meant the elimination of overt discrimination and its effects on present and future generations.

Today, in trying to achieve those dreams, we have to go beyond the efforts of the last three decades and develop for the future a civil rights program that not only preserves the gains of the past, but recognizes that minorities are disadvantaged not because of their desire, but because of a long history of intentional discrimination.

The civil rights agenda for the 1980s must begin with the recognition that the urgent economic plight of black Americans shapes their future, and ours as a nation. As a first step, it must be understood that those who have suffered discrimination will never have a real chance to improve their status without the opportunity for an education that will equip them to compete. They need a voting rights program that will ensure that they have a chance to elect people who are sympathetic to their needs and condition. They need a legislative program that will erase fully and finally the barriers they still face. They need an opportunity for employment that provides a sound economic base for their development. One could say that the anticipated legal struggle underway today is to define new standards of liability and to fashion remedies that would truly help people overcome the effects of past discrimination. New standards are clearly needed to fulfill the dreams of Dr. King—those he set for the nation.

JULIUS L. CHAMBERS is currently Chancellor of North Carolina Central University, Durham, North Carolina. He has been Director and Counsel of the NAACP Legal Defense and Educational Fund, Inc. He has been a lecturer at the law schools of Harvard University, the University of Virginia, and the University of Pennsylvania, and is the recipient of many honorary LL.D. degrees and various distinguished service awards.

Leo Marx

T O SOMEONE LIKE MYSELF, WHO IS INTERESTED IN American cultural history, the unfinished agenda is the perfect title for a celebration of Martin Luther King, Jr. We all recognize, I hope, that the agenda that we are talking about was not just an agenda for King or the Civil Rights Movement or black Americans, but as King understood and kept insisting, it was the agenda of our democracy that was unfinished. The failure of the American people to carry out the agenda of 1863 was the opening theme of King's famous 1963 "I Have A Dream" speech.

I have been struck in the last week or two by television's amiable capacity to trivialize everything by playing too many clips of Martin Luther King saying, "I Have A Dream," and then nothing else. So that the whole meaning of that speech seems to disappear. I want to read the opening sentences.

> One hundred years ago, a great American, in whose
> symbolic shadow we stand, signed the Emancipation
> Proclamation. This momentous decree came as a great
> beacon light of hope to millions of Negro slaves who had
> been seared in the flames of withering injustice. It came as
> a joyous daybreak to win the long night of captivity, but
> one hundred years later, we must face the tragic fact that
> the Negro is still not free. One hundred years later, the life
> of the Negro is still sadly crippled by the manacles of
> segregation and the chains of discrimination. One
> hundred years later, the Negroes live on a lonely island of
> poverty in the midst of a vast ocean of material prosperity.
> One hundred years later, the Negro still languishes in the
> corners of American society and finds himself in exile in
> his own land, so we have come here today to dramatize an
> appalling condition.

Notice how far back the theme of the unfinished agenda takes us. It takes us back to the Emancipation Proclamation of 1863. I wonder how many TV viewers, who in the last few days have seen those clips repeated endlessly, recognize what that 1963 march really was about. King's point was that 1963 was an occasion for Americans to remember the unfulfilled promises of 1863, just as 1863 had been an occasion for Lincoln's generation to remember the unfulfilled promise of 1776. Now it so happens that this theme, America's unfulfilled promise of democracy, is one of the central themes in our classic American literature—a major theme in the work of James Fenimore Cooper, Ralph Waldo Emerson, Henry Thoreau, Walt Whitman, Herman Melville, Nathaniel Hawthorne, Mark Twain, and I could keep going. These writers were haunted by a sense, as Thoreau put it, "of being born in the nick of time." It was a sense that the ideal America with its vision of a just society, a society that aims to narrow the gap between the powerful and the powerless, the rich and the poor, was slipping from their grasp. All of these writers understood that our culture consists, at its very core, of a struggle to adhere to that original democratic agenda. They understood that such an agenda is always in jeopardy, always threatened by those who see it as an obstacle to some private interest. Now in adapting the theme of the unfulfilled agenda to the particular situation of black Americans, King was tapping into the most vigorous and effective, profound and enduring, national tradition of political dissent.

In discussing the Montgomery bus boycott of 1955 and 1956, for example, he acknowledged his debt to Gandhi. "When the protest began, my mind consciously or unconsciously was driven back to the Sermon on the Mount and the Gandhian method of nonviolent resistance." King almost certainly knew, though it doesn't really matter, that Gandhi in turn had acknowledged his debt to Henry Thoreau's essay on civil disobedience, and that's a reminder that ideas flow freely across national boundaries. You will remember that Thoreau, in turn, was prompted to civil disobedience in response to the Mexican War, a war he regarded, like most liberal-minded northern intellectuals, as a naked effort to expand the power of the slave-owning class. He refused to pay his taxes to support that war, with these words: "I cannot for an instant recognize that political organization as my government which is the slave's government also."

It is useful to recall Martin Luther King's kinship with the native American literary and political tradition. It reminds us how much of his power as a leader derived from his command of the language, a capacity for thought and expression and speech that connects him with such gifted writers and speakers on behalf of freedom, as Frederick Douglass or Abraham Lincoln, as well as Emerson and Thoreau. We do not ordinarily think of leaders like King or Lincoln as having been literary people. And yet when you stop and think about it, you realize how much of their power to lead did in fact stem from their power of language, their gift of expression.

King, in the southern Civil Rights Movement, and especially the Montgomery bus strike, taught disaffected Americans a style and language of political dissent. A year after the March on Washington, the Berkeley Free Speech Movement began. The first massive act of civil disobedience by American students was conducted in the fall of 1964, and most of their leaders had been in Mississippi the previous summer. They had learned from the Civil Rights Movement a new style of protest, of nonviolent sit-ins, marches and demonstrations. That kind of protest was to be the chief resource of the anti-Vietnam War movement of the 1960s. I think white America often forgets that the hopeful spirit of the 1960s—that extraordinary, mysterious, elusive feeling we had back then that fundamental change was possible without violent revolution—was taught to us by King and his fellow civil rights activists of the early 1960s.

But this is 1985 and that spirit of possibilities seems far away— as much a part of ancient history as 1863 or 1776. Martin Luther King is now referred to as a symbolic figure who connects us with the best, the most hopeful and generous and human aspects of our past. By now he represents one of those effervescent moments in our history when the old democratic agenda was reactivated and the country success- fully completed one or two items on its long deferred list of promises. But then we quickly relapsed into another period of complacency and inertia where we find ourselves now.

We haven't time today to consider all the possible explanations for this most recent relapse, but I think it is important to take stock of our situation and see what lessons can be learned from the condition, from

King's life and death. Where are we now? As John E. Jacob, president of the National Urban League said in his annual report released two days ago, "The social and economic status of black Americans today is very grim." In that report Jacob describes some of the gains made during the 1960s—gains that peaked in the 1970s, and then he says, "In virtually every area of life that counts, black people have been sliding back ever since." Black unemployment, to take just one example, is now at 16 percent—more than double the 6.5 percent for whites. And he compares that with ten years earlier, when black unemployment was less than double that of whites. Now one lesson we learned from King and his colleagues is that the situation of black people, of the poor and powerless in America, is a pretty accurate gauge of the condition of the society as a whole. Here, of course, I am not thinking of employment conditions, or even economic conditions as a whole, but rather the sense of society's overall direction, its prevailing moral or spiritual condition. Those are much grimmer indicators of America's situation today than unemployment figures. I am thinking about the widening gap between the rich and the poor, the powerful and the powerless, the relentless militarization of our allegedly peace-loving democracy.

After the integration of the 1960s and 1970s, the seeming hardening of social as well as class barriers, the decline of public services, especially education and low-income housing, and the deterioration of life in our cities, all suggest a decline in American society. I am thinking also of that familiar terrible downward spiral that many deprived young people follow—the spiral that begins with lack of self-esteem and education and leads to drugs and crime and prison and an early death. We are all aware of these things, I know, yet it is important to remind ourselves that at the same time, millions of Americans are extremely well-off. They are rich and getting richer, and our country as a whole is immensely prosperous and powerful when compared with most of the world's nations. It is not the dismal situation of black people in isolation that is appalling, it is the combination of that economic disaster and all its moral confusion, with the prevailing crime of cheerful, even callous lack of concern fostered by our popular president. Even more revealing than what our leaders do and say is what they fail to do and say. How rarely, if ever, we hear them express interest in the problems of social justice that stood at the top of Martin

Luther King's unfulfilled agenda. We would be deceiving ourselves if we did not admit that those problems are not the primary concern of most Americans these days, perhaps never have been. But that does not explain why America is so quiet right now.

Where are the people of principle of the 1960s? Where are those famous white liberals who marched with King in the 1960s? I am not sure I know the answer. But the question reminds me of an episode in the nineteenth century. It's a story about the defection of one white man of presumed principle, Daniel Webster, senator from the Common-wealth of Massachusetts. He had been regarded by New England intellectuals like Emerson as an exemplary politician, a practical man of principle and the embodiment of the nation's democratic anti-slavery conscience. But then in the Congress in 1854, Webster helped negotiate a compromise with the slave power that shocked all liberal-minded intellectuals. As part of the bargain, he voted for the fugitive slave law, a law that required every citizen to assume responsibility for helping to capture escaped slaves. Failure to do so meant prosecution. It was a terrible moment. And Emerson, who had kept his distance from the abolitionists, felt compelled to speak out in a brilliant, angry, savage lecture on the fugitive slave law. He asked the same sort of question I have just asked.

How did the country sink so low? His answer is worth listening to:

> The way in which the country was dragged to consent to this, and the disastrous defection and the miserable cry of union of men of letters, of colleges, of educated men, nay some preachers of religion, was the darkest passage in our history. It showed that our prosperity had hurt us and that we could not be shocked by crime. It showed how the old religion and the sense of right had faded and gone out. And that while we reckoned ourselves a highly cultivated nation, our bellies had run away with our brains and the principles of culture and progress did not exist.

That's powerful language. Our prosperity had hurt us and while we reckoned ourselves a highly cultivated nation, our bellies had run away with our brains. Could this be what's happening to us again? Perhaps. But I suspect that the problem is not so much that people of principle, like Webster, have defected, but that the potential coalition of 1963, for all sorts of complicated reasons, fell apart.

In conclusion, let me suggest one or two possible lessons. They are really hypotheses to be drawn from this recent history. We have been reminded of the fact that the problem of civil rights is a problem for all Americans, not the minority alone, and that only a black-white coalition can possibly hope to fulfill the old agenda. We all remember that in the darkening days of the late sixties and seventies, when the Civil Rights Movement was splitting apart, fragmenting into separatists and militants, Muslims and moderates and Black Panthers, the white liberals became a convenient target for many activists, and may well have deserved a lot of the charges leveled against them. But, however self-serving and inconstant, however unreliable many white liberals may have been in those days, and I am prepared to conceive the worst, I think we have rediscovered lately that there is something worse than an inconstant white liberal. And I don't think we need to spell out what it is. The voting record of black Americans in the presidential election in 1984 makes this point more eloquently than anything I can say.

Martin Luther King understood that fulfilling the agenda of American democracy involves a struggle—*that there is an enemy*. King was a believer in nonviolence, to be sure, but he took pains to emphasize his belief in the need for active and militant nonviolence—resistance. "Nonviolent resistance is not a method for cowardice," he said. It is not a method of stagnant passivity. The phrase passive resistance often gives the false impression that this is a do-nothing method in which the resister quietly and passively accepts evil. But nothing is further from the truth.

Yes, 1985 is a bad time. Mr. Jacob says, "It is a very grim time." He was talking just about the situation of black Americans, but I think that it's a grim time for anyone who takes the promises of American democracy seriously. 1854 was also a bad moment, when Daniel Webster lent his support to the fugitive slave law. Few people at that time would have imagined that the Emancipation Proclamation was only nine years away. I take a little hope from that. There also is at least one truly hopeful feature of the current political situation in the United

States as it affects minorities, and it is implicit in two facts about the election of 1984:

1. The extraordinarily bold and innovative, and in many ways successful, campaign of Jesse Jackson—that was a contribution to American political history that has yet to be fully understood. He showed that the hope of fulfilling the King agenda is still an immensely powerful mobilizing force in American politics. And that black and white voters will respond to it.

2. The relative weakness, the virtual intellectual and moral bankruptcy of the Democratic Party between the time of the convention and election day, their failure to establish anything like a genuine commitment to the agenda we have been talking about. And so when Democrats do not address themselves to revising the agenda, to bringing it up to date, so that we can speak of it as new, they have no power. I think the election of 1984 told us something about the weaknesses and needs of the Democratic Party.

I want to end with this observation: The forces represented by Jesse Jackson, and the forces represented, however imperfectly, by Walter Mondale, need each other. Without the other, each is impotent in the present climate of American society. Neither has a chance alone. Together, they may help us shake off our dangerous and discouraging lethargy.

 LEO MARX is Professor Emeritus at MIT, where he was the William R. Kenan, Jr. Professor of American Cultural History in the Program in Science, Technology, and Society. Dr. Marx has held a fellowship from the ACLS, has been a Phi Beta Kappa National Scholar, and has had two Guggenheim Fellowships. He is author of several books, including *The Machine in the Garden: Technology and the Pastoral Ideal in America*.

Michael R. Winston

SINCE THIS PROGRAM IS IN HONOR OF THE MEMORY of Martin Luther King, Jr., it may be worthwhile to begin by observing that it is quite possible for a society to honor a positive symbol of a reform movement, and simultaneously reject the substance of its claims for fundamental social change. To one type of public moralist, this is rank hypocrisy to be condemned forthwith. Some others may cite this as a so-called "contradiction" to be expected in certain types of societies. For a social scientist, however, such social behavior would reflect a deep and unresolved conflict between certain civic values and quotidian social action.

In the United States, I would venture to say, the most obvious unresolved conflict of this kind is between the values of a just and democratic society and the many deeply held racial beliefs and practices embraced by the American rank and file.

Martin Luther King is perhaps the most apposite symbol in current American race relations. He not only attacked the overt brutality and exploitation of segregation in the former slave states and its more subtle but effective counterpart elsewhere in the country, he also articulated a radical, ethical doctrine that social justice, racial equality, and economic reform were achievable in our society through successful appeal to the conscience of the individual. He believed that despite the accretion of a historical experience that reaches back to nearly two and a half centuries of American slavery, it is possible to ascend to a higher plane in human relations, without violence or other forms of coercive force. In the tense racial conflicts of the late 1950s and 1960s, many hardheaded pragmatists of the Civil Rights Movement regarded Dr. King's belief in nonviolence and the transforming power of aroused conscience as naive at best, and at worst, a deceptive detour from the more direct remedy of a change in the power relations between the races. To a historian with a long (and perhaps too long) view, the

183

jury is still out on this case. In any event, the 1980s present us, in John Gardner's words, "with a series of great opportunities brilliantly disguised as insoluble problems."

Many of those well disguised opportunities, in my judgment, derive from our society's rejection of the appeals to conscience and action that the Civil Rights Movement had generated for decades, from the Reconstruction era protests of Frederick Douglass, through the period of W. E. B. Du Bois's Niagara Movement, to the half century of advocacy by the NAACP's Walter White and Roy Wilkins. Yet, it would clearly be an error to claim that some significant progress has not taken place in these remarkable decades of change since World War II.

We find ourselves currently in a period of ambiguity and frustration, at least in part *because* of that progress. Expectations of social justice raised in the last two decades remain unfulfilled, while at the same time some changes that would have seemed scarcely probable in 1964 are now commonplace. This is particularly true of the narrowly defined civil rights issues that were hallmarks of the struggle to eliminate statutory segregation in public accommodations—hotels, restaurants, buses, and trains—or in publicly supported institutions such as libraries, schools, colleges, and universities. An even more significant rupture with the past was the dramatic increase in voting by blacks, who had been denied this fundamental right of citizenship before the passage of the Voting Rights Act of 1965.

In historical terms, in a relatively brief time the nation abandoned segregation as public policy once enforced at all levels of the government. But beneath the surface of the civil rights advances, fundamental processes that govern the distribution of economic opportunities and social benefits continue to be shaped by motives that had their origins in the racial conflict that has scarred American history since the seventeenth century.

That this country could experience what was rightly called a civil rights revolution in the early 1960s, and yet remain resistant to the larger goal of racial justice, came as a surprise to many civil rights advocates. This occurred because segregation had come to be thought of as a self-contained system buttressed by a legal structure. It was widely thought that if the segregationists' legal structure was over-turned, a new equalitarian legal order would produce segregation's opposite, what has come to be known as integration. The experience of recent years made it clear, however, that statutory segregation was merely a means to what was unabashedly defined in the 1880s as white supremacy. What must now be understood is that white supremacy, as doctrine and social fact, can be maintained without the cumbersome and internationally embarrassing apparatus of statutory segregation. In other words, it is clear that civil rights *battles* can be won and the *cause* of a racially just society still be lost.

This perspective is important to keep in mind because my principal assignment today is concerned with race and equity in higher education in the 1980s. Higher education, I would maintain, is a particularly sensitive barometer of social equity in modern industrial-ized societies. It is, by its nature, selective in varying degrees and a critical element in the selection of the society's leadership as well as its professional, technical, and bureaucratic personnel.

There is a remarkably close nexus between higher education and the flow of trained talent from various social strata to careers that offer full participation in the benefits of American society. Because higher education is relatively selective depending on the type of insti-tution in question, the system as a whole, as heterogeneous as it is, still reflects the way in which the society provides the means for differenti-ated population groups to enter the system or not. For this reason, it is not possible to develop a clear picture of the real prospects for blacks in higher education in the 1980s unless we examine the entire system of education, from elementary school to the graduate and professional schools.

It is more important, perhaps, to recognize how the economic and social systems affect opportunities for blacks and other disadvan-taged minorities to succeed in the educational process. The preponder-ance of evidence demonstrates that socioeconomic status affects to a significant, and in some extremes, determinative degree, the probabili-ties of success or failure in the education system. If this is so, then certain trends suggest that there may well be a dramatic reversal of the educational gains made by black Americans since the early 1960s.

Let's first look at the gains. It should be said at once that in comparison with the early decades of this century, when statutory segregation prevailed, the base year of 1960 represented an enormous improvement in the educational opportunities of black youth. In most of the former slave states, for example, while public high schools were provided for whites, there were no public high schools for Negroes in most jurisdictions. A city as large as Atlanta did not have a single public high school open to Negroes until 1924.[1] All Negro education above the eighth grade was private. In those decades, there was a disparity of several years between the educational attainment of whites and Negroes, with the Negro average at seven years of school.

In the years between 1920 and 1940, the high-school completion rate for blacks improved dramatically, but not nearly as rapidly as in the next thirty years. In 1940, only one in every ten blacks ages twenty-five to thirty-four was a high-school graduate. By 1969, the proportion had increased to three in ten, but by 1975, it had reached seven in ten. Since 1960, the percentage of both black and white males twenty-five to thirty-four years old who have completed four years of college has almost doubled. In 1960, only 4.1 percent of the black population in this age group had completed four years of college, compared to 11.9 percent of the white population.

In 1974, 8.1 percent of the black population and 21 percent of the white population had completed 4 years of college.[2] Between 1965 and 1975, black enrollment in colleges increased from 4.8 percent to 9.8 percent. But blacks continue to be underrepresented when compared to their share of the fourteen to thirty-four year old population.[3] Between 1950 and 1975, there was a 380 percent increase in the number of black males who had received four or more years of college: In 1950, there were approximately 839,000 black males, compared with 1,451,000 in 1975.[4] Furthermore, between 1960 and 1980, blacks made dramatic gains in higher education. For example, in 1960 there were 200,000 black college students, in 1970 there were 500,000, and by 1980 there were 1 million.

Even though there are qualifications and caveats that must be factored into this data, such as a comparison of the graduation rates, distribution of degree programs, and relative access to high quality

The three panelists who spoke at the 1985 MLK Celebration, seated from left to right: Leo Marx, Michael R. Winston, and Julius L. Chambers. The moderator, Helen G. Edmonds, is at the podium. To the right of the podium are Clarence G. Williams, Nathaniel A. Whitnal, Michael Lipsky, and Herman Hemingway.

programs, the progress registered in the years between the first student sit-ins in Greensboro, North Carolina in 1960 and the election of 1980 is impressive.

On the other hand, if one looks at certain social and economic indicators for the last decade, there are warning signals that the educational gains cited thus far may not be sustained for the age cohort that will be entering higher education between 1985 and 1995. Among the more ominous facts are the following:

1.   Years of high school completed does not translate into preparation for higher education, particularly in a period in which admissions standards are rising. According to the United States Department of Education, 42 percent of black seventeen-year-olds are functionally illiterate.[5] Moreover,

only 61 percent of blacks are in college preparatory programs as compared with 78 percent of whites.[6]

2. If it is true that high-school students whose family incomes
    are below the poverty line have a decreasing chance of
    entering higher education, then there will be a significant
    drop in black enrollment in higher education. According to
    a recent report from the Children's Defense Fund, the
    National Urban League, and the United States Bureau of the
    Census: (a) fifty percent of all black children are poor;[7] (b)
    70.7 percent of black children in female headed families are
    poor, and there are 4,600,000 black children in such house-
    holds;[8] (c) one in every six black Americans is unemployed,
    and only 61 percent of all black males are now in the labor
    force, compared to 89.7 percent in 1955;[9] (d) as black male
    unemployment has soared, their participation in two other
    sectors of the society has increased—they constitute 20.1
    percent of the armed forces, and 46.8 percent of the prison
    population;[10] (e) in 1950, 8.3 percent of black families were
    headed by women, which rose to 20.7 percent in 1960, 30.6
    percent in 1970, and 46.5 percent in 1982, a rate three times
    that of whites. The economic impact of the latter trend is
    clear when you consider that the median income of black
    women is half that of white men.[11]

When these facts are considered in terms of probable trends—
especially in unemployment and its corrosive impact on families,
increasing social disorganization, and arrested academic development—
there is ample room for pessimism.

It is true, of course, that individual institutions of higher
education have limited capacities to intervene in a social process
controlled by forces far beyond their control. But the system of higher
education in the United States, as differentiated as it is, has the organi-
zational capacity to maintain policies that mitigate some of the academic deficits of large numbers of minority students who have been
trapped by the residual effects of institutionalized discrimination and
the economic disaster that has struck black Americans in the last
decade.

Especially important in the next ten years will be a redistribution of black students by academic discipline and level of studies undertaken. In spite of the increases noted in gross black higher education enrollment, as John Egerton has pointed out, in all but a few graduate and professional fields, the percentage of black students has never risen higher than 2 percent. This can be attributed to the fact that nearly half of the black students in higher education are enrolled in two-year institutions that collectively have a poor record of preparing students for advanced degrees.[12] Even when black students earn advanced degrees, they tend to be clustered in certain low demand fields. In 1979, for example, 53 percent of all the doctorates earned by blacks were in education. This may be compared with 1.6 percent in engineering, and 4.6 percent in the physical sciences.[13] In 1981, there was only one doctorate in computer science granted to a black American.

Equally perturbing to some observers of black graduate and professional enrollment is the decline that has been reported since 1980 by most large research-oriented universities. The trend in law schools and medical schools generally parallels the pattern of these graduate institutions. As the number of black graduate students declines, so do the prospects for any significant increase in the number of black faculty and academic administrators in higher education, whether at historically white or historically black institutions. Of even greater concern to me is the fact that there has not been an increase in the number of black scholars and university scientists commensurate with the increase in the number of black Ph.D.'s.

In a world transformed by proliferating new technologies and intensified international competition, one of the major questions before us as a nation is: Can we have equity and excellence simultaneously in American higher education? For many leaders in education, there is a chasm that cannot be bridged. Anyone who experienced the turbulent 1960s in higher education may perhaps be pardoned for believing that this is so. There were many flights from academic integrity, as institutions and individuals with deservedly guilty consciences debased the intellectual coin of the realm as the price for greater equity. That was a great, if understandable, mistake. But it should not be allowed to obscure the fact that most institutions have only recently begun experimenting with methods to address equity issues in higher education. It is too soon, therefore, to conclude that there is an inherent incompatibility between more fairness and high academic achievement.

The 1980s are likely to be a time of severe social stress for America. And as the domestic economic implications of intensified international competition become clearer, there will also be greater pressure exerted to abandon all efforts to achieve greater equity in higher education and society at large. This will have to be resisted not only because it would be wrong ethically, but also for the practical reason that in the new global system that is emerging, no world power will be able to afford a laissez-faire attitude towards its economically or socially disadvantaged citizens. We will need to abandon our inherited social superstitions about race, class, and intellectual achievement. Dealing with the mounting educational problems that our social system produces will require new thinking about the central purposes of our educational institutions, as well as about the incalculable capacities of individual human beings. It may be that in the stress of the 1980s, we may discover for the first time the significance of Martin Luther King's role as a social prophet and ethical teacher. We may as a nation discover for the first time the genuine and universal core of the Afro-American idiom that he exemplified, which has its intellectual and spiritual anchor in the still unfulfilled promise of this country as a new nation founded on justice and opportunity. If we can preserve the best in American education's social diversity, while attaining equality—genuine equality of results—for all students regardless of class, sex, or race, then we will usher in a new era that will help create a model for the future of man—a free, productive, and just society.

Notes

1. Meyer Weinberg, *A Chance to Learn: The History of Race and Education in the United States* (New York: Cambridge University Press, 1977).

2. U.S. Congressional Budget Office, *Inequalities in the Educational Experiences of Black and White Americans* (Washington, DC: Government Printing Office, 1977), p. 26. [Report prepared by Steven Chadima and Richard Wabnick.]

3.   *Ibid.*, p. 25.

4.   James E. Blackwell, "Demographics of Desegregation," in Reginald Wilson, ed., *Race and Equity in Higher Education* (Washington, DC: American Council on Education, 1982).

5.   *The Washington Star*, July 27, 1980. Education Vertical File, Moorland-Spingarn Research Center, Howard University.

6.   "1982 Report of the College Entrance Examination Board," *The Washington Post*, October 6, 1982, p. A3.

7.   Children's Defense Fund, *American Children in Poverty* (Washington, DC: Children's Defense Fund, 1984), p. 22.

8.   *Ibid.*, p. 23.

9.   *Ibid.*, p. 24. For adults 20-24, as of October 1983 there was an unemployment rate of 30.4 percent for black males and 32.5 percent for black females, compared to 11.4 percent for white males and 9.6 percent for white females. See National Urban League, *The State of Black America, 1984* (Washington, DC: The National Urban League, 1984), p. 3.

10. *The New York Times*, November 20, 1983.

11. *Ibid.*

12. John Egerton, "Race and Equity in Higher Education," in Wilson, *op. cit.*, pp. 3-4.

13. Blackwell, *op. cit.*, p. 57.

MICHAEL R. WINSTON served as Director of the Moorland-Spingarn Research Center from 1973 to 1983, and Vice President for Academic Affairs at Howard University from 1983 until his retirement from the University in 1990. He is co-author of *The Negro in the United States* and co-editor of *The Dictionary of American Negro Biography*. In 1993 he became President of the Alfred Harcourt Foundation.

Montgomery, Alabama, March 19, 1956—Rosa Parks being escorted up the Montgomery County Courthouse steps by E. D. Nixon, former president of the Alabama branch of the NAACP.

Living the Dream: To Believe and Achieve

Shirley Ann Jackson

"**L**IVES OF GREAT ONES ALL REMIND US, WE CAN make our own sublime, and departing leave behind us footprints in the sands of time." Today is particularly significant for me because I was a child of the King era. I literally grew up during that time. I was a careful watcher and student of his activities, and a believer in his principles. And it was his assassination on April 4, 1968, which caused me to remain at MIT for graduate school. Allow me to digress a bit and personalize for a moment.

In 1968 I was a senior at MIT in physics. I had applied to a number of physics graduate schools, among them the University of Pennsylvania. Now Penn had invited me to visit their physics department at their expense, to try and convince me to attend their graduate program. I visited Penn on April 4, 1968. And it was as I was being driven by a friend back to the Philadelphia Airport, after my day at Penn, that the announcement came on the car radio that Dr. King had been assassinated in Memphis, Tennessee. My friend and I almost wrecked the car when we heard that. And I began to rethink my plans. It was Dr. King's death and subsequent events at MIT which, in fact, caused me to stay. I was going to go to the University of Pennsylvania. I felt that MIT was an excellent graduate school, that it was and is an institution important to the world. And more importantly for me at the time, it was one which I felt that I and other black students could have some impact on.

In his August 1963 "I Have A Dream" speech at the March on Washington, Dr. Martin Luther King, Jr. said that he had to "face that one day we could all sing with new meaning 'My country 'tis of thee, Sweet land of liberty, Of thee I Sing, Land where my father died, Land of the Pilgrims' Pride, from every Mountain side, Let freedom ring.' " We know that Dr. King knew that America was his and his people's country, too. He wanted it to be a land of liberty for all. It was the land of his ancestors, his father, his father's father and many more before that. It was and is the land of the pilgrim's pride. They were pilgrims, too. Not free ones, but pilgrims nonetheless. Let freedom ring.

Now, 366 years after the advent of the first black pilgrims, America is pausing to remember, and hopefully honor, this black American with a national holiday honoring his birth. This man who was a prophet and who died for it. This is a day for reflection, to reassess where we are as a nation relative to the evils which Dr. Martin Luther King, Jr. sought to stamp out—racism and all which goes with it: poverty, illiteracy, unemployment, denial of self-fulfillment. We must remember, however, that Dr. King never lost hope. He believed and he achieved.

Since a historical perspective is always instructive, let us reflect again on certain aspects of the life of the Reverend Dr. Martin Luther King, Jr., and on the recent history of blacks and other minorities at MIT. Dr. Martin Luther King, Jr. was born in Atlanta on January 15, 1929, the second of three children of the Reverend Martin Luther King, Sr. and Mrs. Alberta Williams-King. He attended Atlanta public and private schools, skipping two grades and entering Morehouse College at the age of fifteen. He was ordained as a Baptist minister just before his college graduation, and went on to attend and graduate from Crozer Theological Seminary. He married Coretta Scott on June 9, 1953. He began his ministry as a pastor of the Dexter Avenue Baptist Church in Montgomery, Alabama, in 1954, the year of the famous *Brown vs. Board of Education* case, in which the Supreme Court ruled that segregation in public schools was unconstitutional. And that ruling, in fact, affected my education because the schools in Washington, DC, where I grew up, were then desegregated, at least for a time. The year of 1955 was especially significant to Dr. King. He received his Ph.D. from Boston University, his first child was born, and he had his date with destiny.

Rosa Parks refused to give up her seat to a white man and move to the back of the bus. And from that, the Montgomery bus boycott by blacks began. It lasted a year before the segregation of the city buses was declared unconstitutional, and the buses were finally integrated. During this time, Dr. King was arrested a number of times, harassed, and had his home bombed. Between 1957 and 1958, Little Rock (Arkansas) Central High School was integrated with protection provided reluctantly by the Arkansas National Guard, federalized by the 101st Airborne Paratroopers Division of the United States Army. Again Dr. King was arrested and harassed during this period. He was even stabbed in Harlem while autographing one of his books. During the period 1959 to 1963, Dr. King visited India to reaffirm his belief in Mahatma Gandhi's nonviolent principles. He left Alabama and the Dexter Avenue Baptist Church to become co-pastor with his father of the Ebenezer Baptist Church in Atlanta. He participated in a number of sit-ins in Atlanta and throughout the South and was harassed by the states' governments. It was also during this period that the freedom riders began their attempts to integrate interstate buses, and they were continually attacked, especially in Alabama. Dr. King was involved in a number of civil disobediences aimed at integrating public facilities, and, of course, in August of 1963 the March on Washington occurred, bringing together a quarter of a million people at the Lincoln Memorial to demand the inalienable rights of blacks to life, liberty and the free pursuit of happiness.

In November of that year, President John F. Kennedy was assassinated in Dallas, Texas. In 1964 to 1965, the Civil Rights Act guaranteeing access to public accommodations regardless of race, and the Voting Rights Act of 1965, were signed into law. In December of 1964 Dr. King received the Nobel Peace Prize. In February of 1965 Malcolm X was assassinated in New York City. In 1966 Dr. King moved his struggle to the north to Chicago. During that period, he protested America's involvement in the Vietnam War. In 1967 race riots occurred in various cities in the United States, among them Newark, New Jersey and Detroit. These race riots continued for a number of years, and a number of blacks died in them. In March of 1968 Dr. King went to Memphis to support a strike of sanitation workers. On April 4, 1968 Dr. King was shot and killed while standing on the balcony of the Lorraine Hotel in Memphis. Dr. Martin Luther King, Jr. believed and achieved.

During the years 1955 to 1968, there are a number of things to be noted. There were tremendous changes in the rights of blacks to public accommodations, to integrated and equal public education, to vote. In general, there was a breakdown of the obvious vestiges of hundreds of years of enslavement and discrimination. It is important to note that the period 1955 to 1963 was characterized by massive civil disobedience by blacks and others, along with mass arrests, including several arrests of Dr. King as he led the way in these assaults on racism. Beginning in about 1963, with the assassination of President John F. Kennedy, with the killing of four black children in the bombing of a Sunday School in the Sixteenth Street Baptist Church in Birmingham, and interestingly with the push for legislation outlawing certain obvious disenfranchisements of blacks, the level of violence escalated. A number of people involved in the civil rights struggle were killed, among them Medgar Evers, the NAACP leader from Jackson, Mississippi, and Mrs. Viola Liuzzo, who was the wife of a white Detroit Teamster's Union business agent. It is also interesting to note that Dr. King was killed just as he was beginning to espouse a global perspective on poverty and racism, as was also the case with Malcolm X.

Now let me reflect for a minute on the history of blacks at MIT since 1968, because I think 1968 was a pivotal point in MIT's history. After Dr. King was assassinated, a group of black students who had been at MIT for a number of years—juniors, seniors, and graduate students who were later joined by a dedicated group of freshmen—did a number of things. We founded a Black Students' Union. We worked on and presented to the MIT senior administration a list of demands: proposals to change the character of MIT, to increase the number of black students through recruitment, financial aid incentives and a summer transitional program which is now Project Interphase. In the summer of 1968, MIT had a program called Project Epsilon. Note that epsilon in mathematics means a small quantity. As a forerunner to

Project Interphase, Project Epsilon was meant to be a ramping program for five American black students and one Native American student from high school to their freshman year at MIT. Our demands also included an increase in the number of black and other minority faculty, administrators and staff. A Task Force on Educational Opportunity comprised of MIT faculty, administrators and black students was immediately created in response to these demands. It was chaired by Dr. Paul Gray, who was then Associate Provost.

This was a difficult, yet exhilarating period. Our sessions were always serious, animated, often heated, sometimes nasty. People studied each other, studied books about black Americans, argued and slowly believed and achieved by hammering out a comprehensive program initially oriented to increase the number of minority under-graduate students at MIT, especially blacks, through recruitment, financial aid, and Project Interphase. Many of us who were students spent tremendous amounts of time and energy preparing for Task Force sessions. We developed proposals and went on recruiting trips, sometimes for a week at a time, and although we took time out from classes, we were sure to do our academic work. As a consequence of these efforts, the number of entering black freshmen went from around five per year to fifty-seven in the fall of 1969. The first real Project Interphase occurred in 1969, in the summer, with faculty members as instructors and black and white students as tutors. Now today, there are approximately 300 black students at MIT, 114 Mexican-American students, 86 Puerto Rican students and 23 Native-American students. The first black to graduate from MIT graduated in 1892. There is no record of when the first black woman graduated from MIT, although there was a black woman here in 1908.

The Black Students' Union tutoring program was initiated, and progress was made in hiring minority administrators. Faculty hiring has always been a hard issue. It apparently still is, as there are only fourteen black faculty here today of which nine are tenured, out of a total faculty of 1,100. That's a little over 1 percent. You see more black administrators, but none is running the Institute, yet.

As a nation, America has fallen short by Dr. Martin Luther King's yardstick, even though many things have been achieved. In

January 1986—Leading the procession to Kresge Auditorium are, from left to right, Paul E. Gray, Priscilla K. Gray, Shirley Ann Jackson, and Clarence G. Williams.

1955, there were less than fifty black elected officials in the United States. Beginning with the first two black mayors who were elected in 1967, Carl Stokes in Cleveland and Richard Hatcher in Gary, Indiana, there are now over six thousand black elected officials, although they only represent a little over 1 percent of all elected officials in this country. In 1963, at the time of the March on Washington, black unemployment was 10.8 percent. Today, it is greater than 14 percent, and for black youth in some places, it is greater than 50 percent. And, as you have all heard quoted, one half of all black children live in poverty. In fact, the overall poverty rate in America has increased since 1968 from 12.8 percent to 14.4 percent, putting over eight million more Americans into poverty. Now there has been a recent controversial report issued by researchers at the Harvard School of Public Health suggesting that two-thirds of the residents of the poorest counties in the United States who are eligible for food stamps don't get them. Texas was quoted as having the largest number of counties where people were really hungry. Texas also has one of the richest state universities, the University of Texas. And this, perhaps, illustrates an irony to which I will return shortly.

In general, many of the positive areas for black Americans peaked in the 1970s and have shown a downward trend in the 1980s, but there have been many achievements as legacies of Dr. King. There is a larger black middle and upper class, which is wealthier than ever. However, this is tempered by the fact that there is a black lower class which is poorer than ever. There still are hopeful signs. Blacks and other minorities have made assaults on corporate America. There are even a few black captains of industry, such as Joe Black, who is a Vice President of Greyhound Corporation, and progress has been made in middle management for blacks in corporate America, a concept that didn't exist in 1955. According to the Equal Opportunity Commission (EOC), minorities comprise 19.5 percent—that's all minorities—of the private sector work force, and 8.5 percent of officials and managers in private companies. Black professionals are finding niches in many areas, in sales and marketing, such as Vernon Johnson, who is a product marketing manager at DEC, and in research and development. There are even black entrepreneurs, like Mark Hanna, a graduate student at Stanford in electrical engineering, who formed a software development firm with his thesis advisor. And then there are innumerable franchise owners like Craig Wellburne of Philadelphia, who owns a McDonald's franchise.

All of this has happened, and is happening, as America has become a nation of new immigrants, many with extraordinary skills. And unlike just twenty years ago, when more than half of all the immigrants came from Europe, most today are from the so-called Third World: Mexico, the Philippines, Vietnam, Korea, India, Hong Kong, the Dominican Republic, and Jamaica. California has 64 percent of all Asians in the United States. Los Angeles has 2 million Mexicans, and three hundred thousand Salvadorans. They come because they believe in America, or what they feel it represents, and they intend to achieve. But more globally, we live in a dangerous world, witness San Salvador, Afghanistan, the Middle East, and of course South Africa. And South Africa is important to focus on here.

A 1981 report of the Study Commission on U.S. Policy Toward Southern Africa, a commission which was sponsored by the Rockefeller Foundation, noted a number of issues which act to complicate consensus on policy toward South Africa. U.S. companies carry on significant trade with South Africa and have sizable investments there. As of 1981, the U.S. already had $2 billion worth of direct investment in South Africa and trade totaling almost $4 billion. It's much higher than that now. The U.S. imports from South Africa a number of relatively scarce minerals—chromium, manganese, platinum, and bitumen—which are both industrially and militarily important. South Africa has a strategic position on the Cape of Good Hope shipping route.

The U.S. views South Africa as being important in minimizing communist rule in southern Africa. Now communist support helped to end white rule in Angola, Mozambique, and Zimbabwe. But the issue of race makes South Africa important to the U.S. America is a multiracial, multi-ethnic nation, and because of obvious parallels with some of America's domestic history, sustained racial violence in South Africa and discussions of the appropriate responses here could undermine race relations here. Whites and blacks in South Africa are becoming more entrenched in their positions, for example, with respect to one man and one vote. Violence is increasing, and time is running out.

The debate here over South Africa and the divestment movement illustrates an irony in the American character. Americans have always perceived that it is in our hearts and spirits to be concerned for human rights, life and liberty for all. This is evidenced by a haven provided for Salvadorans, by the South Africa divestment movement itself, by the concern for the plight of Soviet Jews, and from a more historical perspective, our involvement in World Way II in fighting the Nazis. At the same time, there have been and are quirks: the imprisonment of Japanese Americans during World War II, the treatment of black GI's in World War II. In fact, there was an official army director telling the French, who fought side by side with black GI's, not to praise too highly the Negro troops for their performance in battle. During World War I, President Woodrow Wilson stated that, "It was a pity to waste good white men in a battle with such a foe. The cost of sacrifice would be nearly equalized were the job assigned to Negro troops."

Closer to today, we have mob situations in cities when blacks move into white neighborhoods, and we have attempts to dismantle affirmative action programs. People tend to forget that affirmative action is a relatively new phenomenon and it is the only mechanism by which black professionals have been given the opportunity to advance in the corporate world. People, particularly in universities, tend to reflect on how blacks prefer jobs in the corporate sector to those in academia. It helps minority firms to get their fair share of projects funded by federal money.

Another irony is reflected in the efforts to raise money to feed those starving in Ethiopia and to aid American farmers, while the level of hunger has risen in this country. One could argue, and this is not meant as an attack, but it is just a statement, that a similar phenomenon occurs when elite schools overlook their own backyards when looking for minority students. Nevertheless, while time may be running out in South Africa, we still have the opportunity for continued change here.

When we Americans believe we can achieve and then we don't, we fall back to petty visions and grievances. So I challenge you to believe again. I challenge you students, particularly minority students, with the following. Because of immigration, because of the electronic age with its rapid flow of information, our society and the world are becoming more pluralistic. This means that a sense of self is impor-tant—who you are, and where you come from. It also means that shared education at a high level is essential to the functioning of a free democratic society and to the fostering of a common culture, as well as the understanding of different cultures and how they can coexist. You have that opportunity here. You also know that those people in our society who do not possess the level of skills, literacy and training essential for the times will be effectively disenfranchised, not simply from the material rewards which accompany competent performance, but also from the chance to participate fully in our national life.

Dr. Martin Luther King, Jr. believed in excellence. He had an excellent mind which he disciplined through study and which he then applied to changing American society. You have the responsibility to fully engage MIT, to fully educate yourselves for life—no hiding in the shadows. If your experience here is not a full one, there is really no point in coming the distance, spending the time and the money being here.

To the faculty and administration of MIT, I challenge you on South Africa, not merely relative to divestment. Now I know many of my colleagues have been involved in activities to bring scholars from other repressive countries to the U.S. to work. You might think about that here. You might think about bringing students here. Some of you might concern yourselves with health issues for black South Africans. I further say to you that the implied social contract, which allows you in pursuing your disciplines to be isolated from the currents of our time, may need to be slightly renegotiated—at least in the sense of facing up to an implied contract with your minority students and colleagues as you have with all students and all your colleagues. Engage them. Seek to increase their numbers. Give them real academic and career opportunity within the Institute. Bring them in.

Now I would like to leave you with some thoughts of Dr. Martin Luther King himself, which I think are germane to my earlier remarks. Dr. King said, "The measure of a man is not where he stands in moments of comfort and convenience, but where he stands at times of challenge and controversy." He also said, "When I speak of integration, I don't mean a romantic mixing of colors, I mean a real sharing of power and responsibilities." He said, "It is wrong to use immoral means to attain moral ends," referring to violence, the use of violent means. But now I must affirm that it is just as wrong, perhaps more so, to use moral means to preserve immoral ends. He also said, "There is one evil that is worse than violence, and that is cowardice."

Finally, let us remember again that Dr. Martin Luther King, Jr.'s greatest legacy to us is that he never gave up hope. As stated by Andrew Young, mayor of Atlanta, "Hope transformed to achievement in his lifetime." He believed and he achieved. After all, his birthday is a national holiday. Remember the Reverend Jesse Jackson's presidential candidacy. After all, you are here, I am here, and now we must believe and achieve. And I ask you to join with me in reaffirming your belief—ask each of you to stand and sing the words to what has been called the black national anthem, written by James Weldon Johnson and J. Rosamond Johnson.

Lift every voice and sing, till earth and
 heaven ring
Ring with the harmonies of liberty;
Let our rejoicing rise, high as the
 listening skies,
Let it resound loud as the rolling sea.
Sing a song full of the faith that the dark past
 has taught us;
Sing a song full of the hope that the present
 has brought us.
Facing the rising sun of our new day begun,
Let us march on till victory is won.

 SHIRLEY ANN JACKSON is a theoretical physicist of
international renown. She has worked at the AT&T Bell
Labs, and has been a lecturer at the NATO Advanced
Study Institute of Antwerp. Dr. Jackson is the first black
woman in the United States to receive the Ph.D. in
physics, and the first to earn a Ph.D. from MIT. She has
served on the MIT Corporation for nearly twenty years,
and is the recipient of dozens of awards and honors.

Newark, New Jersey, March 27, 1968—Martin Luther King, Jr. spreading his hands over a group of admiring children on arrival in Newark for a tour of the city's riot areas.

Introspection, Outreach and Inclusion: Achieving Pluralism at MIT

Samuel D. Proctor

I NTROSPECTION, OUTREACH AND INCLUSION: Achieving Pluralism at MIT. Let's put this in the frame of reference of the King legacy to see how these things are connected. Anyone as old as I, who lived in the pre-Martin Luther King era and who has remained active for a good while in the post-Martin Luther King era, will recognize what his legacy bequeathed to us.

In 1955 when all of this began, black folk had negotiated some kind of a peace with the whole issue of racism in America. In those days a black community was fitted out with all the paraphernalia that it needed to remain adjusted to what seems now to have been a perfectly abominable situation.

When I was a boy in Norfolk, Virginia, we had black grocery stores on almost any corner in a black community. The man who brought ice to my home had a great big orange and green ice wagon with the healthiest looking horse you ever saw, and we would love to ride on his ice wagon all day long on a Saturday to be with that big handsome horse and just watch Mr. Petty collect his money—a black businessman who delivered ice throughout our entire community. The vegetable man, Mr. Hackett, was a black man. My dentist was black. My physician was black. My bandmaster was black. My football coach was black, the principal of the high school, the biology teacher, the English teacher. No white person touched my life, except a used car salesman, when I was growing up in a black, segregated, dusty hollow called Huntersville in Norfolk, Virginia. Do you know what it means to have that kind of environment? I had become accustomed to seeing competent black people functioning in every aspect of life.

We were not arrogant about it. We were not filled with hostility about it. We didn't hate anybody. There was a negotiated settlement, and only God knows how long that might have lasted. We had fraternities and Masonic lodges, great big stone churches, big choirs— we had them all fitted out to accommodate every need that we could anticipate. There was a lot of poverty, but most of us had no working definition of poverty, so we didn't count ourselves among the poor. We just lived it out some kind of a way. That's what it was like in the pre-King era. Why, we even had debutante balls every spring, and Greek-letter fraternities and sororities. Martin Luther King, Jr. was a part of it; you couldn't have found anybody more middle-class and more deeply submerged in the black community.

He used to tell me about his home, where they had telephones on every floor and two bathrooms in the house—most people had only one, and that was out a little distance from the house. He was never poor. In all of my conversations with him, I can never remember him talking about having a job when he was a boy. When he was up here in graduate school at Boston University he had an automobile, and that was rare. King was a part of this well organized, neatly designed black community.

This young man who brought such rich endowments—from his home, from his education—found himself in a position, therefore, to invest himself in the enormous movement for social change. King used to tell me how when he was a boy, people would come to his house to stay, because black folks could not stay in the hotels and motels.

Whoever had a great big house, like a black Baptist preacher or a Methodist bishop or presiding elder, was obliged to open up his guest rooms, and his wife was obliged to serve dinner to all of these dignitaries who came through. King would say to me, "You know, Sam, the door bell would ring, and there would be Mordecai Johnson from Howard University, Howard Thurman, Mary McLeod Bethune, or Thurgood Marshall." All of these illustrious people would be using the King's household as a stopover place. And so King began to hear ideas about the dreams and aspirations of black people right from the fountain, when he was a little fellow. Then he would sit on the edge of his grandfather's pulpit and hear these thunderous Baptist preachers just roar rhythmic tones, all about the great eighth-century prophets and the Sermon on the Mount, and the Great Hymn to Love by the Apostle Paul. So when you heard King speak, you heard these echoes from that kind of a past.

Then he went to Morehouse College. Morehouse is not like a college, Morehouse is more like a "cult." I was down there one day for the Charter Day ceremony and when I finished my talk, President Gloster got up and said, "If there is a mountain," and the whole Morehouse family responded, "We'll climb it." Then he went on. "If there is a river." "We'll cross it." "If there is a disease" "We'll heal it." And he went on with this little antiphonal ceremony, and I thought to myself, "This is not a school, this is a religion; this is a cult down here." But you see, there were personalities like Benjamin Mays and Charles Hubert, people who were deeply committed to seeing to it that these young men defied every stereotype, that they killed every rumor about black people, and that they ascended to the heights in whatever field they entered. All over the world you'll find them in places of influence—the Morehouse people.

King went on to Crozer Theological Seminary, and at that seminary they did not sit down and memorize Bible verses. The first thing you did at Crozer was to study the oriental background of the Old Testament. You had to know all the Babylonian and the Egyptian and Assyrian influences that poured into ancient Judaism. And then when we studied the New Testament, we started off with Alexander the Great. We had to put the Greco-Roman world together, like a jigsaw puzzle, then see how later Judaism was fitted into the world of the Greco-Roman influences; and then see Jesus of Galilee against that background. Then King came here to Boston University, a Methodist institution that emphasized heavily the social aspects of Christian gospel.

Now I have gone through the pains to put these things together so that you would understand who this person was who came on the scene at that fortuitous moment when Rosa Parks refused to give up her seat. The Montgomery Improvement Association put him out front, and he went on to pursue his career which is so familiar to all of us now. How well this legacy embraced his awareness and concern for the poor and the helpless, his deep commitment to community in America, and his passion for justice in matters social, economic and political.

How does this relate to the pluralism and community that you seek at MIT? I have the suspicion that universities and colleges are now at the point of taking a fresh look at who they are, what they stand for and why they are here. We have been so terribly embarrassed by educated people in high places with no sense of purpose, that schools and colleges will have to look again at what it is they're trying to do.

Our nation, with all of its wealth and all of its technological success, has now in New York City 23,000 people with no homes at all. Many parts of New York City have been bombed out; they look exactly like German cities after World War II. And nobody has the genius for funding or designing the replenishment of housing in big cities all over America. With all of the things we can do, we cannot find a way to rebuild the cities of America. The only thing we can do about crime is to build bigger and bigger jails; we haven't figured out any kind of a way to rehabilitate people who have gone with lives of crime. We don't know how to take a kid twelve years old who has not been parented at all and institute a program of surrogate parenting. All we know to do is to let that kid grow up to be an adult criminal. Very fundamental things about our society have been left unattended, while our fine educational institutions continue to thrive and grow.

What it says to me is that there is no theme or purpose to all of this. There is no plan that we want to see pursued in higher education.

If we all succeeded at what we are trying to do in our universities and colleges, then what on earth would the world look like? I am afraid to answer that question. I am afraid that we do not have anything we can count on except that our young people want to get out of here and make all of the money they can make as quickly as they can make it, and head for early retirement. Where is the idealism? It vanished somehow. What do we stand up and sing anthems about anymore? We have a vague sort of thing that we call academic excellence, but what a deceptive sort of thing that can be. You can spend a long time asking the wrong questions and keep on getting the wrong answers.

I remember going to Yale for graduate school back in 1946 and Dean Weigle saying to me, "Mr. Proctor, I am confused about colored students from the South." In those days, we weren't black. (I am so old I've been everything, you know.) I have been black about twenty-four months. I was colored at that time. He said, "Mr. Proctor, I have your Graduate Record Examination score before me. You have been here one semester, and you have made very strong grades. What confuses me is that this record shows that in the verbal and social sciences and some of the other areas, you are way up above the national norm, but in mathematics and chemistry and physics and the fine arts, you are off the bottom. Tell me about that." I said, "Dean Weigle, had you attended the inimitable Booker T. Washington High School in Norfolk, Virginia in the days of the Great Depression, your score would look the same way my score looks." He said, "But how can you do so well in some other areas?"

I said, "Dean, I have had to learn how to live out the answers to questions that you haven't thought of yet. There is a whole range of knowledge in my life, existential knowledge that I have, that has never occurred to you. What would you do if you went to a water fountain and they had two faucets there? One that you use with your right hand and one that you use with your left hand. You, being right-handed, sought a right-handed drink of water, and somebody hollered, 'Hey boy, that ain't your fountain. Use the left-handed one.' I am not left-handed. I turned the left-handed fountain and water squirted all in my face. I couldn't control it. Then I walked away from that thing and said, 'Who thought that up?' You would walk away from that thing asking the same thing. I remember having to walk away from experiences like that over and over again. So I have had no rehearsal for answering these kinds of quantitative questions that are on this test, but there is nothing wrong with my mind. I can be taught all of that. I can think. I can comprehend." He began to understand why it was that many of the students who came from what they called "limited backgrounds" were not limited at all in those fundamental things to which they had been exposed and through which they had to live.

I say that it would be a great moment now, for colleges and universities to lead this country in acknowledging our pluralism—not to be embarrassed by the past, but to acknowledge it. Talk about it. Sing about it. Write plays about it. Standing on the great promises of the Declaration of Independence, standing on the Constitution, and standing on our Judeo-Christian traditions, we have here a reservoir of values that guide us in creating genuine community out of what we had. We will discover that hidden beneath the veneer of poverty, there are persons who have the ability. With enough care and enough treatment by true professionals in education, these persons can be brought forward into real accomplishment.

I had a young man come into the Peace Corps office one day, a football player from Virginia State College. When I was President at Virginia Union, he was their fullback. He used to run through my team all the time. He came to this Peace Corps building and said he wanted to be a Peace Corps volunteer. I thought right away that he was not academically strong enough for the Peace Corps, and I said, "Tell me what was your average in college before we go any further." "Oh, Doc, don't go into all of that. I was a kind of C minus fellow, but I managed to graduate." As I talked with him, I decided to let him talk with somebody to see if we could find a place for him. We did. You know where we found it? In an athletic program in Iran, of all places. So we sent this great big, heavy, fast, agile, active, C minus fullback to Iran to teach the fellows baseball and basketball. He could teach all of these sports. Later we started a program for Iran and we couldn't find anybody to teach Farsi language to Peace Corps volunteers. We ended up bringing that C minus fullback from Iran to put in one of our fine colleges over here to teach the Farsi language. We did not have enough people in America who could teach it, and he had gone over there and had learned a very, very complicated language sufficiently to teach it to these volunteers. When he left there, he went on to Nairobi to prepare the Kenyan Olympic team for the Olympics.

For all of these thirty-nine years that I have been in education, I have seen one case after another. Beneath all of this veneer of poverty and deprivation, there are minds and spirits and personalities. I wish the universities of this country could stop being so lukewarm and half-hearted about it and take this great challenge of teaching and pedagogy and decide that you can induct persons who have had very little rehearsal in their early years into the life of the mind. That is not too much to ask.

The King legacy calls us to just that kind of a response. King wanted to see community developed. King turned down all of those persons who asked him to talk violence, to speak mean and ugly terms about the condition of black folk. King believed that in the long run the nonviolent, positive goodwill would overcome evil.

You could never guess where I got the news that King had died. I got off a plane in Dallas to go to a conference down there. And a young white cab driver with a tiny bit of a stump of a cigarette, tattoos all on his arm, dirty hair hanging down his back, smelling bad, said to me in the worst possible English, "Must be, mister, you don't know what done happen today." There I was in the back seat all dressed up, Sam Proctor. Do you know he choked and cried telling me, "They killed Martin Luther King today"? The last person you would expect to have any interest in Martin Luther King. He stopped his cab and held his head as if to say, "It was wrong for that man to have to die like that." That was how I got the news that King had been killed.

Let me tell you what else happened. A white man, a retired missionary from Burma, who worked for the Baptist Retirement Pension Plan, called me one day. "Dr. Proctor, I don't think Dr. King is properly insured, I don't think he has a pension. I have some extra money given to me. I could pay the first premiums for him, if I could get him to sign up." I told him where he might find King. He chased King all over the South, this retired missionary from Burma riding around in an old, raggedy Plymouth with one big crack in the window and slick tires. His name was Martin England. He finally found King down in Birmingham, and he asked all his aides to let him in. They slammed the door and said, "Man get out of here. All you think about is money, stocks and bonds. This man is worried about justice." Martin England called me. "Sam, they think I am a spy or somebody. They abused me." So I told them to see to it that the man saw King. The man had the premium all lined up, put the paper down there, and King signed it to get rid of Martin England, the retired missionary who was following him around.

Within a very few weeks, King was in Memphis and was cut down. Right now his family is being cared for by the M & M board because a tall, thin, liberal, pale, baldheaded South Carolinian white man, a retired missionary, kept following King everywhere. King believed in that. He trusted in the fact that if we could invest enough goodwill into this situation, there would be a response. He turned down every other cheap and vulgar response, and stood on the high ground that he would not ask for change to come in the midst of violence.

Now don't you think it is quite a challenge to the colleges and universities for us to say that you ought to find a way to create this kind of community, to create community out of our freedom and our intellect and make it real? As I close, I can almost hear someone say, "All of that is well and good, but I think we have done enough to last. I don't think we need to do any more for black people to compensate for the disadvantages heaped upon them in 250 years. We have done enough. Let's be equal toward everybody, and let them catch up by being equal. No more compensatory efforts, no more special meetings after hours, no more special committees, no more special deans." This is the atmosphere that is invading our campuses right now—people who ought to know better, people who ought to know history better than they do, people who ought to know more about justice and fairness. Educated folk ought to know how begrudging our existence has been in this country from the very beginning.

Lincoln did everything he could in order *not* to have to free the slaves. General Fremont out there in Missouri made a big blooper. He saw slavery crumbling down all around him and he gave an order to free all the slaves in Missouri in 1861. Lincoln sent a message out there to tell Fremont to put the slaves back into slavery. General Hunter down in Georgia freed all of the slaves in Florida, South Carolina, and Georgia in 1862. The whole system was crumbling all around; slaves were walking off plantations one after another. And Lincoln told Hunter to put them back into slavery. Then he called a meeting of all of the big shot black folk who were free in Washington and sat down with them and said, "I want all of you to lead black folk out of this country. Take them to Liberia, take them to Haiti. I see no way to free the slaves and save the Union. The only thing I can do is to get all of the black people out of the country." Lincoln turned to the right, to the left, every way to keep from freeing the slaves, and finally he had to get his emotions all aligned behind the simple fact that he had to emancipate the slaves to save the Union. What a begrudging way for black folk to begin, and we have been endured and tolerated begrudgingly ever since.

Now wouldn't you think that after all these years the people who populate these sacred walls of these fine universities would say, "What better thing could we do with our intellect, with our resources, than to see to it that this is corrected now?" Shouldn't they want to remove the impediments, to compensate for the damages, to see to it that justice is done and to respond to the legacy of Martin Luther King, Jr.?

SAMUEL D. PROCTOR is Senior Minister Emeritus at the Abyssinian Baptist Church in New York City. Previously he was President of Virginia Union University (his *alma mater*), President of North Carolina A&T State University, Associate Director of the Peace Corps, and Professor at Rutgers University.

Leaders in a Vietnam war protest stand in silent prayer in Arlington National Cemetery, February 6, 1968. Front row, left to right: Bishop J. P. Shannon, Rabbi A. Heschel, Dr.King, and Rabbi M. Eisendrath.

Memphis, Tennessee, March 28, 1968—H. Ralph Jackson, Martin Luther King, Jr., and Ralph Abernathy lock arms during a civil rights march in Memphis.

From Dreams
to Reality

Elizabeth B. Rawlins

T O ADDRESS YOU ON THIS OBSERVANCE OF DR.
King's birthday is a real challenge for me, because I've reached a point
in my life when the years seem to just fly by, to say nothing of the days
and the weeks. As I prepared to respond to this title, "From Dreams to
Reality," it struck me as impossible that on April 4 this year, twenty
years will have elapsed since the death—assassination, really—of Dr.
King. That's a lifetime for many of you. For someone like me who was
a contemporary of this great man and who has many vivid memories
of his life and times, his joys and struggles and fears, it's really difficult
to recall those days and the intervening years without feeling great
ambivalence about today's realities.

I'm a product of the Cambridge Public Schools. I attended high
school here at a time when few black students went on to college. MIT
was that big institution at one end of Cambridge. Nobody I knew came
to MIT. No one I knew even discussed coming here. That doesn't mean
that there were no black people here, but no one I knew came here.
There were no dreams then of inclusion. There were no grants in case
someone had the dream. There were no loans. There was no work
study. And so, in preparation, as I went to my high school, there was

no Upward Bound Program, there was no alternative school, there was no ABC Program, there was no Bridge Program. At the colleges there were no black student organizations or black student unions. In fact there was no Cambridge Rindge and Latin School when I finished. Just Rindge Technical High School and Cambridge High and Latin School.

There was also no Black History Month, so an event such as this would not have occurred. In fact, it wouldn't even have been imagined. But there was Negro History Week, and that did the work that needed to be done in teaching us our heritage. Although we did learn a lot about famous black people in our lives, we learned it from our families or from the ministers in our churches or from the directors and the workers at the community centers. The schools were not the place to learn about our history.

Now, according to the *American Heritage Dictionary,* a dream is the following: either a series of images, ideas, and emotions occurring in certain stages of your sleep; a daydream or reverie; a state of abstraction or trance; a wild fancy or a hope; an aspiration or an ambition; or something that is extremely beautiful, fine, or pleasant. People speak of chasing a dream or they equate it with a nightmare. Langston Hughes, a very famous black poet, wrote of a dream deferred and the consequences of deferring a dream. I have just heard about a dream—the MIT/Cambridge Rindge and Latin School collaborative program. Governor Michael Dukakis said during the presidential campaign that kids should be able to live the dream of a college education and the opportunities it brings. Our dreamer, the dreamer about whom we speak today, proclaimed, "I have a dream." For twenty years now, countless numbers of people have continued to work in a variety of ways to make his dream a reality. It takes hard work to turn a dream into a reality. Along the way, the dream can become a nightmare, but if the dreamer awakens and dreams again, the dream can still become a reality; that is, something extremely beautiful, fine, and pleasant.

The dream of which we speak today was born in a time of intense struggle and hostility. It was born at a time when many felt things would or could not get worse. If you were living in the South, your proximity to all of the terror was much closer and you had a feeling that it couldn't get better. But for the dreamer, if you lived in the North, West or the East, you were affected almost as much as the people who were close to it. You did have a terrible feeling that things could get no worse.

It was a time of contradictions. Number one, I thought hatred reigned, but its expression gave rise to demonstrations of love and support across boundaries of race, class, religion and region. Secondly, violence reigned, but its expression awakened the potential Rip Van Winkles who saw this revolution as a bad dream through which they hoped to sleep. Defiance of the law reigned, but those acts of defiance gave rise to federal intervention and the beginning of the integration of public schools in Mississippi, Arkansas and Alabama, and the beginning of a lot of other things.

I personally have been engaged for several of the past twenty years in looking at the influence that the nightmare of King's assassination had on education, especially higher education in predominantly white colleges and universities. After all, that's where I am every day. Prior to that horrendous night, which was, incidentally, Maundy Thursday or Holy Thursday in the Christian Church's calendar, it would be safe to say that these institutions of learning, acknowledged to be in the minds of many people some of the finest in the nation, if not the world, vied with Christian Churches for top billing as the most segregated institutions in our society. I think that Dr. King addresses this issue in his *Letter from a Birmingham Jail.*

With Dr. King's assassination and the subsequent riots in major northern cities, an increased sense of purpose and a new image of self was born, especially in black students. It was as if people suddenly recognized how ridiculous it was that in institutions dedicated to learning, teaching, research, and service—that's what institutions of higher education are about—there was an appalling lack of learning, teaching, research, and service of, by and about a very significant segment of the American population, many of whose ancestors predated those who were "non-colored." To the degree the situation continued, they felt the progress of American society at large was to be affected.

Folks in the late sixties and early seventies caught the spirit of the dreamer, whose life we celebrate today. We who are Afro-Americans in this audience, in large measure, are here today—that is here in Kresge Auditorium, here at MIT, here at Simmons, here at Boston University, Harvard, and so forth—because of that dream: students, faculty, administrators and staff. Absent that dream, and the statement of it in such eloquent and powerful terms and to such a diverse audience, I doubt seriously that many of the changes of the past twenty years would yet have taken place.

M. Scott Peck, in his book *The Road Less Traveled,* begins by saying, "Life is hard." Understanding and coming to terms with that concept helps to make the difficult possible to handle. One could say that Martin Luther King, Jr. was one of those folks to whom life dealt its most serious blows. That may well have been the reason or the inspiration for his dream speech. He, more than many others, knew that dreams of better times are what makes it possible to weather the harsh realities. Knowing or believing that we will reach the goal or dream provides the impetus to continue the struggle, to do the work, to perform the tasks, to bear the burdens, to smile in the face of adversity, to suffer the setbacks in order to realize the dream.

Now at the risk of appearing to exaggerate profoundly, I'd like to suggest that dreams of a new reality and the ability to dream those dreams and to see them as dreams rather than nightmares, fancies or reveries are responsible for the ability of America's Afro-American citizens to survive in this country. Today's realities, despite the progress made, contain many of the realities of the King years. Listen to a quote from the final chapter, "The World House," of his book called *Where Do We Go From Here: Chaos or Community?* Remember that he wrote it in 1965 or 1966:

> Some years ago, a famous novelist died. Among his
> papers was found a list of suggested plots for future

stories, the most prominently underscored being this one:
"A widely separated family inherits a house in which they
have to live together." This is the great new problem of
mankind. We have inherited a large house, a great "world
house" in which we have to live together—black and
white, Easterner and Westerner, Gentile and Jew, Catholic
and Protestant, Muslim and Hindu—a family unduly
separated in ideas, culture and interest, who, because we
can never again live apart, must learn somehow to live
with each other in peace.

. . . .

From time immemorial, men have lived by the principle
that "self-preservation is the first law of life." But this is a
false assumption. I would say that other-preservation is
the first law of life. It is the first law of life precisely
because we cannot preserve self without being concerned
about preserving other selves. The universe is so struc-
tured that things go awry if men are not diligent in their
cultivation of the other-regarding dimension. "I" cannot
reach fulfillment without "thou." The self cannot be self
without other selves. Self-concern without other-concern
is like a tributary that has no outward flow to the ocean.
Stagnant, still and stale, it lacks both life and freshness.

With the rise in racial incidents on college campuses today, I
want to say as a professor and a dean at a college here and as a member
of the Board of Regents responsible for 29 of them, it really strikes home.
King said the following in response to those sorts of incidents:

When evil men plot, good men must plan. When evil men
burn, good men must build and bind. When evil men
shout ugly words of hatred, good men must commit
themselves to the glories of love. When evil men would
seek to perpetuate an unjust status quo, good men must
bring into being a real order of just.

I think if he were here today he'd say "men and women." Now,
for those of you who would suggest that these situations are less than
serious, who say, "Well, that's not really racial, that's just kids having
a quarrel with each other," this is what King said:

It is interesting to notice that the extreme pessimist and the extreme optimist agree on at least one point. They both feel that we must sit down and do nothing in the area of race relations.

For those of you who have either forgotten or never considered what the role of education should or could be:

Education without social action is a one-sided value because it has no true power potential. Social action without education is a weak expression of pure energy. Deeds uninformed by educated thought can take false directions. When we go into action and confront our adversaries, we must be as armed with knowledge as they. Our policies should have the strength of deep analysis beneath them to be able to challenge the clever sophistries of our opponents.

Dr. King was great and he is remembered because he had a dream. He must have had the dream long before the August 28, 1963 speech at the March on Washington. His greatness is not dependent upon the fact that he won the Nobel Peace Prize, nor is it because of his tremendous skill as an orator. Nor is he great or remembered just because he was assassinated, terrible though that was. It's not even dependent upon the unparalleled leadership role he played. That was the moral leadership that changed the nation, indeed the world.

In my humble view, he was great and he'll be remembered because he dreamed of service and he turned many of those dreams into reality in his very short lifetime. If he were here today, I believe he would have the same dreams and he'd be committed to the same action. However, I believe with Julian Bond, a former state legislator in Georgia, that he'd be addressing international questions and economic questions and homelessness questions and mental illness questions and all of the other social questions as much as he would be addressing race questions.

In the event you lack familiarity with the life and writings of Martin Luther King, Jr., I cannot encourage you too strongly to get in touch with a bit of history whose impact will be felt far into the future.

Then, make his life and work an example for your own. Then we can hope to fulfill his dreams of brotherhood and sisterhood.

 ELIZABETH B. RAWLINS has been Associate Dean of the College at Simmons College since 1984 and a Professor of Education there since 1979. In addition to her work as an educator, Dr. Rawlins has served on the boards of various mental health organizations. She was appointed to terms on the Board of Regents for Higher Education in Massachusetts, from 1980-82 and again from 1985 to the present.

Montgomery, Alabama, March 22, 1956—Martin Luther King, Jr., found guilty of conspiracy in the Montgomery bus boycott earlier in the day, speaking to an overflow crowd at a mass meeting at the Holt St. Baptist Church.

On Behalf of Justice

Gregory C. Chisholm, S.J.

> He has showed you, O man, what is good.
> And what does the Lord require of you?
> To act justly and to love mercy
> and to walk humbly with your God.
>
> Micah 6:8

TO ACT JUSTLY AND TO LOVE MERCY AND TO walk humbly with your God, this is all that the Lord requires of you. On December 1, 1955 Rosa Parks left her job at Montgomery Fair Department store late in the afternoon bound for home. As usual she would ride the public buses used extensively by the African Americans of Montgomery, Alabama. Mrs. Parks worked as a tailor's assistant at the department store and often supplemented her income by sewing for Montgomery families in the evening. She was known throughout the city for the strength of her character and her commitment to the NAACP. Mrs. Parks was both secretary of the local NAACP chapter and director of its Youth Council.

That afternoon her neck and shoulder were sore. She had even sought out a heating pad. Not finding one, she proceeded to the bus. When Mrs. Parks got on the bus, she sat in one of the seats immediately behind the ten rows reserved for whites only. Three stops later the "colored" section was filled; so was the white section, and one white man was left standing. The driver demanded not just one seat in Rosa Parks's row but all four, since the law did not permit colored people to sit next to or across from whites. She refused to move. After she was released from jail she recalled, "I was tired . . . I was not feeling well . . . I had felt for a long time, that if I was ever told to get up so a white person could sit, that I would refuse to do so." The NAACP and the African-American Women's Political Council organized a boycott of Montgomery's buses for the following Monday. That Monday, on the evening of the first day of the United States Civil Rights Movement, Dr. Martin Luther King, Jr., the twenty-six year old pastor of Dexter Avenue Baptist Church in Montgomery, rose to the pulpit of the Holt Street Baptist Church and addressed Montgomery's blacks:

> I want to tell you this evening that it is not enough for us to talk about love. Love is one of the pinnacle parts of the Christian faith. There is another side called justice. And justice is really love in calculation. Justice is love correcting that which would work against love.

Now, to shift gears:

> e to the x du dx
> e to the x dx
> cosine secant tangent sine
> 3.14159
> Square root, integral u dv
> Slip stick, slide rule MIT.
> —*MIT cheer*

That really does say it all, doesn't it? Of course, it could use some updating but it really does capture the Platonic essence of things. When my mother asked me what I would be taking that first year at MIT, I rattled off the following: 2.10, 5.01, 8.011, 18.01, and the obligatory 21.017. "What do they stand for?" she asked. "They are what they stand for," I laughed condescendingly. My first Thanksgiving home, feeling prematurely that I had acquired the wisdom of the ages, I tried to wow the fans again. When my father asked me to say something in Calculus, I rattled off the first two lines of the cheer. We used to use the cheer to encourage each other before crew races. Our freshman coach, a graduate of the boy's college up the river, would stare in awe as we collapsed in laughter. He spoke English, you see. The varsity coach spoke history.

In every sense imaginable MIT is its own world. In the dormitories one would never study electrical circuit theory, one tooled 6.01. Tech has to be the only place on earth where the "all-nighter" becomes a rite of passage. Basketball teams, track teams, baseball teams never hurt for players, they only hurt for fans. IFC president, tiddlywinks star, UMOC—it was all the same at MIT. The real stars could find the direction of steepest ascent on a curved surface, realize an FIR filter in a computer code, or optimize the motion of a robot arm. MIT is about science and technology. It is a celebration of science and technology. Everybody knew that and fell over each other trying to survive it. During my freshman year, all things were intuitively obvious or you just couldn't cut the mustard.

MIT is crazy, tough, fun and sometimes dangerous to your health. The professors were overwhelmingly white, hardworking, eccentric, busy, difficult, and important. The students were over-whelmingly white, aggressive, curious, bright, technical, critical, prob-lem-devouring pranksters.

In 1969 we arrived fifty-seven strong out of one thousand freshmen—woolly hair, high cheekbones, and African grace. From Harlem, the South Side, North Philly, Watts, East Detroit and Jamaica, Queens we came, afraid but not admitting it, curious but not showing it, and bright as hell but doubting it. Martin Luther King's children have arrived at MIT. Suddenly there were tables of black students in the dining halls. Whole rows of young black faces stared from the rear of 26-100. Runkle 5, Burton 3, and McCormick 6 soon became black living groups. Although some ventured out into the fraternities, most pre-ferred the security of the group. The Acid-Rock music blaring from

Bexley Hall onto Massachusetts Avenue soon competed with Earth, Wind and Fire for the attention of the passerby.

Was the Institute ready for us? Well, it thought it was, it hoped it was, but it wasn't. I don't believe anybody knew what would happen. Some people stared, others avoided us completely. Some black students flaked out and denied the reality of MIT. Some burrowed, disregarding both black and white peers. And some jumped in, effecting a kind of accommodation with Tech. Twenty-five or so of our original fifty-seven graduated four years later. A few wanted little to do with MIT ever again. And others, of course, have rarely left.

Ideally, an academic institution would be a place where anyone could fit in and feel at home. That ideal institution would mark as a feature of its greatness the cultural strengths brought by its diverse student body. At MIT, a black student might be curious, culturally identified, technical, aware of the realties of racism, bright, critical, a hope for the future and a problem-devouring prankster. Such fully integrated people are rare. For many individuals, the reality is that you either lose yourself in the majority or stand adamantly against it. For example, as an extreme, a Jew may change his name to avoid identification or a black may join the Nation of Islam. Again, as an extreme , a light-skinned black may pass for white or a Jew may join the Jewish Defense League. For the majority, culture demands that the individual lose himself within or remain forever on the fringes. The law may protect your right to be different, but it is proving loathe to mandate incorporation of your difference.

> I used to live downtown
> 129th Street Convent
> Everything's upbeat.
> Party.
> Ball in the Park.
> Nothing,
> But girls after dark,
> We chill.
> Nobody gets ill
> In the Place.
> —Kool Moe Dee, "*Wild, Wild West*"

What has emerged in that nether world between all absolute examples is something that may be unique in African-American history. This new personality can be found in law offices, engineering firms, medical practices and even the halls of academe. This black urban professional is affectionately known as the BUPPY. Perhaps originally from 129th Street and Convent Avenue in Harlem, he or she has other things in mind. Reared on Kunta Kinte, it is with surprise that they watch him out among the stars boldly going where only Uhuru has gone before him. They have seen the plays of August Wilson, collected all of Ernie Barnes's caricatures, and can wax eloquently on the differences between the writings of Alice Walker and Gloria Naylor. Jesse Jackson was the candidate and the Chicago Bulls the basketball team. But beyond the hype, black professionals are bright, hardworking, politically aware, success-oriented, careful, fun-loving and sensitive to the prerogatives of race. They are concerned with success, money, happiness and job satisfaction, tenure, safe and secure living and racism. They are not unlike their white peers, if considerations for racial *realpolitik* are excluded.

There are tensions in such a world, believe me there are. After all, we are not on welfare, but many who look like we do are on welfare. I don't use crack, but it is destroying the place I used to call home. Is Willie Horton an object of fear or a point of identity? When the NCAA debates academic preparation among minority athletes, do we run to total our SAT scores and high-school grades? Are we as afraid of violence from black people as our white colleagues? Can we remember the beauty of our negritude in the face of mass negative press coverage?

The truth is that there is no running away from these questions, white folk will not let you. Whether you ever wanted to be free of us or not, your past and future are a part of a legacy rooted in something as accidental as the color of one's skin and as malicious as racism. I believe we will never be free of the dilemma until we are all free.

> But . . . when you see hate-filled policemen curse, kick,
> brutalize and even kill your black brothers and sisters
> with impunity; when you see the vast majority of your 20

million Negro brothers smothering in an air-tight cage of
poverty in the midst of an affluent society; when you are
harried by day and haunted by night by the fact that you
are a Negro, living constantly at a tiptoe stance, never
quite knowing what to expect next, and plagued with
inner fears and outer resentments; when you are forever
fighting a denigrating sense of "Nobodiness"; then you
will understand why we find it difficult to wait.
—Martin Luther King, Jr., *Letter from a Birmingham Jail.*

When Dr. King began his journey, many of the "race" men were
on the ropes. Black Zionist Marcus Garvey had been jailed and
deported. Historian W. E. B. Du Bois was eased out of the moderate
ranks of the NAACP, dismissed from Atlanta University and ultimately died an expatriate. Singer, actor, statesman Paul Robeson was
labeled communist and prevented from traveling freely by our State
Department.

Segregation was supported by both law and American predis-
position. Integration was rare and admired with awe by many African
Americans in the forties, fifties and sixties. Jackie Robinson played his
first season with the Brooklyn Dodgers in 1947, Harry Truman desegregated the armed services in 1948, Sammy Davis, Jr., Sidney Poitier
and Harry Belafonte were moving into the mainstream of entertainment. The Supreme Court had struck down segregated education only
to find that the executive branch did little to enforce the ruling.

Since the Civil War, African Americans had been forced into
their own society, setting up their own schools, colleges, churches,
newspapers and entertainment. There was even a social stratum which
mimicked white society. Education, sex, property and skin color
established one's place in that society. One of the arenas where a black
man in America could be master of his fate and respected by his peers
was in the pulpit of a black church. Of course, the minister could not be
better prepared than by having been educated at Morehouse College.

As measured by the rules of black society, Martin Luther King,
Jr. was heir-apparent to a remarkable legacy. He was the son and

grandson of renowned Baptist pastors. As a graduate of Morehouse and the son of graduates of Morehouse and Spelman Colleges, he was at the pinnacle of Atlanta's society. Like so many of today's privileged graduates of American universities, his path was laid in the direction of maximum success. He was a preacher and a scholar following the formulas defined by the lives of Howard Thurman, Mordecai Johnson and Benjamin Mays. He could see himself celebrated by black Americans, as a statesman/preacher ensconced in a comfortable position as, perhaps, president of Morehouse. But the greatest plans of mice and men often go awry.

King was a student of the Social Gospel movement, which saw racism, segregation, and classism as antithetical to the teachings of Jesus. And, as a follower of Reinhold Niebuhr, he also saw that human institutions can be inherently evil. It was Niebuhr, the theologian, who asserted that the white race would not admit black Americans to equal rights if it was not forced to do so. He suggested nonviolence as a strategic means of battling the oppressor if the oppressed is "hopelessly in the minority."

And so from his place of privilege, caught up in indignation over the segregation of his people, thrust forward as the standard bearer of a religious, social, political revolution, Martin Luther King began to fight violence with nonviolence. He did so for twelve years, until his death in Memphis, Tennessee.

I was sixteen years old when Dr. King was killed. His death, though disturbing and disruptive, did not have the effect on me that it would have in later months and years. In 1968 my imagination was consumed by thoughts of attaining my dream of going to MIT. While the City of Detroit came face to face with the reality of racism in its midst, in devastating police actions and community revolts, my peers and I pondered the relative merits of higher educational institutions. I was then not aware how much my thoughts and actions reflected the effects of race and racism. Being blissfully ignorant of what was not possible, I thought all things were possible. An African American could be president or the senator from the state of New York. On Broadway, Cleavon Little gave words to this sense at the conclusion of the musical *Purlie* in which he starred. "May your dreams be your only boundaries," he sings. "Yes," I said, and yes again.

My education for survival in these United States began here at MIT. I woke up when standing at Massachusetts Avenue across from Building 7, waiting to cross. A car of young white men unknown to me yelled "nigger" as they sped past. I woke up when I saw the unnecessary jealousies and rivalries among some of my black peers. I woke up when a black professor of engineering called me into his office in my sophomore year and told me to wake up. I woke up when my best friend failed out of MIT and returned to North Philadelphia, lonely and demoralized. From within us and outside us there were forces operating of which I had never before been aware.

In her Pulitzer Prize winning novel, *Beloved,* Toni Morrison summarized the awakening of Sethe, her principal character. Sethe says, "Anybody white could take your self for anything that came to mind. Not just work, kill or maim you, but dirty you. Dirty you so bad you couldn't like yourself anymore." Fortunately for Sethe, at least, there is an apotheosis.

In what I believe are more dramatic ways than were evidenced in my youth, or at least in ways of which I am more aware, the state of our community in 1988 is critical. The pervasiveness of crack and its concomitants—violence and larceny—is devastating black urban communities. There is an increase in the presence and activity of white hate groups throughout the country. Twenty-five percent of the national AIDS caseload is black, although we are barely 12 percent of the general population. Government decided in 1980 to begin limiting its role in civil rights. Fifty percent of black high school students drop out before graduation and the public education system in some areas is considered a disgrace. The chances of an Hispanic or Asian with a third-grade education finding integrated housing is better than for a black with a Ph.D. Sixty percent of black families are headed by a single parent, usually a female. Nationally, blacks are rejected for home loans twice as often as whites. In Boston blacks are rejected three times as often as whites. The number of black males on college campuses is double the number of black males in federal and state prisons, while their white peers number twelve times as many in college as whites in American prisons. The Supreme Court has begun to roll back some municipal set-aside programs, even though for every African American making $36,000 there are twelve who are at or below poverty.

My people are under siege. We are besieged from within by a gradual disintegration of the communal network. We are besieged from without by fear, prejudice and racism both overt and covert.

There are many African Americans who do not sit idly by watching this occur. I recommend them to your consideration. Some of our traditional black churches have formalized what was informal practice for decades and have attempted to form networks of support for black business development. In Boston the Multi-Cultural AIDS Coalition is attempting to bring more aggressive AIDS education to the black and Hispanic populations. Organizations like the National Center for Neighborhood Enterprise in Washington, DC, and the Granville Academy in Princeton, New Jersey are black sponsored efforts directed at teaching, legal training, foster care and business development training. The Richard Allen Center in New York and One Church, One Child in Chicago encourage adoption of unwanted black children by black people. Non-blacks are also present in our community in hospitals, drug rehabilitation centers, literacy volunteer programs, as well as religious high schools and grammar schools.

The fear is that the forces without and within may increase in strength faster than our best efforts to deal with them. As a student of our history, however, I know that we have survived much. Nothing about our lives in this country has been smooth. The melting pot doesn't burn hot enough. But survive we will. Maybe one day we will even thrive.

Watch and listen. It is in the flight of Michael Jordan, and the art of Romare Bearden. It is in the wisdom of Barbara Jordan and the grace of Judith Jamison. It is in the literature of James Baldwin and the politics of Ron Brown. It is in the business acumen of John Johnson and the sensitivity of Danny Glover. It is in the analysis of John Hope Franklin and the science of Joseph Francisco. It is in the remarkable life of astronaut Ron McNair. Through them we can see what is possible.

I challenge you on behalf of justice, MIT. Can MIT buck the national trend and stand uniquely among its great peers as an institution where any man or woman on earth can find encouragement and support in pursuit of an education? Can you see that true greatness lies in incorporating the unique gifts of many and diverse people? We are diminished when any group is marginalized.

White men and women at MIT, I challenge you on behalf of justice. In your offices and labs and classrooms and living groups, is there a place to grow for all people, black, brown, yellow and white? Is there encouragement to be a fully integrated man or woman, not a dual personality or soulless human being?

Black men and women at MIT, I challenge you on behalf of justice as I challenge myself. Is there an area of concern in which you are uniquely qualified to lend assistance to our needy community, whether in education, business, day care, drug rehabilitation, athletics or jobs? Can you teach your children with pride about their African ancestors, their journey through slavery, the fight against Jim Crow, Martin Luther King's dream and love of self?

> He has showed you, O man, what is good.
> And what does the Lord require of you?
> To act justly and to love mercy
> and to walk humbly with your God.
> —*Micah 6:8*

On December 1, 1955, Rosa Parks left her job at Montgomery Fair department store late in the afternoon bound for home. When Mrs. Parks got on the bus, she sat in one of the seats immediately behind the ten rows reserved for whites only. Three stops later the "colored" section was filled; so was the white section, and one white man was left standing. On the evening of the first day of the United States Civil Rights Movement, Dr. Martin Luther King, Jr. said:

I want to tell you this evening that it is not enough for us to talk about love. Love is one of the pinnacle parts of the Christian faith. There is another side called justice. And justice is really love in calculation. Justice is love correcting that which would work against love.

 GREGORY C. CHISHOLM , S.J. was ordained into the Roman Catholic priesthood in 1993, and earned his Ph.D. in mechanical engineering at MIT that same year. He earned his bachelor's and master's degrees in mechanical engineering at MIT during the 1970s, and worked at AT&T Bell Laboratories and the U.S. Department of Transportation before returning to MIT to continue his studies.

Memphis, Tennessee, April 3, 1968—Martin Luther King, Jr. and his aides being served papers by a U.S. marshall. A federal restraining order prohibited Dr. King from leading any mass marches.

Montgomery, Alabama, December 21, 1956—Ralph D. Abernathy and Martin Luther King, Jr. were among the first to ride the bus after the Supreme Court's integration order went into effect.

The Dream and Hope, the Nightmare of Reality: Closing the Gap for Our Youth

Nikki Giovanni

YOU ARE CHILDREN, IN CASE NOBODY HAS mentioned that to you lately. You do not know everything. I have a child and I like him. He's now twenty years old. He'll soon be grown; I accept that. I want him to go on and live his life. He is not my best friend. I never trust the parents who say, "My child is my best friend." You know, my best friend gets in trouble with her Mastercard, but she doesn't call me.

My best friend loses her wallet and she doesn't call me, but my son just did. He just went to college and I tell you, the reason that you go to college is that it makes your mother so happy. It does. Thomas is enrolled in a real school working for a degree. I could not be happier. Why? Because I don't want a dumb child sitting around the house. I never wanted a dumb child, and I'm sure your parents don't either. I would rather not understand him. I would rather send him off to MIT and not know what he's talking about. "What are you all studying?

What are you talking about?" When I don't know what they're talking about, I smile.

I would rather not understand them than understand them all too well. "They're out to get me, Mom." No, they don't know you. And they don't care, whoever they are. If they don't shoot you, you don't die, they don't care. Your job in life is to do something with your life for the people who do care. Your mother cares. If you're lucky, your father does, too. Your brothers and sisters might get interested, they might not. It depends. So don't get used by those people just because they're kin to you. Do something with your life. I know that greed is not acceptable. I'm not going to recommend greed, but I am going to recommend that what you want you get. Because if you really don't do what you think you need to do to be happy, I can tell you right now, you will not be. Those of you who are sitting there saying, "If I just had a Mercedes Benz, I'd be happy," I can give you a Mercedes Benz. You are still going to be a miserable son-of-a-gun because things will not make you happy. It is better for you to have the things and know that, because then you can deal from the same point of view. Am I making you sick this morning? If you will understand that, that what you have coveted is not worth coveting, then you will understand that because you have it, you should come together to build something else. I am not a materialist. There is a limit to what material goods can do.

I want you to understand. It is better to have a good job than a bad job. Because why should you work hard, get dirty, and smell bad when you come home, when you can wear a good suit, soft shoes, and have a car to pick you up? Why shouldn't you go for the easy thing? There is something about the black community that tickles me. We always think if you're not sweating, you're not actually working. Get rid of that notion. The easier you can make your life, the better it's going to be. Think, work with your head. Strength comes from the shoulders up. I'm a sports fan. It delights me to see tall black boys shoot balls. They should make lots of money doing that. And when their knees give out, and they will, they should have something to show for it. I am speaking as their mothers. It will break my heart if Michael Jordan ends up poor and on drugs and selling tennis shoes or something to earn a living. This boy should be rich. So should you.

Now we're MIT people here, so we're technologically inclined. Some of you might go to law school, or you know somebody who does. Some of you are going to become investment bankers or know somebody who does. There are many people in Boston who are going to need your help. Am I making sense? If you are black and you want to be a professional the first thing you'd better learn is keep your mouth shut about your class. We who are professionals have to be professional, we cannot be black. We have to be professionals.

I like the teaching profession, I want to recommend teaching. To all of you who are saying, "What should I do with my life?" I say, teach. Somebody needs you. It's no fun. Some of you out there are teenagers, you know you're no fun, nobody wants to be bothered with you. You don't want to be bothered with yourself. It is not fun, but we need you. We need black males, really. We need you in the classroom. We need you in kindergarten.

I love the guys. "I can't handle no baby." Yes, you can, because you've got it. You can change his diaper, you can wipe his dribble, and you can teach him ABCDEFG. Not for all of the time, but for a little while. Think about teaching. Some of you are getting your doctorates. You're going to go out into the real world, you're going to make money. You're going to find yourself fifty or sixty years old, you're going to say, "What can I do?" Teach. We need people to be involved with people.

In 1990 on planet earth, it is not fun. Am I making sense here? It's not fun. Somebody says, "Life should be about happiness." What's happy about being alive? But it's hard to be born, and it's going to be hard to die. You don't remember being born, that's the only difference. Your mama does. It's hard to be born, it is difficult. Those of you who are teenagers, you don't know what we go through. We used to be teenagers, we hated it. We don't admit that to you, there's no fun to being sixteen. You've got all of these hormones raging. It's hard.

I do have insight, because I do have a twenty-year-old. I know that mothers want their sons married, we don't care if our daughters never do. Mothers want their sons married, no matter what. If you're a woman keep this in mind. We want our sons to hook up with any good woman, because a son without a woman is uncivilized. It is men who invented marriage. I don't have to develop that further, but I've learned that. Because I look at my kid and I think, "If he doesn't get a wife soon he's not going to have any reason to build something." It's true. Why am I excited about that? Because it's going to happen whether I like it or not. I would say this to my daughter though, "Get your degree, do not reproduce yourself, get yourself a good job." Somebody would say, "Huh, she's too independent, she won't get a man." There's a man out there. I get so sick of hearing that. Look at the numbers in the black community: we have a shortage of black men. You don't have to settle for some damn prisoner because you're an educated woman. That's ridiculous. If he's not black that's too bad, go get someone.

The one thing that I do love more than anything is space. If you looked out the other night, there was a full moon. It was wonderful. It was a nice thing to be alive in 1990 for one specific reason. We have finally crossed the end of the power of the yellow sun. We have Voyager II that has crossed beyond that which is even imaginable for us. I love it. We know that the dog star, in fact, has to be beyond the power of the yellow sun. It is too far out. What does that mean? It means that the cosmic loneliness of earth is not real. There is life in space because, if nothing else, we are in space. But we know that there has to be something beyond space. We are earthlings. We are a small ball in a small universe and we now have to envision a universe beyond. What does that have to do with anything? It puts our lives in perspective. I will be so happy when a three-headed purple monster comes to earth. I will. Because human beings are such skitterish people. Human beings are so nervous that the first thing they'll do is pull together because something that they don't understand has come upon them. It would be good for us. It's like any other tragedy.

Think about tragedy. Now obviously, you all are much too young to remember Hurricane Camille. Some of you may. Remember Hurricane Camille came up through the Gulf of Mexico, came up all the way to Mississippi? We had a bad situation. All of a sudden, in a state where black people and white people kill each other all the time, all of a sudden we had a "Let's you and me stop this hurricane." I love it. All of a sudden we didn't have any racism. I love a tragedy for that, because people rise to the occasion. My question is, why do we always have to

January 1990—Leading the procession to Kresge Auditorium are, from left to right, Priscilla K. Gray, Paul E. Gray, Nikki Giovanni, and Royce N. Flippin, Jr.

have a tragedy to do it? If we had a fire right now, some of the most militant people in this room would stop and help an old white lady because it's a fire and we're trying to get out of here. If a plane crashes, somebody will grab the baby and it won't be a question of what color, what race, or what religion. It will be a question of, "The plane crashed, I didn't die. Who can I help?" Am I making sense? Why do we have to wait for a tragedy for this to happen?

If we contemplate earth, and you must contemplate the system in which we live—the solar system—you know that we are a small part of a small system. What can it mean? It means that there is something else. It means that I will rise beyond that which we know and that which we see. How do we know that? We educate you. And how do we educate you? Through books. There is no substitute for reading. You are not too busy. Somebody says I can't read *The Brothers Karamazov* because it's too big. You eat, you can read. You go to the bathroom, you can read. Am I making sense? You can read. Put a book every place that you are. You are on the East coast here, you don't necessarily have to drive—which is lucky, because most of you here in Boston do that very poorly.

Read while you are on the bus. I cannot substitute what books do. Audiovisuals will not do that. Public Enemy cannot do it, and I'm beginning to like Public Enemy. It has enlightened me about rap. I used to not be able to stand it because it's loud, first of all. And they say the same blah, blah, blah. But nothing takes the place of a book. If we do not know the novels of Toni Morrison or the poetry of Langston Hughes and Gwendolyn Brooks, I submit that we cannot continue to educate our white youngsters to the idea that the world is white. We're doing a disservice there, you and I know that. We who are black know that we not only have to have our contribution, but we have to be aware of what other people have done. You cannot be black and decide that you are not going to read Henry James because after all he doesn't speak to you. No.

You're going to do it all because planet earth is making a change, and we are no longer black, we are no longer white. We are not really effectively men and women anymore, because the body is an insignificant thing. It houses our soul and our mind. The body is insignificant if you're not actually doing some sport. It is unimportant. What is important is that we are earthlings. And being earthlings, we share that with our basic whales, with our basic wolf, with the basic snake, with the marigolds. We share life on this planet with life on this planet.

I will share the sad news because I wear a sign, for those of you who have been close to me today, that says "Militant Smoker." Somebody said, "Ms. Giovanni, you shouldn't smoke because you'll die." I said, "Is that the reason I'm going to die?" Because I would quit smoking if that would be the reason that I'm going to die. But I was born, and that's why I'm going to die. If you were born, you're going to die. And I think that's something we ought to remind people. To be an American, to be a human being today, you're going to die. Now should you die soon? I hope not. But will you die later, who knows? So don't worry yourself about how long you will live.

We've been quoting King today. He said longevity has its charm. I'm sure it does. But it's not the longevity of our lives, it is what we do with them. You have to assume in this world that you will not be here tomorrow. You have to do today's job today. I come from an over-qualified generation. We were more than able to do everything that the world threw at us. We could handle it because we were always over-qualified. We talk about the gift that Dr. King had of speaking. Perhaps it was a gift, but I know this. He was a well-educated man. He went to the best schools available to him, and he put his time in. He was a Ph.D. That's not a gift, he worked for it. King worked hard. He didn't wake up one morning and say, "I think I shall quote Aristophanes." He studied. And you must also. I want to remind us as we are getting reminded. It is a joy to be alive. I would recommend it. I think life is fascinating. I don't want to be your age anymore, I'm glad to be finished with it. I'm forty-six, I recommend the forties an awful lot.

For any of you who are sitting around saying things like, "Oh, I think I'll commit suicide, I can't handle being eighteen," get through it. Get to your twenties, get to your mid-twenties, get to your thirties. Because the thirties start to smooth out really nicely. But in the forties it's really mellowed and to tell you the truth, I'm looking forward to my sixties. I understand the fifties can be a little iffy. I want to recommend life, because those of us who are caring, those of us who are thinking, those of us who are sensitive to some of the needs, we have got to survive to make the changes. "Living well," somebody said, "is the best revenge." I want to remind those of us who are suicidally inclined, living is a good revenge.

Survive and find your purpose. You are not going to have to tell yourself at twenty-five, "I should know what I'm doing." Because in most of these cases, we have made it easier for you. I think it's good. I never liked people who said, "I had a hard time. They're going to have a hard time, too." I don't believe in suffering. The fact that you were born and the fact that you die means that you will suffer. I don't believe that we have to add to that. I don't think that we need to put people on the streets and some other people will say, "Well, I've got a home, I should be grateful." Why should you be grateful that there is a roof over your head? It is a necessity, it's not an option. Why should you be grateful that you ate dinner last night? Why are we trying to make people grateful for basic things that we know we have to do? And we've got to get the homeless off of our streets, because I hate it. It's tacky, it looks bad, it smells bad, and I don't think any nation that calls itself civilized can afford to have that. You go to Washington, DC, and people are sleeping on the grates. I don't care how we get them off. I don't. People say, "How are we going to pay for it?" The same way we pay for everything else—we put it on George Bush's American Express.

When we want to buy a missile we buy it. Why is it so difficult to buy a house? Somebody will say, "I don't see why I should buy a house, they ain't buying me a house." I don't care. Nobody is ever going to give me anything in life, from a glass of water to the house I live in today. I come from a generation that was given nothing. We fought for everything we had from simple dignity. You, who have had it a lot easier, ought to be a little bit more supportive. I want the homeless to have a home. I think that there is nothing more stupid than building shelters for the homeless. It already doesn't make sense. If they were shelterless, then let's call them that. They're not shelterless; they are homeless. Build a home and put an air conditioner in it. And put a cable box in it so that they can watch ESPN. Make them whole and let them be productive. Somebody says, "Well, why should we sacrifice?" Because you're here. It's the luck of the draw to be born. But don't sit there and say the homeless love it, they've chosen to live on grates. No. Feed and clothe these people.

I love it that we're a Christian nation. It was Eisenhower that put that "one nation under God." I remember that, because I had to learn the Pledge of Allegiance again. I'm not picking on the Christians, but if we're so busy being Christian, wasn't there something basic? Jesus was not a complicated man. He said things like, "Feed the hungry, shelter the homeless." He didn't say homeless, he said "those without," and "clothe the naked." If I paraphrase him, I'm sure there's somebody in this room that knows it. That's all. He didn't say a whole lot. He said, "Love one another." That's not difficult. We don't need a theologian to say, "what he actually meant was . . ." He said, "Love one another."

Don't close your eyes to agony. Don't close your eyes to joy. You have a right to be proud of yourself. I met some people this morning who were attending MIT. That's not easy. I teach at Virginia Tech; that's not easy either. But you have a right to be proud that you came to MIT. You have a right to be proud that you graduated from high school, those of you who have. You have a right to be proud that you get accepted at Virginia Tech or MIT or Harvard or anyplace else. You have a right to be proud of what you have achieved. You must take pride in what you are and what you have achieved. You must look in a mirror and say, "I may not be the greatest, but I am all right." And sometimes you have to look in there and say, "I *am* the greatest." You've got to take some joy in your own being; a part of you belongs to us.

A part of you is the public life that you lead. We expect things of you. But I want to remind you that a part of you belongs to you. A part of you says that you can enjoy your life, that you can build something in it. James Baldwin speaks of a floor on which you dance. You must have an inner floor on which you dance. There must be something for you called your life.

I simply wanted to share this morning with you that there are still dreams to be dreamed. We are still looking for you to do things. We are looking for you to ask us to help you. This is a partnership on earth, we all come together. The intelligence of mankind must be used to further the goals and the joys of mankind. We go forward because it is all we know how to do. I would hope that we go forward in love, in peace and with joy of being a human being. But no matter what, we will go forward. I recommend that you look around and you look inside your heart. I recommend that you, too, have a dream.

NIKKI GIOVANNI is a poet and professor of English at Virginia Polytechnic Institute and State University, and has taught black studies, English, and creative writing. She has written and recorded a large body of poetry, and her work has appeared in numerous anthologies over the years. Several honorary degrees have been bestowed on Ms. Giovanni, and she has been selected a life member of the National Council of Negro Women.

Memphis, Tennessee—Martin Luther King, Jr. with Jesse Jackson and Ralph D. Abernathy on the balcony of the motel where he was shot.

Linking the Civil Rights Movement to MIT and Dr. King's Dream: Reality— Closing the Gap

Benjamin L. Hooks

APRIL 3, 1968 WAS A VERY BAD DAY, WEATHER-wise, in Memphis. Rain was falling incessantly, thunder roaring ominously, fitful flashes of lightning were playing a nimble game of hide-and-seek across the dark sky, and one of my dearest friends had died. I had gone to the memorial service and had planned to hear Dr. King speak later that night. The meeting where Martin Luther King, Jr. was to speak was being held at Mason Temple, a large building seating perhaps 7,500. It is owned by the members of the Church of God in Christ. The occasion for the speech was a strike by sanitation workers in Memphis seeking simple decency, fair play, justice, and equity, after years of frustration and heartbreaking efforts to redress these griev-ances. Whatever racial harmony or pretense of racial harmony that existed in the city was shattered. It was late, it was wet, it was getting cold and I wanted to go home, but since Dr. King had come to be with us, it would be a tragedy not to attend.

In spite of the dreadful weather, there must have been almost 2,500 people present. The auditorium had a tin roof and you could hear the rain falling. The brown-stained glass windows of the place revealed the flashes of lightning still playing across the skies. The thunder roared like a thousand hungry lions behind the mountains. Every time the door opened, the wind howled and shrieked. It was so ominous that my nerves were on edge and I felt a sense of tension.

I was a member of the board of directors of the Southern Christian Leadership Conference. It had been my pleasure and privilege to work with Dr. Martin Luther King, Jr. through much of his public life in the Civil Rights Movement. I'd heard him speak all over the nation—in the great religious institutions and small chapels, in board meetings, on informal and formal occasions. But, as I sat there that night, I thought I had never heard him speak with such pathos, power, and passion. In fact, I had been at the March on Washington and I thought that not even there had I seen this kind of gripping urgency.

The thing that was rather strange was that we thought we had come a long way. We had achieved a great deal of progress. And yet, on that night, Dr. King talked about dark and difficult days ahead. As he continued in that marvelous speech and talked about the conditions past, present, and future, he did not leave us in despair or hopelessness, but toward the end, he raised that magnificent voice and declared, "I have been to the mountain top, I have seen the promised land. I may not make it there with you, but I've seen the promised land." And then, as he finished that speech, tears were literally running down his face and lapping under his chin. He took his seat and we were transfixed and transfigured by the power of this marvelous man. I had no way of knowing that this would be the last speech that he would deliver on this earth, and that, within twenty-four hours, he would be killed by a cowardly assassin.

Since that day, I've thought about that speech twenty-some years ago, and I can tell you that there have been dark days and these are difficult days, and that that speech enhances the feeling that I have that Dr. King was not only a preacher, but a prophet sent from God. He was trying to prepare those who would be left behind. Think about it. Twenty-two years ago we were on the verge of euphoria. We had seen the passage of the Voting Rights Act and the Civil Rights Act. We had seen barriers fall and signs saying "colored" and "white" come down. Many perhaps felt that we had overcome.

These are some difficult days. Think of all the things we've had to face—the fighting about Ronald Reagan, and Jesse Helms running a racist campaign in the state of North Carolina and resorting to the dirtiest tricks that we've known in politics. Look at David Duke, a psychopath from all I've read, who received 60 percent of all the white votes cast in Louisiana in his race for the Senate.

I look at the college campuses where the best and brightest are now resorting to all kinds of tricks and demagoguery, where crosses are being burned, the Ku Klux Klan is being revived, and in the name of free speech, we trample upon the rights of minorities, Jewish people, and women—those whose color of skin or religion or background is different. And if it happens here, if it happens at these marvelous colleges and universities where our minds are being trained for the future, what is the hope for those who live in the filth and squalor of the alleys of economic deprivation, where there's too little for too many? What is the hope of America?

I see a Supreme Court that has apparently lost its collective mind. If you took the brains of a majority of the present Supreme Court and put them in the head of a bird, that bird would fly perpetually and forever backward. Do you have to be a Rhodes Scholar to understand that this nation has a history of racial and sexual discrimination that is rooted in wrong and injustice? Does someone have to teach us all over again about 244 years of slavery without a payday; and a hundred years of second-class citizenship; and that there must be steps taken to remedy the mistakes of the past?

Let me say to all of you that the holiday for Dr. King does not have to deal with his perfection. Don't come telling me about what you heard about him. I could tell you about a Thomas Jefferson who allegedly had a mistress—a slave, and had illegitimate children, who did not free his slaves even when he died. Don't tell me about the mistakes of people. I could talk about Ben Franklin and George Washington, and their alleged escapades. They were not perfect, but we honor their memories as great Americans.

And I can go up and down the list of human frailties, but when we honor Dr. Martin Luther King, Jr. it is not simply him alone. We honor the contributions of those millions of black people, crammed in slave ships like cattle, who crossed the turbulent waters of the Atlantic, and yet as they landed from the mystic deep, came upon the shores where the flora and fauna were different, and somehow built the highways, picked the cotton, planted the tobacco, and helped build this nation. They fought in every war, and yet, when the wars were over, were still told to sit in the back of the bus.

When we come to the celebration of Martin Luther King, it is not only him, but a people who have been able to go through everything, who took nothing and made something. Who was it that showed people what a hog chitlin could do? Who was it that discovered that you could not only eat pork chops, but you could eat pork ears, hog heads, and hog feet? Who was it that took nothing and made something? It was black folks sitting back there who cried out in the depth of all the degradation, discouragement, despair: "Over my head, I hear music in the air, there must be a God somewhere."

Now, my brothers and sisters, let me just stop here and tell you one thing so you can understand where I come from. I make no excuse whatsoever. I don't apologize for the fact that this nation needs affirmative action. If it spent all of these years keeping blacks and women out, it is high time that we spent some time bringing them in. And therefore I make no excuse for affirmative action, I'm not afraid of it. And yet they have somebody telling me, "Well, if you get a 'minority' scholarship, they won't know whether you're dumb or smart." They don't know *anyway* whether you're dumb or smart. Hey, friend, just because you're at MIT doesn't mean you're the brightest person in the world or that you can set the world on fire. It's not being here that counts, it's getting out that counts, and with grades that are worthwhile.

I'm a veteran of World War II and I received benefits from the GI Bill of Rights. I went to school at government expense. I didn't know what tuition was at law school, I never saw it, and I have never been sorry or ashamed. Nobody can make me feel guilty because, under the GI Bill of Rights, I got $65 every month, I kept my insurance, and I would have bought a house if I'd had the down payment. There are ten million veterans who got all those benefits. Have you ever heard any of them saying, "I'm so ashamed I got certain benefits when all my brothers and sisters who were not veterans couldn't get them"? It's a damnable lie to say that when this nation tries to make amends, somehow we've got to drop our head in shame.

MIT is graduating some black engineers and we shall be looking for more, not less. We shall expect and demand that for all the years the doors were closed, they'll now be opened—not to take unqualified people, but to give people a chance, an opportunity to demonstrate what they can do.

Dr. King, on that night, talked about the difficult days ahead. Believe me, my friends, I have witnessed those difficult days. I have seen the resurgence of the Klan, a backward moving Supreme Court, a timid Congress, and a George Bush as president not measuring up to his full potential. When he became president, it wasn't necessarily my choice, but he was a welcome relief from Ronald Reagan. When Carter was president, I went to the White House often. I even went upstairs in the presidential quarters and had tea and crumpets. After Reagan became president, I was in and out so fast I didn't know I had been there. Bush became president and I was one of the first black people he met with. I thought that we were going to go far.

But then came the Civil Rights Bill, the first litmus test. He had us on a merry-go-round for six months as we worked with that Civil Rights Bill. And then, when he could have signed it and gone down in history as favorable to civil rights, he became one of only three presidents of the United States of America who has ever vetoed a Civil Rights Bill. He joined the disappointing ranks of Andrew Johnson and Ronald Reagan. I still have hopes that he will do better.

Think about the war in the Persian Gulf. Whatever your feeling is about the war, it is a tragedy that almost 30 percent of the combat troops will be black. Men and women who have been denied the fullness of opportunity in this country, will die for it, come back in body bags. Those who live will come back to a country where the president refused to sign a simple Civil Rights Bill to correct mistakes that have been made. These are dark and difficult days.

I'm talking now to my own black brothers and sisters because there are some things that we have to do for ourselves. The late Elijah

Mohammed used to say—and I believe that he was right, "Nobody can save us from us, but us." I want you to understand that I don't believe that my destiny is in the hands of any single white man or woman in this world. I believe that my destiny is finally in the hands of God and my own people, and so I am calling us to look at some of the things that are happening.

Violence is at an all-time high. The leading cause of death among young black men is to be killed by another young black man. Society has so twisted our minds and warped our imagination and twisted our thoughts that we turn *on* each other instead of *to* each other. AIDS is sweeping our community, teenage pregnancy, babies having babies, women are becoming grandmothers before they're thirty years of age. In Baltimore, the city where I live now, 80 percent of all the babies born in the black community in 1989 were born to single mothers. Think of the tragedy, the economic and social conditions that will rob many of those young people of a chance to live a decent life.

Dr. King talked about the dark and difficult days, but he did not leave us without hope. He said, "I have been to the mountain top, I have seen the promised land." And so, in spite of the darkness, in spite of the difficulty, in spite of the heartache and the disappointments, there is still hope.

In spite of all we've gone through, I rejoice in the fact that when I go to Los Angeles, California to see the mayor, I walk into the office of a black man. In New York City we have a black mayor and we had a Harold Washington in Chicago, we have a Coleman Young in Detroit, an Andrew Young and Maynard Jackson in Atlanta, down in Birmingham a Richard Arrington, and down in New Orleans an Ernest Morial. We've come a long way: 7,000 elected black officials, a million black young people in post-secondary education. This is the bright side of things that make me happy. When I look at young people, and I see you with your books rubbing against your side as you rub your heads against the post of knowledge trying to achieve educational excellence to make a better world, then I am happy. When I see these dedicated professors trying to open a way for those who've not had a way opened for them, I rejoice.

I look out and see a people who have a $250 billion GNP. We have a lot of money, but we've got to teach our dollars to have some sense and we have to say to business, "We're not going to spend our money where we cannot get jobs and respect." We can take those dollars and make them open doors that have been closed in our face. I'm happy and proud to see a people who have done so much with so little. When I look at what we have accomplished, such as the grandson of slaves being sworn in as the governor of the Commonwealth of Virginia, in the former capital of the Confederacy, I know we have a lot to be proud of. I'm proud of Louis Sullivan, Secretary of Health and Human Services, the largest department of the government other than the military, who speaks up. They've tried to shut him up, but he speaks up anyway.

Now four things, and I'll be through. And the first is that, in spite of whether it's dark or whether it's light, there are some things we must do. And the first thing, my brothers and sisters, as we try to close the gap, is that we must build coalitions. There is no sense in people going around hating white people because they're white, or white folk hating us because we're black. Most of us had absolutely, positively nothing to do with how we came here. We didn't choose to be black or white, male or female; you didn't have much to do with naming yourself. You didn't pick your mother, didn't pick your father.

And I think on balance, we ought to just accept it. If you get mad every time you look in the mirror, you're not going to make much progress. I hear Martin King saying, "If you can't be a mountain, be a hill, but be the best hill that ever stood. If you can't be a mighty river, be a stream, but be the best stream that ever ran. If you can't be a mighty oak, be a little bush, but be the best bush, be the best of whatever you are." That's all that God requires of us. Not everybody can be a President Charles Vest, but whatever your name is, you can be the best that there is. You can give it your best. And when you give it your best, somehow God can transform that. So let us build coalitions, not get mad at people, not turn on each other, but turn to each other, black and white together. We have been put on this planet earth, in this nation called America; let us therefore work to make it as good as we can.

Secondly, we must get rid of envy and jealousy. No matter what happens, we can't afford to get so mad that we forget the objective for which we work.

And then we've got to exhibit a sense of pride. Somebody said a long time ago, the early bird gets the worm. I don't particularly care about getting up early, everybody knows that, but I get up. I've never missed a plane in my life because it left too early. If you plan to lay around in bed till twelve or one o'clock, and then by four o'clock come and look for a job, nobody's going to hire you. Too late. Put your shoes on your feet; don't walk on them, walk in them. Got a cap? Wear it like I used to wear mine; put the bill in front so folk will know you know where you're going, don't turn it around backwards.

Let everybody know that you understand where you're going. If you're in school, it's more than play and fun and fashion—it's study, it's understanding. Don't let anybody fool you and tell you that geology and physics are for white folk, and that you ought to be studying the pathology of the black ghetto and black English. All these folk who talk about black English want their children to speak standard English. And if you think we can't do it, listen to Martin Luther King, Jr., who mastered the English language. Someone has said that of all the speeches made in America, only the Gettysburg address and King's address to that mighty crowd in Washington couldn't be improved.

If you think we can't master the intricacies of the English language, listen to the majestic voice of a Langston Hughes saying, "I've known rivers, ancient dusky rivers, my soul has grown deep like the rivers." And that other great poem among many, mother to son: "Life for me ain't been no crystal staircase." Listen to all of these great people, look at the life of Henry C. McBay, whom you honor as the first Martin Luther King scholar. Whatever it is that has to be done, we as black folk have proven that we can do it. Let us not be unfaithful to the legacy of the past and let us be up and doing!

Finally, as I close today, don't forget God. I would be untrue to the deepest tradition of my being if I did not tell you that I believe with all my heart there is a God who rules above, hand of power and heart of love.

Young people, I understand that you are here in this great prestigious institution where science reigns, but behind the dot that produced the big bang, stood God within the shadows. And in my own life I've seen God moving and working. In spite of all that has happened, and is happening, I'm confident that we shall overcome. I sat there in Brown Chapel in Selma, Alabama; saw the troopers, tear-gas, dogs; heard people singing, "We Shall Overcome," and somehow we did. I watched them with their massed armies, with their tanks, and all the implements of federal government and state authority, saw a little ragtag band of black and white people who believed in freedom. I saw the manifestation of the glorious will of God transcending human force.

I was a public defender in the courts of Shelby County, Tennessee. It was alleged that one of the judges didn't even want me to practice in his courtroom, but he died. The governor called me up and asked me to serve on the bench. A black judge in Shelby County in Memphis? In 1965? There were no black judges anywhere in the South, and only a precious few in the North. I said, "Mr. Governor, if you will appoint me, I will accept it."

On the first day of September 1965, I put on a black robe and went into the courtroom, the same courtroom, behind the same bench where that judge did not want me to practice law, and raised this right hand and swore to uphold the laws of the State of Tennessee and of the United States of America. People were sitting there crying because they never thought they'd see a black judge. I'm just trying to say to you, ladies and gentlemen, young men and young women, what God can do in your life.

We shall overcome: black, white, young, old, priest, rabbi, nun. In my heart I do believe we shall overcome someday. The Lord is on our side today. Thank you, Martin, thank you. I do believe we shall overcome someday.

PEACE—POWER.

BENJAMIN L. HOOKS served as Executive Director of the NAACP from 1977-1993. He is a noted attorney, ordained minister, and public servant, and has received many honorary degrees and awards. In the early 1970s, he served as the first black member of the Federal Communications Commission, and is a former member of the Board of Directors of the Southern Christian Leadership Conference.

Chicago, Illinois—Martin Luther King, Jr. at a press conference in September 1966.

The Dream and Reality: Closing the Gap

Margaret A. Burnham

MARTIN LUTHER KING, JR. WOULD HAVE BEEN but sixty-three years old on January 15, 1992, had he not been struck down by a bullet in Memphis. Sixty-three. The age of our neighbors, our colleagues, our fathers and mothers, our teachers, mentors, and leaders. Not an old man. Our contemporary. It's perhaps this nearness that makes Dr. King's birthday celebration so unique and so different from the other national heroes' days that we as a country commemorate. Martin is still very much flesh and bone to us. Bone and fiber. Tears and sweat. He has only just left us. His deep, baritone voice is still an echo in our ears, much like a room freshly vacated.

Even if only through the pages of our daily newspapers, many of us in this hall knew Martin Luther King, Jr. Some of us who are here walked down the same roads he walked down. Others who are here may have scorned his methods as too conciliatory, even as we were uplifted by his spirituality and his perseverance. Others of us also here today may have raised our eyebrows at strokes that seemed too bold and too risky for a country only just getting accustomed to the end of Jim Crow.

Most of us who are here were alive on April 4, 1968, and shuddered and then moaned together as a country as Martin faltered and then collapsed on the Lorraine Hotel balcony. So fresh, so raw and haunting is the memory of Martin's death, his blood spilling out over his colleagues Ralph Abernathy and Andrew Young and James Bevel, that the birthday we mark every January seems as much funereal as celebratory.

In a sense, then, when we come together to honor Martin, we also come together to walk back into our own lives, as much as to reflect on Martin King's short but rich sojourn with us. It is an annual journey in quest of the answers to two interlocking questions: the meaning of his life and time, and its bearing on our own lives today.

Thus, January 15 has never been a static memorial to a dead and fossilized hero. Nor can we permit the story of Dr. King and the Movement he represents to be co-opted and diluted, commercialized and canonized under the undifferentiating spotlight of a national holiday. It is still our Movement, and it is we who must define it.

It is far too soon to wrap up our Martin Luther King celebrations in rigid rituals commemorating an untouchable icon of a bygone era. First of all, because the history we commemorate today is the story of what happened just yesterday. And the details have yet to be fully unfolded. And secondly, because Dr. King's vision—what school children have been taught to call the King dream—was meant to be a yardstick against which we might measure our progress as a people, and as a nation.

Surely the realities of our lives have vastly changed since the 1960s, but in ways that seem to render the vision of the Movement a distant mirage. Even while we as a people take on new shape and form and visibility on the American landscape, we African Americans are at the same time both more empowered and more impoverished now than we were then; and surely, we must ask about that contradiction.

Let me return to the first question: what was the Movement of which Dr. King was a part? What was his role in that Movement? How did he come into the leadership of that Movement? Would that Movement have taken a different shape had he not been there at all, or had he not been assassinated when he was? Would the picture of the

Movement have been altered if King had not been so much a part of that picture? What were the unique dimensions of the relationship between this individual of powerful and universal voice, himself a very reluctant leader, and a Movement that sought to lift up those who had been voiceless, and whom few white persons wished to hear, persons very unlike the articulate and dynamic Martin Luther King?

It is this history that scholars are now piecing together. Beginning to emerge is the density and complexity of a grassroots Movement across the South that laid the groundwork for the now-famous campaigns in which Dr. King played so instrumental a role.

Robert Moses likens this Movement to a huge ocean, its waves peaking and then subsiding, over and over again. The peaks were high moments, when the organizing efforts of scores of years would come to fruition. Montgomery, Alabama was such a peak. And only now, in 1992, are we beginning to uncover the layers of Rosa Parks's stance and of Dr. King's emergence onto the national scene in Montgomery.

Through the stories of women like Joanne Robinson, a longtime leader of the Women's Political Council in Montgomery, we've begun to learn about the predecessor Movements to the Montgomery Improvement Association. The Women's Political Council had been protesting segregated buses for several years before the arrest of Rosa Parks. Rosa Parks did not just arise one morning and decide to make history. Rather, she was part of a long Movement protesting segregation on the buses.

We also know now that we are telling our schoolchildren a slightly inaccurate version of exactly what the demands were in Montgomery, with respect to desegregation of the buses. At that time, the practice in Montgomery, Alabama—where 70 percent of the people who rode those buses were black—was that whites filled up all the seats until the middle point of the bus, and then blacks filled up all the seats. If more whites got on the bus, then those blacks who were seated from the rear to the middle would have to get up and give up their seats.

I thought that the demand of the Montgomery Movement was to end segregation in its entirety on the buses in Montgomery. But no, it was a much more modest demand. What those in Montgomery were asking for was an end to the practice whereby blacks had to yield their seats if whites overflowed into their half of the bus. What was being asked for was equal space on the bus—not an end to segregation. And it was that very modest request which was denied, and which led to thirteen months of protest and of walking, and of riding in neighbors' cars, and of car pools in Montgomery, Alabama. That was a wave on the ocean.

The organization of the Student Nonviolent Coordinating Committee (SNCC) by Ella Baker was a wave on that ocean, as was the entire Mississippi Movement—a Movement whose dimensions we are only now beginning to define for ourselves, a Movement so painfully misshapen and misrepresented in the public imagination by the film *Mississippi Burning* some years ago. Charismatic leaders? Martin, yes; but also Bob Moses himself, Fannie Lou Hamer, and—in another context—Malcolm X, were all peaks on that ocean.

Surely Dr. King saw how deep that ocean was, and how wide it stretched, for he prophesied repeatedly that, although he might not see that Movement to its end, its work would nonetheless go on. In his last days, in the speech he gave the night before he died, he told us:

> I don't know what will happen now. We've got some
> difficult days ahead. But it really doesn't matter with me
> now, because I've been to the mountaintop, and I don't
> mind. Like anybody, I'd like to live a long life; longevity
> has its place. But I'm not concerned with that now. I just
> want to do God's will. And he's allowed me to go up to
> the mountain, and I've looked over, and I've seen the
> Promised Land. And I may not get there with you, but I
> want you to know tonight that we as a people will get to
> the Promised Land. And so I'm happy tonight. I'm not
> worried about anything. I'm not fearing any man. Mine
> eyes have seen the glory of the coming of the Lord.

He knew. He knew somehow that he would not be with us, but that the ocean would keep roaring on. One cannot comprehend Dr. King without filling out the pages of the Movement's history book. And if that Movement was an ocean, we have yet to learn what all the forces were that caused it to dry up.

Similarly, as time begins to rest more comfortably on our collective memories of Dr. King, and as we draw back from the shock of his martyrdom, we will be able to look more accurately at the impact of his political philosophy on the Movement and its legacy. Questions abound for venturesome scholars and activists and organizers here. If nonviolence was a way of life for Dr. King, was it ever more than a momentary strategy and tactic for the masses who made up the Movement? Could any differences be drawn between the adherence to nonviolence among those in the South, and Movement activists in the urban North? And if there were differences, what were the moral and religious antecedents of these differing approaches to our struggle? Where, if at all, can the remnants of Dr. King's nonviolent social action be found in today's political life? These are questions to which we have yet to uncover the answers.

With time, too, perhaps the official version of Dr. King's murder will warrant closer scrutiny. It was not until almost ten years after Dr. King was killed that the American public learned the disgusting truth about the protracted campaign launched against Dr. King by the FBI—his hotel rooms bugged, his SCLC staff infiltrated, poisoned letters sent to him, constant visual surveillance, and telephone threats. As Dr. King himself described it, the FBI was, much like the KKK, "Out to break me." We now know, too, that FBI files documented no fewer than fifty threats against Dr. King's life. Finally, the full details of the days leading up to Dr. King's assassination in Memphis have been stingily parsed out, bit by bit. And it cannot yet be said that we have the whole picture.

We know, for example, that among Dr. King's associates in Memphis was an FBI informant, that police plants had infiltrated the Memphis Invaders—a militant group of young men who had precipitated a violent clash with the police at a march led by Dr. King days before he died. And we know also that a young black man, who observed the shooting of Dr. King, and who claimed at the time of the shooting that he was a member of the Invaders, was an undercover member of the Memphis Police Department. He was one of the few people who observed the events from that balcony at the Lorraine Hotel.

We also know that Dr. King deeply despaired of the violence that had broken out in Memphis during the protest demonstration he held there late in March—violence that we now know had been inspired by police infiltrators. Dr. King felt his message of nonviolence was

January 1992—Leading the procession to Kresge Auditorium are, from left to right, Rebecca M. Vest, Charles M. Vest, Margaret A. Burnham, and Leo Osgood.

losing its appeal. And we have learned from an FBI telephone bug of his conversation with a friend that he said, "All I'm saying is that Roy," and I'm quoting Dr. King, "all I'm saying is that Roy Wilkins and others, the Negroes who are influenced by what they read in the newspapers, they will say Martin Luther King is dead. He's finished. His nonviolence is nothing. No one is listening to it." He was deeply troubled and in despair about what had occurred. And indeed, after that march in Memphis, the *New York Times* called the Memphis violence which had led to the death of a young demonstrator "a powerful embarrassment to Dr. King." The *Times* went on to recommend that Dr. King call off his Poor People's Campaign, which he was then in the midst of organizing.

Thus the Memphis violence, which had been generated by the police, had left Dr. King personally demoralized and politically at sea. Nothing could have pleased J. Edgar Hoover more, for this was the result he sought. It was J. Edgar who, you will remember, had widely proclaimed, "Dr. King is public enemy number one."

The Martin Luther King of 1968 was, politically speaking, a far more complex and threatening man than the leader of the Montgomery and Birmingham and Albany campaigns. Having tried to budge the race and class structures of Chicago with his Operation Breadbasket,

Dr. King was now articulating a far broader program. A year to the date prior to his murder on April 4, 1967, at his famous Riverside Church address, he had categorically condemned the Vietnam War, denouncing the United States as the "greatest purveyor of violence in the world today." He later warned black folk, "We can't solve our problems now until there's a radical redistribution of economic and political power in America." And he urged the recognition of the reality that the evils of racism, economic exploitation and militarism are all tied together; and you really can't get rid of one without getting rid of the other.

While today's ear might perhaps not cringe at these stark truisms, Dr. King paid a high price for his embrace of a more radical perspective, especially in regard to the Vietnam War. Public opinion polls at the time showed that 73 percent of Americans disagreed with his opposition to the Vietnam War, and 60 percent believed his position on the war would hurt the civil rights agenda. Moreover, blacks were not altogether enthusiastic about his move onto what they considered to be foreign political turf, either. Only 25 percent of black respondents agreed with Dr. King's position on the war; 48 percent thought he was wrong.

At the same time that his popularity was declining because of his alliance with the peace Movement and his anti-war positions, forces far more radical than Dr. King—the Black Panther Party, for example— were emerging out of the rubble of the 1965 Watts explosion as a challenge on his left. Thus, Dr. King was poised on shifting political ground, reaching out to embrace new coalitions and causes, while holding onto the tenets of nonviolence in the face of urban rebellions in a militant Black Power Movement. Had he been able to enhance his leadership role in these circumstances with his message of economic equality, Dr. King would surely have been an even more powerful force to deal with.

It was the more mature Martin, the more seasoned Martin, the Martin who believed, as he put it, that the "whole structure of American life must be changed," and not just the Martin who dreamed of black and white schoolchildren attending class together, who was killed in 1968. If Dr. King is to be transformed into a national icon, it cannot be accomplished by cutting off the legs on which Dr. King finally stood. Furthermore, although we may yet conclude that his death was not the result of a government conspiracy, it nevertheless seems plain that certain elements of the government were happy to see him go when he did. In light of this political reality, the loose ends still dangling from the several investigations into the King assassination demand honest examination and resolution.

The two questions we explore at a King commemoration are closely related. First, what is our contemporary understanding of Dr. King and his world? And second, how does the vision of the Movement bear on our own circumstances?

We cast an eye back and then, wearing the eyes of Dr. King and of the Movement of that day, we look around at ourselves and assess our own reality. If it accomplished little else, the Movement threw off America's blinders and rendered visible Ralph Ellison's man. The Negro was no longer a silent sufferer; she had a voice and a vision, she could be seen and heard.

Herbert Lee; Chaney, Goodman and Schwerner; Amsey Moore; Medgar Evers; Malcolm X; Martin. What would they see today? What happened after they were all killed for believing that black folk had a right to be seen?

Surely they would see that the civil rights agenda that they had so carefully constructed had indeed been successfully enshrined in the law books: the Civil Rights Act, the Voting Rights Act, and the Public Accommodations Act. But could we blame their curiosity—nay, more likely their anger—when they discovered that the written word, compromised though it had been by a hostile Supreme Court, belied a woeful reality? That we African Americans remain twice as unemployed as whites; that in 1991 we only earned $56 for every $100 that whites earned. That a white who has a high school degree earns more money on average than one of us who is a college graduate. That we are only 3 percent of the Ivy League college enrollment. That less than one of every thirty graduate students is black. That we die younger, and the morbidity gap between black and white is widening. That 56 percent of us looking for housing have to confront and deal with housing discrimination. That six in ten of all the newspapers in the country have no black professionals on their staff. That at MIT only fourteen of 957 faculty members, or only 1 percent, are black. That the African male has joined the condor as an endangered species.

But perhaps more telling than our worsening statistical profile is the palpable despair that has settled over our communities of color—not only African-American, but Hispanic and Native-American communities as well—a deep depression that seems to signal an utter loss of the ennobling and unifying spirit of our old Movement. We witness it in the disdain for human life manifested in the fratricide among our young people, in the violence against African-American women that is so common today, in the nihilistic, self-deprecating and materialistic cultural expression of our young people.

Where, we should ask, is the love of community, the self-love symbolized by our joyful proclamation that black is beautiful, symbolized by our reach for black power fifteen years ago? Where is that love of self, of community?

And what of the backlash of the nineties? Surely Dr. King would strip away the new veneer stretched taut over the old racist "shibboleth." He could see the race-baiting demon of the sixties behind the affirmative action quota/preference debate that provides national politicians with an opportunity to simultaneously distract attention from the national disgrace that passes for an economy, while pointing the finger at African Americans. As well, Dr. King would doubtless see the attack on multicultural education and Afrocentric study as an effort to undermine the campaign to open the university doors to new thinking and to new thinkers.

Those eyes of the sixties Movement glancing forward to the black world of the nineties would no doubt be surprised as well to find deep ideological fissures among black activists and thinkers—divisions that are themselves the reflection of the political disquiet and dissonance experienced by a community that sees itself left in the dust of a technological revolution, and that therefore is turning hard new corners in search of answers. Dr. King, the drum major for peace, would surely be sorrowed to hear America's newest black hero, General Colin Powell, claim of his purported enemy, "First we're going to cut off their legs, and then we're going to kill them." What would he say of the cynical replacement of the Civil Rights Movement's bright light, Thurgood Marshall, with Clarence Thomas, a man who has scorned the civil rights leadership and caricatured them as "a bunch of do-nothing whiners looking for handouts"?

Dr. King went straight to the heart of the matter in condemning the blight of poverty. He once remarked, "Most of the poor people in this country are working every day, but earning so little they cannot begin to function in the mainstream of the economic life of our nation. They're working on full-time jobs, but for part-time pay." And that was in 1965. But could Dr. King ever have imagined that, in the United States of America in 1992 on a cold day in January, scores of homeless people would be strewn across the city streets? That good and decent people, you and I, our brothers and sisters, our neighbors, would train themselves to step gingerly around the women and men in tattered rags, averting our eyes, pretending not to hear their mumbled entreaties, and never questioning where those people went when it was time to go home? What would Dr. King say about that?

Dr. King knew the Ku Klux Klan; he had faced 3,000 Klansmen in 1962. In St. Augustine, Florida in 1963, the Klan had kidnapped the leaders of the local Movement and were on the verge of incinerating them when the local sheriff intervened. In Selma, the Klan openly joined ranks with the state troopers, attacking the marchers. What would Dr. King say about his country in 1992, with an ex-Klansman running for president?

Dr. King had a particularly keen sensitivity to the needs and interests of all children, but in particular of his African-American children, and to their desire to participate in the Movement, in the liberation struggle. In 1963 in Birmingham, Dr. King organized a march of 6,000 children, ranging in age from six to sixteen. And this entire, beautiful crusade of children—from the youngest to the oldest—were all arrested and carted away in wagons as they marched from the Sixteenth Street Church into the town, singing "We Shall Overcome." People all across the country were scandalized and criticized Dr. King for what they called the "use of children." But these critics fell silent when Dr. King asked them, "Where were you with your protective words when, down through the years, Negro infants were born into ghettos, taking their first breath of life in a social atmosphere where the fresh air of freedom was crowded out by the stench of discrimination?"

What would Dr. King say today, in 1992, if we told him that just days ago, two little black children in New York City had their faces painted with white shoe polish by a group of young white people who thought it was funny? That black youth are three times as likely to be unemployed as whites? That one million young black people are out of school? That thousands more are unable to read, to write, to compute? What would Dr. King say about the plight of our children today in 1992? What could a young child say, looking back at the Movement of 1960? A young child with no home, with barely a school to attend—what could such a child say about what that Movement had actually accomplished?

Today is much more than a birthday celebration, although it is that as well. It's a marking of time with a man who is our contemporary, a celebration of the life of a very young man, who began his public life at the age of twenty-six. Think of that, those of you who are nineteen, twenty, twenty-one and twenty-two, who will graduate from MIT and go on to other things. Martin King in Montgomery, when he was called upon to take the leadership of that Movement, was twenty-six. And from that moment on, he gave us all he had—his voice, his dreams, his vision of a new world, a new ethic, a new peace, a new America. All that he had, he gave to us in the twelve years and four months until he was struck down.

We honor Dr. King, not only for that gift, but for lifting us in our despair now and then, and for showing us the way to a greater community. And in committing ourselves to Dr. King and in honoring him, what we commit ourselves to is action.

Dr. King, we pay you the tribute we know you would treasure most by committing ourselves, for all the years we have left, to action. Happy birthday, Dr. King.

MARGARET A. BURNHAM became the first African-American woman to serve as a judge in Massachusetts when she was appointed Boston Municipal Court Justice in 1977. She is currently a partner in Burnham, Hines and Dilday, the first African-American women's law firm in New England. Judge Burnham is also a lecturer in political science at MIT.

Martin Luther King, Jr. speaking at the March on Washington, August 28, 1963.

Where Do We Go From Here: Chaos or Community?

William H. Gray III

W HEN YOU CAME INTO THIS AUDITORIUM today, you saw a film that went back nearly three de- cades, to that great day when over a quarter of a million Americans gathered at the Lincoln Monument to hear the dreamer's dream. I was there along with all of the others in the ninety-degree heat in August, as people of all creeds, all colors, came together to protest American apartheid. I was there when Peter, Paul and Mary sang the hymns of the service. I was there when the great Mahalia Jackson gave the meditation. I was there when Martin Luther King, Jr. went to the microphone to speak.

There was a silence that was unbelievable, considering that we were outside and there were over a quarter of a million people. You could hear the leaves rustling in the wind as everyone strained to hear the speaker, Martin Luther King. For Martin Luther King symbolized a great movement, a nonviolent movement, a revolution that took the country and changed its basic political, social and economic institu- tions. We listened as he told us about the importance of that day.

Now, most of you have seen on television many African Americans speaking to large crowds. You saw Jesse Jackson in '84 running for president, addressing the nation at the Democratic National Convention. You've seen legislators and mayors. You have grown used to the fact that you can see people of color being on center stage. But to understand that moment in 1963, you must try to remember what America was like in 1963.

This was the first time any African American stood on a national stage and spoke to the entire nation through the electronic medium called television. This was the first time that blacks and whites had come together in many decades to protest American apartheid. America was a country where blacks could not go to Duke University, even if they could play basketball. Blacks could not go to the University of Alabama, even if they could run the 40-yard-dash with a football uniform on in 4.1 seconds. Blacks could not go to Georgia Tech to get a college degree. As a matter of fact, they could not even ride on public transportation except in those places reserved for people of color. This was not a phenomenon simply in the South; the virtuous North was not so virtuous. There were no voices back then talking about meritocracies. There were no voices calling for a level playing field. You couldn't stay in the Sheraton, the Hilton, or the Holiday Inn if you were black. That was America.

But one man came along and became the spokesman for the Montgomery bus boycott, and from that was formed the Southern Christian Leadership Conference. From that came a movement of marching feet, of people sitting and praying and swimming, and just confronting racism and segregation and apartheid all across this land, until that day in 1963 when they all came together. The pattering feet of Joshua's army had brought down segregation in America without a shot being fired. A nonviolent movement passed the Civil Rights Bill of '64 and the Voting Rights Bill. You see, blacks couldn't vote in America just thirty years ago.

By 1965, the walls had come tumbling down. The movement started to change. It was no longer a Civil Rights Movement. It moved to an economic and political rights movement, and Martin Luther King became the spokesperson. Most people forget that Martin Luther King, Jr. was not killed in a civil rights march; he was killed in an economics rights march. He was not killed fighting simply for black people; he was fighting for fair wages for all the sanitation workers in that city in

Tennessee, calling for a new economic and political order not just for black Americans, but for *all* Americans. And before that assassin's bullet killed him, he wrote a book, *Where Do we Go From Here: Chaos or Community?* He said, "Our choice is to go back to polarization, conflict, hatred, intolerance, strife, or our choice is to become a community."

Well, it's thirty years later, my brothers and sisters. Where are we today? First, I think Martin Luther King, Jr. would say we've come a mighty long way, because today you can look around and can see the changes that are wrought. This year, as we start a new administration in Washington, there will be forty members of the Congressional Black Caucus, three of them coming from the state of Florida; three of them coming from North Carolina—the very places where Martin had called for a new political order. We not only see progress in politics, but we also see it in other fields. When you turn on the television you see people like Michael Jordan and Oprah Winfrey, who has moved Phil Donahue right off the scale. You see people like Reginald Lewis, who was the chair of a multibillion dollar corporation, Beatrice, and you see people like Bill Cosby, who has become an entertainment and communications conglomerate himself. I know we've come a mighty long way when I come to MIT and look around at this audience and at this campus. When I was going to college, there were hardly any of my kind who were either students or faculty at this institution.

I think Martin Luther King would agree that we have made some progress toward a sense of community. But on the other hand, I believe he would caution us not to be too optimistic, or not to assume that progress will continue, and not to assume that everything is all right here in our country. We have failed to reach community. There is still chaos in this country, still prejudice, racism, bigotry and anti-Semitism. Martin Luther King, Jr. would point that out to you. It is still embedded in the structures of our society: its economic structures, its political structures, even its educational structures.

Last year, the reports of the Census Department and the Labor Department pointed out that in 1992 the black family median income was still only 57 percent of white family median income—exactly where it was in 1968. Even though we dominate the basketball court and the football field, we still haven't gotten into the front office or the coaching ranks of those sports. Even though we've got Bill Cosby, Oprah

Winfrey, and all of those popular shows on television, the fact is that we still haven't gotten into the board rooms of entertainment or communications.

Martin would say we still have a long way to go and he would laugh at those who use his name and his quotations incorrectly, who say, "Didn't Martin Luther King say that one day he wanted to see his children sitting at the table with children of other races, and they would be judged on the content of their character and not on the color of their skin? And didn't he mean by that, that we should get rid of any attempts to redress nearly 400 years of legalized apartheid in this nation, and only twenty-five years of some progress?" They use Martin's words to call for the elimination of affirmative action efforts to integrate faculties and staffs, and diversify student bodies. It is insulting, degrading and downright wrong. You don't level the playing field in twenty-five years for minorities and women after four hundred years of legalized slavery and dehumanization.

I remember when I went to my college. There were five of us in the whole place. I was fairly successful. I was the only four-letter athlete in my high school. I was fourth in a class of 369. I had a 3.76 grade point average in high school, and my SAT scores were pretty good. After I had been accepted and was looking over the campus with my father, the dean of admissions said to my father, "I really don't think he ought to come here because he'll never graduate." Four years later, at the honors banquet, as I prepared to receive the highest award given to a history major in any senior class, guess who was sitting right next to me? The same man who had told me four years earlier that I had no business at that institution. Well, my father looked at him and said, "Aren't you the dude who said . . .?"

We have become confused, and we have lost sight of what the struggle for the beloved community is. The struggle for the beloved community is to open the doorway wider, to build bridges so that those who have been historically disadvantaged will have an opportunity to catch up. I have one question to ask those who argue today that the playing field is level: Are all American women of all colors standing on the same level playing field with white males in America? We've made progress, but don't take a few token deans, a few token professors, a few token achievements in entertainment and in politics, and then conclude

January 1993—Leading the procession to Kresge Auditorium are, from left to right, Clarence G. Williams, Charles M. Vest, William H. Gray III, and Rebecca M. Vest.

that we've struggled long enough. We've come a long way, but we still have even a longer way to have community and avoid the chaos that we see on some of our college campuses, in some of our communities.

Finally, when you talk about where we go from here, you not only have to know the truth of where we came from, but also what we must do now to continue to move towards building community. I will tell you that it is more imperative today than ever before. And let me tell you why. It has nothing to do with good feelings. It has nothing to do with humanitarian, moralistic motives. In a real sense, the desire to build community today is a much greater imperative than ever before, and the reason is there's a revolution going on in America. Let me quickly describe it for you, because it is an economic imperative for all of our interest to move toward community and opportunity for all God's children.

I saw it the other day, when I got on an airplane. I looked in and I saw the captain, hair hanging all down the neck. And I thought, "What happened to rules and regulations? What happened to values?" And then the captain turned around. She was a blond. And then I looked over and I saw the first officer, and he was a brother. Then I looked at the flight engineer, and he was an Asian American. And about that time someone tapped me on the shoulder, the head flight attendant, to tell me I was blocking traffic, and I turned around, and there was Juanita Rodriguez telling me to go sit down. I said, "Oh, Lord, I'm in trouble today." But let me tell you, that was the best flight I have ever had in my life. They flew that plane and landed it magnificently.

That experience symbolizes a revolution that is going on right now, that is creating an economic imperative for the beloved community. It's simply this: that in the next century, 85 percent of all the new workers in America are going to be women, minorities, and new immigrants; and that means that all of us are increasingly going to have to depend upon the productivity, the skills, the excellence of those that we call disadvantaged today. It is in our own self-interest to move toward a community of equal opportunity, or else the prosperity, the strength and the growth of this nation will decline. These are the people who are America's future.

We must move toward community, and in order to move toward community there are four things that I suggest that Martin would want us to do. First, we have to achieve excellence. Don't sit around here at MIT sucking your militant thumb because you find out there may be some residues of racism at this university. What did you expect? There is no difference between the people here and the people out there. Understand that you are here to achieve excellence, and to assimilate all the knowledge, traditions, and information so that you can move forward and build a new world order. Martin Luther King was a strong believer in educational excellence; that's why he had a Ph.D., a Master of Divinity degree, and a Bachelor of Arts degree as well. And if you are to be catalysts for change, if you are to build the beloved community, I don't care what color you are, I don't care what sex you are, I don't care where you come from—you have got to achieve educational excellence.

So, don't get mad and sit around because you find some problems. Did you ever see Michael Jordan say, "Time out," and walk over to the side and say, "Coach, every time I get the ball there are five people trying to stop my stuff." You ever see that? No. Because he knows that the moment he gets on that court, that's the name of the game: somebody is out there to stop your stuff. Therefore, understand that you will never achieve success by sitting around crying about the problem. Run faster, jump higher and shoot straighter than anybody else. And then you, too, will be able to sit at the honors banquet and look the director of admissions in the eye, and say, "Aren't you the dude who told me . . .?"

Second, remember something else. You are put on this universe, on this starship called Earth, not just to take care of you or yours. You are put here to be of service to your community and to the human community. So, if all you do is achieve excellence, and then go out and make as much as you can, and then sit on your can, your name is Swine. But if you go out in life, make as much as you can, and give back as much as you can, then you will be called Blessed. The reason why we remember Martin Luther King, Jr. today is because he didn't sit on his Ph.D. from Boston University, he didn't sit on his Master of Divinity degree from Crozer Theological Seminary, he didn't sit on his bachelor's degree from Morehouse, he decided to do something for a larger cause. You, too, must be willing to give service.

And third, you must have within you a sense of brotherhood and sisterhood that overcomes intolerance, bigotry, anti-Semitism, prejudice of all kind, and sexism. Because they're all sides of the same coin. There are going to be people who will not understand your struggle, who will make you awfully angry. But if we're going to build the community that is beloved, we must begin the revolution within ourselves of loving one another, tolerating one another. Even when other folks hurt us, try to sensitize them and bring them to a new position, not by violent means or by hating them in return, but by showing them that we are better and we know a better way.

I remember one event that will always be framed in my mind about Martin King. You see, not only was I there in 1963, but the King family and the Gray family have been friends for three generations. I used to preach at Ebenezer Baptist Church on many occasions. So did my father. And when Martin Luther King, Jr. went to Crozer Theological Seminary in Chester, Pennsylvania, he often used to come to our home for meals on the weekend, and to practice preaching at Bright Hope Baptist Church, where I am now the pastor. I will never forget one thing that happened that proves something to me about brotherhood, sisterhood, tolerance and love of humanity.

Dance performance at the Martin Luther King, Jr. Celebration, January 1993.

Martin Luther King, Jr. was nearly killed in New York. He was stabbed by a woman with a knife that went so deep into his chest they had to take him to the hospital with it still sticking out to perform the surgery to remove it, because it was so close to his heart. Martin recuperated and went back to the South, but decided that he had to come North and raise money. He came to our home in Philadelphia, because he didn't have the money to stay in hotels—the movement was too poor—and he stayed with the Grays at 1511 North Sixteenth Street for a week as he tried to raise money in Philadelphia. Every evening he would have to put ice on this terrible scar that was still raw on his chest. And all of us would start to talk about the woman, we started calling her names and all of that. I'll never forget to this day that Martin stopped us cold in our tracks, and said, "Don't talk about her that way. No matter what she did, and no matter who she is, she's a child of God." And from that moment on, none of us talked about the woman who nearly killed him.

You see, Martin understood that we are all part of a network of mutuality. We are all brothers and sisters regardless of the color of our skin, regardless of where we live, regardless of where we come from, and it behooves all of us to try to help the rest of us if we are going to have a beloved community. And so, my brothers and sisters, I urge you to have a sense of tolerance, a sense of sensitivity, and create a new spirit of brotherhood and sisterhood within you, because the revolution starts inside of you.

And finally, if we want to move from chaos to community, we must never rest in the fight for justice. We must understand that injustice is often subtle, and that we must stand up against injustice wherever it is found. We must say to our political systems that if they are unjust, they must be corrected. I can't understand a nation that is willing to say, "Give me your tired, your poor, if you are a refugee from Europe. But if you are a Haitian, we have a concentration camp for you." I don't understand a nation that says, "If you're from Yugoslavia or Poland, come on to America. But if you're from Black Africa trying to escape the warfare of Somalia or Ethiopia, I'm sorry, we can't let you in."

There is still injustice in our society, and it is incumbent upon all of us to be vigilant and to continue the struggle. Don't just come here today and remember a dreamer, a historical figure of the past, but go from this place committed to excellence. Go from this place committed to serve your community and your world. Go from this place being more tolerant and creating a sisterhood and brotherhood of all people of all colors and all backgrounds. And go from this place committed that you, like Martin Luther King, will struggle against injustice. One person standing up to the Goliaths of poverty, of militarism, racism and sexism may be able to bring the walls down as he did.

It's not going to be easy. It never is easy. And it won't be any easier for this generation than it was for mine. But let me tell you something I learned a long time ago, which has led my life in giving me direction and strength. It happened in Baton Rouge, Louisiana, where Grandma lived. I'll never forget the day I found out about racism.

I was about five years of age, and I went downtown with my sister in Baton Rouge, and ran around the town. We ended up at a department store—my sister was a little bit older—and I was thirsty and I saw a water fountain and I went over to get a drink. Just as I started to drink, a hand grabbed me and said, "Nigger, you can't drink from that fountain. Go to the one over there." And on the other side of the department store was another fountain with a big sign that said, "Colored Only." Well, the water looked the same to me. But anyway, my sister grabbed me and took me home to Grandma.

My grandmother was a schoolteacher, and she was confronted with the problem that all black mothers and parents have to face, the same problem that all Latino mothers and fathers must face when they have to tell their children that there are people who dislike them simply because of their origin. I guess she had to face that same day that the Irish mother faced in the 1890s here in Massachusetts when her child went out and saw the signs: No Irish Need Apply.

She took me out to the university called the front porch, sat me down in the classroom called the big swing, and she began to tell me about America, about what America was. She also had a way of taking a negative and turning it into a positive, and talked to me about the "Could-Be's" of life. For you see, it's not enough to dwell in the past. It's not enough to dwell in the reality of this moment. Life belongs to those who are always looking at the Could-Be of life, and who are willing to create it. And I'll never forget, she said to me, "Son, you see that mayor, the city council, the state legislature, the governor, the Congress, the courts? It takes all of them to keep you from drinking at that water fountain. That's how important you are." And she told me then that life was never going to be a bed of roses, and that I would have difficulty, and that difficulty would be put there by other people regardless of what I did. My job was to climb the mountain and to overcome the difficulty.

I'm so glad she did. Because, you see, that little boy born in Baton Rouge, Louisiana, who later on went to school in Philadelphia, and North Philadelphia, grew up to be not only a minister, not only a college professor, but in the 1980s he used to sit on the second floor of the White House, and look the most powerful man in the eye, the president of America, Ronald Reagan, and say, "No." I have learned that the only way you get there is by remembering the words she closed the lecture with. I didn't understand then, and I didn't know where she got them from, but I understand now, because they were the words of another black mother to her son. They are the words that I leave with you. I leave it to all of you who are sojourning through this place, whether you are black or white, no matter where you come from—for indeed, the struggle against injustice is a constant one.

> Well, son, I'll tell you:
> Life for me ain't been no crystal stair.
> It's had tacks in it,
> And splinters,
> And boards torn up,
> And places with no carpet on the floor—
> Bare.
> But all the time
> I'se been a'climbin' on,
> And reachin' landin's,
> And turnin' corners,
> And sometimes goin' in the dark
> Where there ain't been no light.
> So, boy, don't you turn back.
> Don't you set down on the steps
> 'Cause you finds it kinder hard,
> Don't you fall now—
> For I'se still goin', honey,
> I'se still climbin',
> And life for me ain't been no crystal stair.

My brothers and sisters, as we celebrate this day in remembering a spiritual giant that God gave to us, and who sojourned and saved our land, we must remember that we are called to climb the stairs. And I urge you here to reach new landings, to turn new corners, and for God's sake, go into the dark, where there ain't been no light.

WILLIAM H. GRAY III is currently CEO of the United Negro College Fund. He is perhaps best-known for his influence in Congress, where he became the first African American to hold the position of majority whip. He served in the U.S. House of Representatives from 1978-91, leaving his mark by implementing economic sanctions against South Africa and by sponsoring the emergency food aid bill for Ethiopia.

January 1994—Charles M. Vest, Coretta Scott King, Rebecca M. Vest, and Leo Osgood leading the procession.

The Movement for Economic and Social Justice: 1994 and Beyond*

Coretta Scott King

I WANT TO CONGRATULATE THE MARTIN LUTHER King, Jr. Day Planning Committee for commemorative activities on this 20th anniversary of your program, and thank you for making possible my participation here today. You have chosen well in making your theme for this program, "The movement for economic and social justice: 1994 and Beyond." I feel this way because I believe that the best way to commemorate Martin Luther King, Jr.'s birthday is to recommit ourselves to his unfinished work for social and economic justice.

Most people are aware that the civil rights movement focused on the elimination of racial segregation. But we were also much concerned about economic empowerment of the disadvantaged and of impoverished people in our communities. My husband once said that "the inseparable twin of racial injustice is economic injustice." In other words, wherever you find racism, you will also find economic injustice.

* Copyright Coretta Scott King. February 11, 1994.

Martin understood that civil rights meant little without economic resources. "What good is the right to sit at an integrated lunch counter," he once asked, "if you can't afford the price of a meal?"

This struggle for economic empowerment was an integral part of every campaign of the civil rights movement, from Montgomery to Memphis. We always pressed for a greater share of jobs, employment training and economic opportunities, even as we struggled against racial discrimination. And let us never forget that Martin Luther King, Jr. was assassinated in a labor union organizing campaign. He felt strongly that trade unions were essential for the economic empowerment of all Americans, and black Americans in particular. As he said, "our needs are identical with labor's needs: decent wages, fair working conditions, livable housing, old age security, health and welfare measures, conditions in which families can grow, have education for their children and respect in the community."

Martin went to Memphis as part of the Poor People's Campaign, which was an interracial coalition he organized to press for fundamental reforms to eliminate the cancer of poverty from American life. Martin understood that there were more white people than black people living in poverty. He felt that a social justice movement had an obligation to help white people, Hispanic, Native American and other ethnic groups who were suffering the ravages of poverty, as well as black Americans.

And even today, more than 25 years after Martin was assassinated in Memphis, economic empowerment is still the central issue we face. We certainly have our work cut out for us in meeting this challenge. Our challenge is now to organize a nationwide, multiracial coalition for job-training, employment, and education programs in our communities. We're not just talking about summer jobs. We want stable jobs at a living wage so people can raise their families in decent living standards. We need tax incentives to make investment in poor communities attractive to business investors, just as we need tax disincentives for corporations that invest in other nations instead of our cities.

We have to be about the business of self-empowerment as well. This means we have to organize cooperative enterprises, so unemployed people will not only have a decent job, but a share in the ownership of the enterprise that employs them. And the same thing goes for housing. Ownership is the key to economic revitalization. Having a stake in the ownership of our homes and places of employment is the beginning of political, social, and economic empowerment. As Andrew Young has said, "the struggle of the 1990s is to integrate the money."

Since it was founded in 1968, the King Center has been active in the struggle for economic empowerment for minorities and working people. The Center played a major role in organizing the national committee for full employment, which was instrumental in passing the Humphrey-Hawkins Act and other legislation to provide jobs. We have lobbied long hours for employment bills and we have aggressively tapped public- and private-sector initiatives to fund job training and employment programs for at-risk young people. The Center has also supported needed increases in the minimum wage, labor union organizing campaigns, tax reforms to benefit poor people, financial aid for education for needy families, and a host of legislative reforms for economic empowerment.

We have a great opportunity to advance the cause of economic empowerment for working people and the poor in this election year. We have to take control of our own destiny by launching a nationwide voter registration drive, followed by the most aggressive voter turnout campaign in history. And remember that political commitment doesn't stop at the ballot box. After the elections are over, we have to do a better job of staying on our elected officials. We have to write to them more often, we have to become better informed about legislation for economic empowerment. We have to meet with them until they are so tired of us that they begin to listen and respond to our concerns.

My most fervent hope is that 1994 will be the year the political system begins to respond to the need for genuine economic opportunity for Americans of all races. Above all, let us keep faith that we *can* do it. With enough creativity and determination, we will be able to create a society where *every* child can have a decent education and a chance for a better life, and where every parent can have a stable job that will enable them to support their families. Let us embrace this common vision and mobilize all of our resources to bring it into being. Let us put hope and economic opportunity for *all* Americans—black, white, red, brown, and yellow—at the very top of the political agenda.

We have witnessed impressive civil rights progress throughout American society since Martin Luther King, Jr. began to lead the civil rights movement. The movement won many great victories, including the desegregation of public facilitates and legislative guarantees of voting rights. Yet racism remains perhaps the single most destructive force in American society. A whole range of social problems, including poverty, urban decay, crime, the failure of our schools, and violence are all aggravated by the persistence of racism. Until America comes to grips with the problem of racism, we will not be able to create the great democracy of Martin Luther King, Jr.'s dream.

Racism not only hurts African Americans, it not only hurts Hispanic, Asians, and Native Americans; it also hurts white people. Racism divides people of all races who would otherwise share common interests. Racism creates a gulf of fear and suspicion between communities in every city. It feeds the cycle of poverty, crime, and violence that is turning many of the nation's urban centers into ghost towns. It prevents our public schools from fulfilling their potential, and it undermines the credibility of U.S. moral leadership.

Equal *economic* opportunity, in particular, has remained an elusive goal. The median income for African-American families is still less than 60 percent of the figure for white families. Nearly half of the African-American children are still living in poverty. The unemployment rate for black workers today is about double the rate for white workers.

My husband was irrevocably committed to diversity in all institutions of society, including the executive suites of America's great corporations and universities. "When I speak of integration," he once said, "I don't mean a romantic mixing of colors, I mean a real sharing of power and responsibility." There has been little progress for African-American executives in the highest echelons of corporate management. Today, only one black American heads a Fortune 500 company, and we are underrepresented in the middle and upper decision-making levels of all but a very few multinational corporations. Women and minorities still encounter the "glass ceiling" when they try to move up the corporate ladder or advance in the academic sector. It is so important for companies and institutions of higher education to make an earnest commitment to go beyond the letter of the law and to make diversity not just a buzzword for their public relations programs, but a real policy that will be reflected at every level of corporate decision-making.

Like many of America's most prestigious colleges and universities, MIT has not done so well in making its faculty and administration representative of the community it calls home. It doesn't have to be this way. MIT can become a national leader in promoting diversity by setting up more scholarships for minorities, by reaching out to help needy people get a decent education, and by awarding more tenured professorships and higher administrative positions to minorities. This will not only benefit minorities and women; it will also benefit white students and the entire university community by helping to prepare them for living in a multiracial society.

A commitment to improving race relations can help prevent further racial conflict. If we can build such bridges of knowledge and understanding between people of all races and religions, we will sow the seeds of a new unity in America.

I include religious diversity because I think any of us who claim to be followers of Martin Luther King, Jr. have a moral obligation to deplore the recent expressions of anti-Semitism that have polluted our society. Anti-Semitism is as reprehensible and contemptible as racism, and anyone who supports this form of bigotry does a disservice to their country. As my husband said in a speech he gave just a month before he was assassinated, "for the black man to be struggling for justice and then turn around and be anti-Semitic is not only a very irrational course but it is a very immoral course, and wherever we have seen anti-Semitism, we have condemned it with all of our might."

He saw America not as a melting pot, but as a vibrant mosaic of people of all races, religions, and ethnic groups. We need not surrender our group identities, he felt. Instead, we could weave them into a cooperative and mutually supportive framework.

He understood that equal rights can be legislated to a great extent, but genuine brotherhood cannot, for it comes from the heart. We have learned that there is nothing automatic about good race relations. Instead we must consciously work to build interracial trust and cooperation.

If we are serious about fulfilling Martin Luther King, Jr.'s dream of a nation united in justice and peace, somehow, some way, we have to find a way to live together. As Martin said, "Like life, racial understanding is not something that we find, but something that we must create . . . The ability to work together, to understand each other will not be found ready-made; it must be created by the fact of contact." Such a commitment can help prevent further racial conflict. If we can build such bridges of knowledge and understanding between people of all races and religions, we will sow the seeds of a new unity in America.

During the civil rights movement, it was college students like you, students of all races and religions, who provided crucial leadership for social change. Young people like you are always the vanguard of any social movement, setting an energetic tone of courage and commitment which compels an aggressive spirit of social change.

Never doubt that you have the power to provide leadership for social change. College students provided decisive leadership for ending the Vietnam war. College students were there in Birmingham and Montgomery and Selma and all of the campaigns of the Civil Rights Movement. And now we need you to lead us once again to a higher and more noble destiny.

So I want to appeal to you today to rise up and lead a new revolution for social change. I appeal to you to reject the easy road of apathy and indifference. Reject materialism and drug abuse and all of the other selfish concerns, and lead your generation to a better America, where every person can lead a decent life in peace and harmony and with justice for all.

We must take a more proactive approach to challenging racism. Through intensive workshops, the King Center in Atlanta, which I serve as President, has also trained thousands of people from all walks of life, including teachers and students, in applying Dr. King's teachings to eliminate poverty, racism, war, and all forms of violence. Americans of all races must now begin to live and work together with the faith that we are all brothers and sisters in the great human family. The King Center in Atlanta is making a contribution to this effort by educating and training people of every age group about the values of love and compassion and the methods of nonviolent conflict-resolution that empowered Dr. King in his leadership of the Civil Rights Movement.

We feel strongly that this training is urgently needed to address the crisis of violence that is destroying the hopes of America's young people of all races. Alcohol and drug abuse, handguns, unemployment, disintegrating families, inadequate educational opportunities and media glorification of violence—all contribute to pervasive alienation, despair, and hopelessness among young people. All of these problems are interconnected. All reinforce each other to create a destructive mix of conditions that make frustration, anger, and violence among young people all but inevitable. We have to keep working for a more just society, but we can't afford to wait for the day when it finally becomes reality, because we are losing too many young people to the war in our streets.

At the King Center in Atlanta, we feel strongly that *now* is the time to follow the rhetoric of concern with the force of *action*. The Center is a memorial, research, and educational institution. It is a people's lobby for sanctions against South Africa, gun control, and amnesty for political prisoners. We are working for nuclear disarmament, and for legislation to protect voting rights, to eliminate job discrimination, and to put people back to work, to name just a few issues of continuing concern. Our staff and volunteers have been involved in almost every major social change coalition of the last quarter of a century.

We believe that education in the values and virtues needed to help create a more loving and decent society must begin as early as possible. Thus, our early learning center is pioneering curricula for pre-school age children that teaches them the power of nonviolent conflict-resolution. We think it is time to demand that public schools become partners in moral development. We're not asking that they get involved in religious controversy or engaged in church and state conflict.

But we must insist that they create programs to teach young people the virtues that empowered Martin Luther King, Jr.—honesty, tolerance for diversity, self-respect and respect for others, love, forgiveness, compassion, sharing, and most all, the *moral courage* to resist peer group pressure and to stand up for what is right.

To help meet this challenge, our "model project for teaching Dr. King's nonviolent principles in schools" helps teachers integrate the principles of nonviolence and moral values taught by Dr. King into public school curricula across the nation. These curricula can help educate our young people about the values and responsibilities of democracy. We teach them about moral courage. They learn how to challenge violence without doing injury to adversaries, that peace is the way, not just the goal. They learn about the self-discipline that is needed to practice nonviolence at the personal and social level. They learn how to cope with interpersonal conflict in a creative, constructive way.

This July, our annual youth workshop on nonviolence will bring young people from across the nation to Atlanta for an intensive training program in applying Dr. King's philosophy and methods to addressing current social problems. The Center also has a scholars-internship program, which provides a fully accredited course on Martin Luther King, Jr. and the Civil Rights Movement for undergraduate and graduate students. We hold an annual college and university student conference that brings together students from all across the nation to develop nonviolent strategies for correcting social and economic injustices. We also have training workshops for law enforcement personnel, including police chiefs and officers, as well as correctional and administrative staff. To date, more than 900 law enforcement personnel have completed this training.

Recognizing that Martin Luther King, Jr. had a *global* dream of peace and brotherhood, the King Center extends its training programs to other nations. The African National Congress has asked the King Center to help coordinate from the American side a nonpartisan voter education training program for the people of South Africa. We have accepted this invitation to assist with the transition to democracy in South Africa, and we have already sent teams of American students to South Africa as part of this program. We are also working with the

Johannesburg King-Luthuli Transformation Center, which is training young South Africans for leadership in the new South African government and business, as well as for nonviolent action campaigns for social and economic justice after apartheid has ended. We have trained and certified 80 South Africans in Dr. King's teachings in nonviolent, nonpartisan voter education, and voter turnout techniques. By April, when South Africa holds its first free elections, these trainers will have trained an estimated 150,000 more South Africans.

If you apply Martin Luther King, Jr.'s nonviolent philosophy and strategies with courage and determination, I believe we will see a great nation being reborn in justice and brotherhood. I see a nation where every child is safe and secure from the mayhem of deadly weapons and the scourge of drugs. I see a nation that nurtures its children and protects their precious innocence with compassion and caring. I see a nation where every child is enrolled in a good school that has all of the resources needed to teach them to love learning. I see a nation where young people can get as much education as their minds can absorb and a full range of cultural opportunities to enrich their spirits. I see a nation where families are once again restored to wholeness, where parents can find employment adequate to create a decent living for their children. I see beloved community where children need look no further for positive role models than the faces of their own mothers and fathers.

We *can* create the beloved community that Martin Luther King, Jr. envisioned. Let us now dare to embrace this common vision and mobilize all of our resources to bring it into being. Let us build a society based on hope, and let us not only dream, but *create* a new national unity, unburdened by bigotry and strengthened by a conscious commitment to prosperity through interracial brotherhood and sisterhood.

I conclude today with some words from one of Martin Luther King, Jr.'s last sermons, delivered in Ebenezer Baptist Church in February of 1968. In the sermon, he called for a new commitment of sacrifice and service from his followers. The sermon was entitled, "The Drum Major Instinct," and I think the challenge he presented is more relevant to our times than ever before. Martin said, "there is deep down within all of us, an instinct. It's kind of a drum major instinct—a desire to be out front, a desire to lead the parade, a desire to be first. And it is something that runs the whole gamut of life. . . . and the great issue of life is to harness the drum major instinct. . . ." And Martin went on to say, "If you want to be important—wonderful. If you want to be great— wonderful. But recognize that he who is greatest among you shall be your servant. That's your new definition of greatness—it means that everybody can be great because everybody can serve. You don't have to know about Plato and Aristotle to serve. You don't have to know the second theory of thermodynamics in physics to serve. You only need a heart full of grace, a soul generated by love and you can be that servant."

Martin Luther King, Jr.'s words provide an urgent challenge to all of us to become peacemakers. I hope you will become drum majors in those areas of lasting value. Be a drum major for human rights. Be a drum major for love and justice. Be a drum major for peace. Be a drum major for the beloved community with all of your heart and soul, and you will be that servant.

Thank you and God bless you.

CORETTA SCOTT KING, civil rights activist and widow of Martin Luther King, Jr., received her A.B. degree from Antioch College, and her Mus.B. and Mus.D. degrees from New England Conservatory. She has received numerous awards and honors. Until recently, Mrs. King served as President of the Martin Luther King Center for Nonviolent Social Change, Inc.

Appendix

Martin Luther King's Open Letter to Newt Gingrich*

A. Leon Higginbotham, Jr.

I AM PLEASED TO BE HERE, NOT ONLY TO SPEAK OF Martin Luther King, Jr., but equally important, to say "thank you" to MIT for its extraordinary support of young people who have great intellectual talent, but limited financial resources. I am speaking of the dreadful case that began in 1991, when Attorney General Richard Thornburgh, with much publicity and fanfare, just before resigning to run for the United States Senate, filed a civil antitrust suit against the Massachusetts Institute of Technology and the eight Ivy League colleges. In 1958, these colleges committed themselves to providing sufficient financial assistance to ensure that every student admitted to these schools would be given all the aid needed to attend the school of his or her choice. To that end, the agreement featured two main points: (1) financial aid would be awarded exclusively on the basis of need; and (2) a common formula would be used to calculate that need. The Department of Justice took the position that the agreement, which

* This speech was presented at MIT's 21st Annual Martin Luther King, Jr. Celebration, February 10, 1995. Copyright A. Leon Higginbotham, Jr. All Rights Reserved. No portion of this speech may be reproduced in any fashion or quoted without written permission of the author.

benefited minority and poor students, constituted price fixing because it restrained the colleges from bidding for other students, whether those students needed the aid or not.

Many in the education community deplored the MIT antitrust suit and described it as an anti-civil rights case.[1]

Faced with the threat of costly and protracted litigation, the Ivy League schools entered into a consent decree with the Justice Department and agreed to suspend critical portions of the Overlap Agreement. MIT stood alone, profoundly concerned about present and future students. It resisted the blatant misuse of the antitrust laws and, despite the fact that its talented lawyers had made arguments for dismissal that were irrefutable, the case was lost in the district court. Barely a week after this decision was issued, *The New York Times,* in an editorial dated September 6, 1992, wrote: "A federal judge in Philadelphia has struck a heedless, unpersuasive blow to the scholarship hopes of poor, black college students. . . . This decision is more antisocial than antitrust."

Fortunately, the judgment of the trial judge was reversed in the Court of Appeals, and I was privileged to argue *pro bono publico* on behalf of all of the *amici* in support of MIT's position.[2] As MIT stood firm in its resolve to aid needy students, as it refused to be intimidated by the awesome power of the federal government, you were implementing the core of Martin Luther King's dream.

When one talks about honoring Martin Luther King, it is not the public relations spin or rhetoric that makes the difference—it is the day-in and day-out hard policy choices for the weak, the poor and the powerless, the times when the ambit of opportunity is expanded, that pay tribute to Dr. King. Today, I want to pay tribute to MIT for its steadfast stand in that historic antitrust case. I pay tribute to the leadership of Dr. Vest, the MIT Corporation, and to someone whom I came to admire greatly, the late Constantine B. Simonides, who gave his heart and soul to this important case and who tragically is no longer with us. I was privileged to play a minor role in this case, and one of the most precious mementos I have from that litigation is a letter from an antitrust lawyer who heard me argue the case. I had concluded my comments before the court by saying there is no correlation between brains and financial affluence, and that the elite colleges should not be reserved solely for the Kennedys, the Rockefellers and the Lodges, but that they should be open to all persons of talent who are admitted but do not have the funds to meet their costs. The antitrust lawyer said that in the future, many poor white kids will get into Ivy League schools, and they will not recognize that this option was made possible partially because of the arguments a black lawyer and the Congressional Black Caucus made on behalf of MIT before the Court of Appeals for the Third Circuit and the Department of Justice for *all* of the poor kids in America. We meet here today to acknowledge that Martin Lather King's legacy was not merely to aid black people or brown people. His legacy was one that embraced *all* people.

A Perspective of 1983

Twelve years ago, I spoke here at MIT at your annual tribute to Martin Luther King. At that time, Ronald Reagan was in his first term as President. No one knew then that Dan Quayle did not know how to spell the word "potato," and William Jefferson Clinton was not known outside of Arkansas. The Soviet Union was still a formidable adversary, and Nelson Mandela was serving the 21st year of his lifetime sentence, breaking and chipping stone at the oppressive Robben Island prison. In 1983, I thought that conditions for many poor and powerless Americans would grow increasingly bleak and would not be helped by Ronald Reagan's rhetorical "safety net." I felt then, as I do now, that—to use Justice Holmes's phrase—a page of history is worth a volume of logic. Thus, I conjured up the fantasy that, because of the talents of the extraordinary MIT Department of Earth, Atmospheric, and Planetary Sciences, we were able to do something that had never occurred before. We were able to eavesdrop electronically on a conversation in Heaven between Thomas Jefferson and Martin Luther King. I hypothesized what King might say to Jefferson:

> Mr. Jefferson, since we have such equality here in Heaven,
> do you mind if I call you Tom? Now, Tom, how is it that
> individuals who are as philosophical and profound as
> you, and as brave as George Washington, and as eloquent
> as Patrick Henry, could treat an entire group of people—
> black people—with such special harshness and cruelty
> solely because of the color of their skin?

After reflecting on the King-Jefferson dialogue, I concluded that if, in 1983, we were to rekindle the spirit that Martin Luther King symbolized, he would want us to focus on basic issues, such as dignity, peace, hunger, and jobs, rather than simply pressing the nation to honor him by creating a Martin Luther King Day. I suggested that King would want us to recognize that verbal platitudes about justice and equality are deceptions and venal machinations, when a nation is not committed to, and does not ensure justice and equality for all.

Yesterday, while reflecting on my speech of twelve years ago, I had another experience that I would like to share with you. I do so with some trepidation, since I know most of you will be skeptical. Yet I choose to expose myself to your incredulity, because I feel it is important for me to relay to you the messages with which I have been entrusted.

Another Mystical Experience

I was reading the paper in my study. The television was on and I distractedly listened to the news on CNN while I read the newspaper stories on the O. J. Simpson case. I gradually became aware that the TV had stopped transmitting its usual images. Instead, the screen was pulsating with a bright light while emitting an eerie sound. As I tried to fine-tune the screen with the remote control, the image suddenly became clear and a series of scenes began to unfold.

First, I saw the image of a golden gate in front of a huge marble slab on which had been chiseled the words "Welcome to Heaven." The camera focused on a cathedral-type white building, framed with columns and surrounded by greenery. The camera zoomed down a corridor and focused on a door which had a brass plate marked, "The Abraham Lincoln and Thurgood Marshall Seminar Room." The door swung open as if by some mysterious force. Inside was a small seminar room; on the blackboard, written in huge block letters, were the following words: "Seminar at 11:30 Today—Martin Luther King, Jr., Speaker; Thurgood Marshall, Moderator; A. Leon Higginbotham, Jr., Transmitter at MIT." I could not believe my eyes: Martin Luther King at a podium shared with Thurgood Marshall, lecturing to an extraordinary assemblage of my human rights heroes. I barely had time to scan some of the faces in the audience: Sojourner Truth, Earl Warren, Charles Hamilton Houston, William Henry Hastie, Abraham Lincoln, Frederick Douglass, Ida B. Wells, Fannie Lou Hamer, Charles Sumner, Eleanor Roosevelt, Rabbi Joachim Prinz, Dag Hammarskjold.

At that point, I was not the least bit interested in the O. J. Simpson case. All I could think about was whether I was having a mental breakdown because I had been working much too hard lately, or whether I was truly having a mystical experience? But before I could make any coherent sense of the thoughts that were racing through my mind, my fax machine began to beep furiously as it received a transmission.

On the first page were words in fonts larger than any I had ever seen on my printer. It read *"From Heaven,"* and below it in smaller type was the byline *"From Martin Luther King, Entering Class of 1968."* The printer was going so fast that the paper was almost ablaze; it was so hot that I could not hold it comfortably in my hand. Nevertheless, I read every word, and just after I finished the last line on the last page, suddenly all of the ink print disappeared and the paper disintegrated into ashes. The TV screen reverted to its usual images, and a smiling and cheerful woman was trying to convince everyone to come to McDonald's.

Dazed and confused, I rushed to my desk and started writing frantically about the miraculous events I had just witnessed. Unfortunately, I cannot provide any corroboration of the fax I received or the events I observed from Heaven on my TV screen. There is no video tape of what I saw, nor is the letter in the memory of my computer or fax machine; the ashes of the fax cannot be reconstructed in paper form. Nevertheless, I am confident that through the television I saw Martin Luther King speak, and that through the fax I received a letter from him that he wants me to transmit to you and to Newt Gingrich. It was exactly what I would have expected to see and hear from Dr. King and his colleagues, who had been so actively involved in the Civil Rights Movement. Let me describe to you exactly what I saw on my TV screen yesterday, and exactly what I read on the fax.

Martin Luther King's Open Letter to Newt Gingrich

As Dr. King approached the podium in the seminar room in Heaven, he looked like the young, vigorous orator I had seen on so many occasions. He started his lecture as follows:

My dear brothers and sisters, I have prepared my commentary for this afternoon as an "Open Letter to My Fellow Citizen of Georgia, Newt Gingrich," and I am hoping that my old friend, Leon Higginbotham, will forward it to him soon and deliver the substance of my comments at his lecture today at MIT. More importantly, I hope thoughtful Americans will recognize the tragic hoax and potential cruelty of what Mr. Gingrich calls his "Contract With America."

As a former citizen of Georgia, first, Mr. Gingrich, I want to congratulate you on your election as Speaker of the House. This is an extraordinary opportunity for you to increase the quality of justice and fairness for all Americans. At the same time, it also provides you with the opportunity to further polarize our nation, to make us meaner than we have ever been, and to disregard the plight of the weak and the poor, who do not have political clout. I write you because it is within your power to make our nation either fairer than it has ever been or meaner to some of the most powerless persons in our nation. I have read every page and every line of your book "Contract with America." The back cover notes that the "pressing issues" addressed in this "important book" are:

Balancing the Budget	Strengthening National Defense
Stopping Crime	Cutting Government Regulations
Reforming Welfare	Promoting Legal Reform
Reinforcing Families	Considering Term Limits
Enhancing Fairness for Seniors	Reducing taxes

Of course, I agree with some of your premises. I am against crime, and I favor fair law enforcement. I favor the work ethic, and most black people favor the work ethic. I believe that there have been some abuses of welfare and that welfare should be reformed to deal with the abuses. Tragically, I did not see any specific provision in your contract, which was stated as a pledge, to support vigorously a concept of eradicating racial, gender, religious, and ethnic discrimination in America, and to deal with the consequences caused by decades of oppression in those areas.

Though you stress that one of your important concerns is "enhancing fairness for *seniors*," you never mention enhancing fairness for *children*. Unfortunately, children have no voting clout, but Mr. Gingrich, aren't they also entitled to fairness? You do not use the terms "equity" and "fairness" for the weak and the poor, which would have suggested that your contract assures justice even to the powerless. Nowhere did I see any recognition of the great injustices which were imposed on so many of "us" in the good old days, nor any concern about eliminating the unjust consequences of those good old days. Let me give you a couple of simple examples which make my point.

The Good Old Days

I trust that you will recognize that, from the days that they arrived here on slave ships, African Americans have often been skeptical about some of the contracts with America implemented by adroit politicians, statesmen, and even revered forefathers. Today, many African Americans and all other persons of good will are hoping that your "Contract with America" will not constitute a turning back, a return to the denial of justice for the weak, the poor, the powerless, and minorities. I trust that you will reflect on how much worse our state of Georgia and the nation were a century ago, and even three decades ago, for African Americans. I trust that you will not try to bring back the same brand of conservatism that opposed the passage of the 1964 Civil Rights Act, which prohibits discrimination on the basis of race, gender, religion, and national origin in employment, public accommodation, and other areas, and that opposed the 1965 Civil Rights Act, which prohibits the continued disenfranchisement of many African Americans. Let me cite you some other examples of my concerns.

In 1899, the United States Supreme Court had a simple case of invidious discrimination against blacks in Richmond County, Georgia.[3] The School Board said they had to close the high school for blacks because they could not afford a high school for blacks and at the same time provide elementary education for 400 black children. The Board made certain that all white children had options for a high school education; it provided opportunities for all white girls and subsidized education within the county for all white boys.

While there were always public high schools accessible to whites throughout Georgia, there was *not even one* public high school for blacks until the 1920s. Thus, Mr. Speaker, perhaps the distant past was relatively good for the whites who didn't care about excluding their fellow citizens from equal options, but those days were profoundly tragic for blacks and the poor. And, in many ways, even today we are suffering the consequences of the devastating inequalities that have been imposed by an educational system that short-changes blacks generation-by-generation-by-generation in thousands of school districts. Are you sufficiently concerned, Mr. Gingrich, about dealing with those past inequities to spend even disproportionate amounts of revenue to aid those who are weak and poor and who have experienced the maximum disadvantages in our society?

I hope that in your heart and mind you have the capacity to empathize with those who have been victims of racism, sexism, and oppression in our state of Georgia and throughout the nation. You have never had the anxiety and the tension of asking to be served a bottle of soda and a hot dog in a Woolworth 5 & 10¢ store, and of being told that—because of the color of your skin—you can't eat at the store counter. Newt, you have never had to march from Selma to Montgomery to assure *whites* the basic and fundamental right to vote. And what concerns me most is my uncertainty as to whether you have the sense of equity and fairness that recognizes the necessity of all the legislation which has been passed to ensure equal public accommodations, to eliminate discrimination in employment, and to ensure the right to vote. I ask you these questions because, in the 1960s, at the time in which it was most critical for black people to get the support of the white community, many of your fellow Republicans opposed the Civil Rights Acts and judicial acknowledgments of the Constitution's requirement of equality of treatment for citizens regardless of race.

It was primarily the conservatives who attacked relentlessly the Warren Court because of its *Brown v. Board of Education* decision declaring state-imposed segregation unconstitutional, and who objected to almost every measure to ensure gender and racial advancement. For example, on March 11, 1956, ninety-six members of Congress, representing eleven southern states, issued the "Southern Manifesto," in which they declared that the Brown decision was an "unwarranted exercise of power by the court, contrary to the Constitution."[4] Ironically, those members of Congress reasoned that the *Brown* decision was "destroying the amicable relations between the white and Negro race"[5] and that "it had planted hatred and suspicion where there had been heretofore friendship and understanding."[6] They then pledged to use all lawful means to bring about the reversal of the decision, and praised those states which had declared the intention to resist its implementation.[7] The Southern Manifesto was more than mere political posturing by Southern politicians. It was a thinly disguised racist attack on the constitutional and moral foundations of *Brown*. Where were your conservatives in the 1950s when the cause of equal rights needed every fair-minded voice it could find?

At every turn, the conservatives, either by tacit approbation or by active complicity, tried to derail the struggle for equal rights. In the 1960s, it was the conservatives, including the then-senatorial candidate from Texas, George Bush;[8] the then-Governor from California, Ronald Reagan;[9] and the omnipresent Senator Strom Thurmond;[10] who argued that the 1964 Civil Rights Act was unconstitutional. In fact, Senator Thurmond's 24 hour 18 minute filibuster during Senate deliberation on the 1957 Civil Rights Act set an all-time record.[11] He argued on the floor of the Senate that the provisions of the Act guaranteeing equal access to public accommodations amounted to an enslavement of white people.[12]

Do You Care About Children?

Since you talk about fairness to seniors, I must cite you some data, based on U.S. Government statistics, which I believe have profound implications. I must ask whether you believe in equity and fairness for the poor children of America.

Health care for all children and their families is a necessary investment in their future and in society's future. But this country's record on child health—especially for lower-income children—is dismal:

- A higher proportion of babies are born at low birthweight in the United States than in 31 other countries, including Romania, Greece, Turkey, and Portugal. Such children often require costly neonatal care or experience a lifetime of disabilities.

- The United States ranks 19th among developed countries for infant mortality rates.

- The United States ranks 17th among all nations in the percentage of one-year-olds who are fully immunized against polio, behind Romania, Albania, Greece, North Korea, and Pakistan. In some American cities, only 10% to 42% of children starting school receive critical immunizations on time. Our polio immunization rate for children of color ranks 70th in the world.[13]

- The number of people living in poverty was reported in October 1993 to have risen to 14.7% of the entire population for 1992, a rise for the third straight year.[14]

- The poverty rate then reported among African Americans was 33%, and for Hispanics over 29%.[15]

- One of four American children lives in poverty.

- In the third quarter of 1993, the national unemployment rate was 6.6%; for African Americans the rate was 12.6%. And these poverty and unemployment figures may be understated, according to the National Urban League's Hidden Unemployment Index, which notes that official government figures do not count discouraged workers and involuntary part-time workers, and which measures total unemployment at 13.1% and African-American unemployment at 23.2%.

The Wisdom of Barbra Streisand

I suggest that for the good of the country you tone down your meanness, and I ask you to reflect on the eloquence of Barbra Streisand's recent speech at Harvard. She said:

> I am worried about the direction in which the new Congress now seeks to take the country. I'm worried about the name calling, the stereotypical labeling. I want to believe that these people have good intentions, but I think it was dangerous when Newt Gingrich developed a strategy in the last campaign of pitting President Clinton against so-called "normal Americans." Just last week, the Speaker attacked again when he said, and I quote, "I fully expect Hollywood to have almost no concept of either normal American behavior, in terms of healthy families, healthy structures, religious institutions, conservative politics, the free enterprise system."
>
> We are all normal Americans, even with our problems and complexities, including people in my community.
>
> This notion of "normal Americans" has a horrible historical echo. It presupposes that there are "abnormal Americans" who are responsible for all that is wrong. The new scapegoats are members of what Gingrich calls the "Counterculture McGoverniks."
>
> I'm disappointed that I've read so little in defense of McGovern. Was McGovern countercultural? This son of a Republican Methodist minister has been married to the same woman for 51 years and flew 35 combat missions in World War II. Isn't it odd that his patriotism be disputed by a person who never served in the military and whose own family history can hardly be called exemplary? But then again—*no one* should have to conform to some mythical concept of the ideal family—not even Mr. Gingrich.
>
> I'm also very proud to be a liberal. Why is that so terrible these days? The liberals were liberators—they fought slavery, fought for women to have the right to vote, fought against Hitler, Stalin, fought to end segregation, fought to end apartheid. Thanks to liberals we have Social

Security, public education, consumer and environmental protection, Medicare and Medicaid, the minimum wage law, unemployment compensation. Liberals put an end to child labor and they even gave us the 5 day work week! What's to be ashamed of? Such a record should be worn as a badge of honor!

I agree with Barbra Streisand's remarks, and I trust that you will try to de-escalate your impugnment of those many human beings who disagree with you.

The Shame of Silence

Some years before my death I wrote:

Was not Albert Einstein right when he said: "The world is in greater peril from those who tolerate evil than from those who actively commit it"?

Will the nation ever forget the searing impact of Rabbi Joachim Prinz's admonitions, as he spoke at the March on Washington in 1963: "When I was the Rabbi of the Jewish Community in Berlin under the Hitler regime, I learned many things. The most important thing that I learned in my life and under tragic circumstances is that bigotry and hatred are not the most urgent problems. The most urgent, the most disgraceful, the most shameful, and the most tragic problem is silence."

A great people which had created a great civilization had become a nation of silent onlookers. They remained silent in the face of hate, in the face of brutality, and in the face of mass murder.

How will we, in 1995, as individuals and in our institutions, respond to the retrenchment of the increasingly conservative Congress? Will we remain silent to the debacle that goes on daily before our eyes? Will we have the courage to seek the truth, to speak out against those practices that fall short of our ideals? Will history say that because of our values and priorities, the poor, the disadvantaged, and the weak were needlessly harmed, denigrated, and ignored? Or will historians say that, because of our priorities and values, we understood and strove as valiantly as we could to achieve the kind of world my colleagues and I envisioned when we said, "[We] have the audacity to believe that people everywhere can have three meals a day for their bodies, education and culture for their minds, and dignity, equality and freedom for their spirit."

Newt, I know that you are on a political roll. Just as Governor Wallace did in Alabama, Faubus in Arkansas, and Barnette in Mississippi during the 1950s and '60s, you may continue to mobilize significant support in direct proportion to the meanness you convey in your political rhetoric. Last week, in one event alone, you and your colleagues may have raised eleven million dollars for the Republican Party.[16] With that kind of funding, it seems hypocritical that you would delete the modest funding Congress provides for the Congressional Black Caucus and the women's and Hispanic groups which might never have the easy access to the millions of dollars that you and your colleagues possess. I believe that the American people must condemn this hypocrisy.

If we remain silent to the steady diminution of basic justice for the weak and the poor, we will fail to understand the wisdom of Langston Hughes's poem:

> There is a dream in the land
> With its back against the wall.
> By muddled names and strange
> Sometimes the dream is called.
>
> There are those who claim
> This dream for theirs alone—
> A sin for which, we know,
> They must atone.
>
> Unless shared in common
> Like sunlight and like air,
> The dream will die for lack
> Of substance anywhere.
>
> The dream knows no frontier or tongue,
> The dream no class or race.
> The dream cannot be kept secure
> In any one locked place.
>
> This dream today embattled,
> With its back against the wall—
> To save the dream for one
> It must be saved for all.

Notes

1. In an editorial dated May 3, 1992, entitled "U.S. v. Needy Students," *The New York Times* described the suit as a "destructive claim, unworthy of litigation." *The Washington Post,* in an editorial dated May 6, 1992, stated: "the case against the Ivy League and its friends may be good sport, but its bad policy." The *Los Angeles Times,* in an editorial on May 24, 1992, described the antitrust suit as "lunacy." *The Boston Globe* on May 24, 1992, characterized it as a "twisted interpretation of the Sherman Act," and the *Philadelphia Inquirer,* on May 19, 1992, remarked that the idea of an antitrust suit against the colleges was "strange." These respected newspapers, in one way or another, all agreed with *The Washington Post* when it remarked in a May 24, 1992 editorial: "The Justice Department looked the other way at the merger mania of the 1980s only to scrutinize the practices among universities with extraordinary effort and at high cost."

2. The *amici* included: American Council on Education, Association of American Medical Colleges, Association of American Universities, Association of Catholic Colleges and Universities, College Board, Council of Independent Colleges, National Association of Independent Colleges and Universities, National Association of State Universities and Land Grant Colleges, National Association of Student Financial Aid Administrators, National Association of Student Personnel Administrators, United Negro College Fund, School District of Philadelphia, Urban League of Philadelphia, Greater Philadelphia Urban Affairs Coalition, Hispanic Bar Association of Pennsylvania, Barristers Association of Philadelphia, Inc., Asian American Bar Association of the Delaware Valley, National Bar Association Women Lawyers Division, Philadelphia Chapter, Association of Alumni and Alumnae of the Massachusetts Institute of Technology, and Rockefeller Brothers Fund, Inc.

3. *Cumming v. County Bd. of Educ.,* 175 US 528 (1899).

4. 102 Cong. Rec. 4255, 4515 (1956).

5. *Id.* at 4516.

6. *Id.*

7. *Id.*

8. See Doug Freelander, "The Senate-Bush. The Polls Give Him 'Excellent Chance,' " *Houston Post,* Oct. 11, 1964, § 17, p. 8.

9. See David S. Broder, "Reagan Attacks the Great Society," *New York Times,* June 17, 1966, p. 41.

10. See Charles Whalen and Barbara Whalen, *The Longest Debate: A Legislative History of the 1964 Civil Rights Act.* (Washington, D.C.: Seven Locks Press, 1985), p. 143.

11. *Id.*

12. Senate Commerce Comm., Civil Rights—Public Accommodations, S. Rep. No. 872, 88th Cong., 2d Sess. 62-63, 75-76 (1964) (Individual Views of Senator Strom Thurmond).

13. *America's Children At Risk: A National Agenda for Legal Action* (Washington, D.C.: American Bar Association, 1993), p. 35. [A Report of the American Bar Association Presidential Working Group on the Unmet Legal Needs of Children and Their Families.]

14. *The State of Black America, 1994* (New York: National Urban League, 1994), p. 30.

15. *Id.*

16. Jill Abramson and David Rodgers, "Shifting Fortunes: As G.O.P. Tries to Shrink Government, Coffers Swell With New Money," *Wall Street Journal*, Feb. 9, 1995, p. A1; see also Kim Masters and Roxanne Roberts, "Vested Interests: G.O.P.'s Fete Cats: The Rewards of Mixing Business With Politics," *The Washington Post*, Feb. 10, 1995, p. B1; "Fund Raiser Pulls In $11 Million for G.O.P.," *The Plain Dealer*, Feb. 11, 1995, p. 7A.

 A. LEON HIGGINBOTHAM, JR. is Chief Judge Emeritus (Retired), United States Court of Appeals; Public Service Professor of Jurisprudence, John F. Kennedy School of Government, Harvard University; and Counsel to Paul, Weiss, Rifkind, Wharton & Garrison.

Index

Note: Page numbers in italics indicate illustrations.

Thurmond, Strom, 297, 302n12
Trotter, Monroe, 102
Truman, Harry, 228
Truth, Sojourner, 150, 293
Tse, Mawuli, *xi*
Tubman, Harriet, 150
Turner, Nat, 150
Tutu, Desmond, 166
Twain, Mark, 177
Tyler, Margaret Daniels, *xii, xiii*

Uhuru, 227

Vest, Charles M., *vii, vii, ix, xi, 29, 32,* 251, *260, 271, 278,* 290
Vest, Rebecca M., *260, 271, 278*

Wabnick, Richard, 190n2
Wadleigh, Kenneth R., *83*
Walker, Alice, 227
Wallace, George Corley, 43, 108, 143, 301
Warde, Cardinal, *xiii*
Warren, Earl, 43, 131, 293
Washington, Booker T., 102
Washington, George, 110, 137, 140, 247
Washington, Harold, 250
Washington, Joseph E., *83*
Wasiyo, Khaitsa, *xi*
Webster, Daniel, 180, 181
Weigle, Dean (Yale), 209
Weinberg, Meyer, 190n1
Wellburne, Craig, 199

Wells, Ida B., 293
Whalen, Barbara, 302n10
Whalen, Charles, 302n10
White, Walter, 184
Whitman, Walt, 177
Whitnal, Nathaniel A., 17, *187*
Wicker, Tom, 112, 113
Wiesner, Jerome B., *xi,* 3, *6, 32, 66*
Wilds, Chandra, *xii*
Wilhelm, Sidney M., 53n14
Wilkins, Roy, 65, 92, 184
Williams, Adam Daniel, 130
Williams, Alton L., *xiii*
Williams, Clarence G., ix, xi, 1–35, 6, 27, 66, 74, 83, 93, 121, 187, 198, *271*
Williams, Clarence G., Jr., xi
Williams, Edward Bennett, 168
Williams, Mildred Cogdell, *xiii*
Wilson, August, 227
Wilson, Woodrow, 200
Winfrey, Oprah, 269–270
Winston, Michael R., 16–17, 183–191, 187
Wrighton, Mark S., *vii–x, xi,* 28, *29,* 33, 35n43

Yeates, Michael W., *xii*
Young, Andrew, 202, 250, 256, 281
Young, Coleman A., 69, 250
Young, Whitney M., 64, 65, 92

Zinn, Howard, 84